DATE DUE

A Pr
Guid
Entr

*To six remarkable women and two men without
whom my life would be different; alphabetically:*

*Bernard Charles Morris
Eleanor Jane Morris
Frances Clare Morris
Hilda Morris
Elizabeth Rose Pohler
Felicity Sophia Pohler
Stuart Pohler
Bridget Mary Smith*

A Practical Guide to Entrepreneurship

How to turn an idea into a profitable business

Michael Morris

KoganPage

LONDON   PHILADELPHIA   NEW DELHI

Publisher's note

Every possible effort has been made to ensure that the information contained in this book is accurate at the time of going to press, and the publishers and author cannot accept responsibility for any errors or omissions, however caused. No responsibility for loss or damage occasioned to any person acting, or refraining from action, as a result of the material in this publication can be accepted by the editor, the publisher or the author.

First published in Great Britain and the United States in 2012 by Kogan Page Limited

120 Pentonville Road	1518 Walnut Street, Suite 1100	4737/23 Ansari Road
London N1 9JN	Philadelphia PA 19102	Daryaganj
United Kingdom	USA	New Delhi 110002
www.koganpage.com		India

© Michael Morris, 2012

The right of Michael Morris to be identified as the author of this work has been asserted by him in accordance with the Copyright, Designs and Patents Act 1988.

ISBN   978 0 7494 6688 6
E-ISBN   978 0 7494 6689 3

British Library Cataloguing-in-Publication Data

A CIP record for this book is available from the British Library.

Library of Congress Cataloging-in-Publication Data

Morris, M. J. (Michael John)
  A practical guide to entrepreneurship : how to turn an idea into a profitable business / Michael Morris.
    p. cm.
  Includes bibliographical references.
  ISBN 978-0-7494-6688-6 – ISBN 978-0-7494-6689-3   1. New business enterprises–Management.
2. Entrepreneurship.   I. Title.
  HD62.5.M676 2012
  658.1'1–dc23
                                                                                    2012020103

Typeset by Graphicraft Limited, Hong Kong
Printed and bound in India by Replika Press Pvt Ltd

CONTENTS

ACKNOWLEDGEMENTS

With thanks to Tim Morris for prompt and helpful responses to strange enquiries, and to Julia Swales, my editor, for inspiration, sage advice, guidance and patience.

Introduction

Why *this* book?

This book gives the reader a framework for the study of entrepreneurship together with the necessary information to translate course-work directly into the production of a business plan – whether for real-life application or solely for academic purposes.

Who this book is for

This book is written for the student of entrepreneurship who seeks a practical guide to the subject which could, if he or she so chooses, lead to setting up a business on sound foundations.

Features of this book

A Practical Guide to Entrepreneurship is much more than just another book on enterprise. It features:

- a step-by-step guide through the main issues faced by the new entrepreneur, working down from the big picture to essential detail;
- a strong emphasis on the need for rigorous, integrated planning on paper, to be followed cyclically by review and modification;
- 20 bite-size case histories of start-ups from around the world, showing that the task of starting a business faces the same challenges anywhere on the globe;
- appendices, including a draft set of legal terms and conditions of sale, a simple self-instruction example of building a cash-flow forecast and information on starting a 'green' business;
- a glossary;
- a template enabling the production of a business plan suitable for consideration by managers and potential investors;

- a set of learning resources both within the text and on the Kogan Page website, which include:
  - discussion and learning notes on the case histories;
  - sample questions and answers, with indicative marking schemes;
  - over 350 PowerPoint slides, covering the entire book, chapter by chapter;
  - links to Durham University's highly-respected GET (General Enterprising Tendency) test for assessment of entrepreneurial potential and to the University of Kent's free leadership styles test.

Above all, it is rich in the practical detail needed by new entrepreneurs, from the pros and cons of costing systems, through how the VAT system works, to the legal implications of the choice of trading name, as well as the need to take two pens when visiting a customer (because one always runs out). To ensure its usefulness it draws on the long-running Kogan Page publication *Starting a Successful Business*, a practical handbook now in its seventh edition.

A greatly respected writer on organizational matters was the late Peter Drucker. Among his famously pithy dictums is: 'Plans are only good intentions unless they immediately degenerate into hard work'.

I wish you well with your planning, as well as its degeneration into work which, though it may be hard, ought to be richly rewarding.

Michael Morris

PART 1:
Entrepreneurship

01
Entrepreneurship today

In this chapter

LEARNING OUTCOMES

By the end of this chapter you should be able to:

- understand the nature of the environment for enterprise;
- recognize international comparisons;
- see that public attitudes and policy towards enterprise are changeable.

Starting a business today may be more difficult than at any previous time in history. In mediaeval times people who made pots, pans and other household items made their goods, popped them in a bag and trudged round selling them door to door. Nowadays, within any developed economy there is a multitude of regulations to observe. In the UK they range from health and safety ('have you been trained to place items in bags, Sir?') to the Cancellation of Contracts made in a Consumer's Home or Place of Work etc Regulations 2008, and plenty more besides.

That does not seem to act as a deterrent for, despite all the obstacles placed in the way of the new businessperson, people continue to form new enterprises – and it is important that they should do so, since small firms account for most of the new jobs created as well as for an astonishing number of inventions and new ideas. It is difficult to overstate the importance of small business to free-market economies the world over. In the UK, the Office of National Statistics estimates that in 2011 there were 3,580,215 self-employed people with no staff (Shaw, 2011), and many more who did employ people.

For the individual, the reasons for entrepreneurship are obvious: either exploiting a potentially lucrative opportunity or responding to the fact that no other reasonable possibility of earning a living exists. At the level of the whole economy, the sum of all these self-interested decisions agglomerates into a socially useful phenomenon. Writing in 1942, the economist Schumpeter echoed earlier scholars by writing of 'creative destruction', the force exercised by entrepreneurship which causes old models to fall and others to rise from the ashes. (Unfortunately, perhaps, for the right-wing economic theorists who have more recently seized on this dictum, he also went on to predict the demise of capitalism.) Creative destruction, in its current interpretation, is seen as a good thing, reallocating resources away from those who use them less efficiently and towards those who use them better.

Schumpeter is given support from the ranks of the entrepreneurs themselves. In an interview with Emily Maitlis in *The Sunday Times* on 4 December 2011, Mark Zuckerberg (founder of Facebook) enjoins the world to 'move fast and break things'.

Moving fast is something that entrepreneurs are doing constantly. Consider consumer music recordings: from the 1920s to the 1950s the sole medium was the 78 rpm disk, superseded in the 1960s by the 45 rpm and 33 rpm extended-play and long-play records; the eight-track tape came in and was, in turn, knocked out by tape cassettes. Next came the CD, sales of which are stalling as MP3 players take over. Creative? Certainly. Destructive? Just look at the pile of obsolete technology in lofts all over the world. Whole industries have risen and fallen in the space of half a century. Why? Because of the restlessness of entrepreneurs in organizations large and small as they vie with the existing order to make something better and make the future better than the past, at least in their tiny corner of the world economy.

There is an international dimension to entrepreneurship. Given that the basic challenges of starting a firm – finding customers, getting orders, getting paid and making profits – are the same the world over, it might be thought that the situation for entrepreneurs is the same in every country. Not so. The World Bank and the International Finance Corporation researched the situation in 174 countries and found startling differences; for example, a fairly random selection of the time taken to comply with official requirements and to organize a start-up is shown in Table 1.1.

This suggests that an entrepreneur should scrutinize the situation in any territory in which the new firm might be located. Where the possibility of choice exists, the entrepreneur should pick the most benign location available.

Other tables in the same publication compare countries on a wide variety of dimensions: for the possibly mobile entrepreneur they are a good read; for anyone faced with cross-border competition they point to where the opposition might be sited. They hold some surprises, for instance: 'The economies that improved the most in the ease of doing business in 2010/11 – with improvements in 3 or more areas of regulation measured by *Doing Business* – are Morocco, Moldova, FYR Macedonia, São Tomé and Príncipe, Latvia, Cape Verde, Sierra Leone, Burundi, the Solomon Islands, Korea, Armenia, and Colombia' (The World Bank/International Finance Corporation, 2011: 2).

The pace of change is quickening, and generally in favour of the entrepreneur: 'Worldwide, 125 economies implemented 245 reforms making it easier to do business in 2010/11, 13% more than in the previous year... The pickup in the pace of regulatory reform is especially welcome for small and medium-size businesses, the main job creators in many parts of the world' (The World Bank/International Finance Corporation, 2011: 2).

TABLE 1.1   Time taken to set up a business, by country

Country	Days taken
Brazil	119
Brunei Darussalam	101
China	38
India	20
Indonesia	45
Kenya	33
Korea	7
Liberia	6
Malaysia	6
Mexico	9
Nicaragua	39
New Zealand	1
Singapore	3
Suriname	694
Timor-Leste	103
United Kingdom	13
Venezuela	141
Vietnam	44

SOURCE: The World Bank/International Finance Corporation (2011)

This increasing liberalization can be contrasted with the situation in one advanced economy a generation ago. There was a time, during the 1960s and 1970s when the UK was trying out the idea of an increasingly powerful state with big government seen as the answer to, rather than the cause of, many of the country's economic ills, that anyone admitting to running a business was seen as something of a social outcast. Large scale was the god: between 1966 and 1971 there was even a government organization (the Industrial Reorganisation Corporation) devoted to encouraging mergers between companies 'in the national interest' (of international competitiveness) more or less irrespective of the effect on domestic competition. Under this gigantist model the ordinary employee was expected to see his or her interests as being best served by an equally large trade union, and the history of that period is remarkable for the enormous number of industrial disputes. While the titans of ownership and labour were clashing far above his or her head, the small businessperson was seen as greedy, dishonest, a bad employer and generally prepared to grind the faces of the poor into the dust in the interests of profit. No doubt there were such businesspeople then as now, but it cannot have been accurate to typify all as if they were the few. In its manifesto for the 1979 general election, the Labour Party's prescriptions for economic growth continued its commitment to central planning and nationalized industry with these ideas: 'To ensure that private industry plays its full part in the drive for prosperity and full employment, we shall conclude planning agreements with the major industrial companies...'; 'We shall expand the work and finance of the National Enterprise Board, using public ownership to sustain and create new jobs...' (*Labour Party Manifesto*, 1979).

But change was in the air. In the same year the winning Conservative Party's manifesto had stated: 'The creation of new jobs depends to a great extent on the success of smaller businesses.'

New businesses came to be seen as the engine room of the economy, where new ideas would overturn the old and outdated, forging a new future for the country. That future was to be dominated not by the great industrial dinosaurs of yesteryear (many of them in government ownership), their managements defeated by deeply conservative workforces and powerful trade unions often opposed to any change at all, but by a far more diverse and ever-changing population of businesspeople whose personal prosperity would depend not on warfare against their employers, but instead on the perceptiveness, ingenuity, imagination and energy of a large and ever-changing army of brave new entrepreneurs. Much rhetorical hot air was dispensed in that direction, not without some effect, though it did little to offset the dire loss of small businesses in that government's early years. What helped business best was not moral support but the general economic prosperity which was, eventually, delivered.

The pro-enterprise mood proved so powerful that when the Labour Party came to power in 1997 its manifesto had said: 'We see healthy profits as an essential motor of a dynamic market economy, and believe they depend on quality products, innovative entrepreneurs and skilled employees.' Yet only 10 years earlier its manifesto's sole mention of small enterprises was as cooperatives: 'We will... encourage the establishment and success of co-operatives of all forms' (*Labour Party Manifesto*, 1987).

All of this suggests a pattern, whereby the attitude to entrepreneurship has moved through a cycle.

Conclusions

- Social attitudes move in cycles; even when things seem static they are changing, sometimes quickly sometimes not, but always on the move.

- Entrepreneurship is currently fashionable and acceptable; this, too, will change in time, probably once it is perceived as not having delivered against the excessive expectations at present placed upon it. Governments rightly recognize the vital part played by entrepreneurs in job creation (the primary element in economic success that is directly recognized through the ballot box) but do not dare deregulate to allow them to breathe. Consequently, they continue to be suffocated by red tape. It is possible that the disillusion, when it comes, will be not only with newer businesses but with capitalism as a whole, in which case entrepreneurship will be faced by a wide range of new challenges.

- Whatever the vagaries of fashion, enterprise is important to an economy. New businesses need to rise to replace those lost to the constant churn of economic events and old businesses need to reinvent themselves. Darwin saw in nature that a constant supply of variations offered organisms the chance to adapt to changing environments: as with nature, so with the firms within an economy.

02
Becoming and being an entrepreneur

In this chapter

LEARNING OUTCOMES

By the end of this chapter you should be able to:

- describe entrepreneurs' special characteristics;
- assess your own propensity to entrepreneurship;
- decide whether attitudes to enterprise vary with gender;
- decide what sort of firm to start.

Characteristics of entrepreneurs

Entrepreneurs are often thought of as special people with exceptional personal characteristics. Dr Sally Caird at Durham University Business School has done a great deal of research into what makes them tick. She has developed a test, the General Enterprising Tendency test, that takes about 10 minutes and gives a potential entrepreneur a score out of 100, with subsidiary scores for what she sees as the five different components that make up the whole, namely:

- need for achievement: wanting to be a winner;
- need for autonomy: wanting to answer to oneself, being free to do things one's own way;

TABLE 2.1   Tests used to differentiate between employed and self-employed

Test	Factors
Control – who holds control over task, mode, means and timing?	Duty to obey orders, discretion on hours of work, supervision of mode of working
Integration – how integral is the work to the business?	Existence of disciplinary or grievance procedures, inclusion in occupational benefit schemes
Economic reality – where does the financial risk lie?	Method of payment, freedom to hire others, providing own equipment, investing in own business, method of payment of tax and national insurance (NI), coverage of sick pay, holiday pay
Mutuality of obligation – what evidence is there of formal subordination to contract terms?	Duration of employment, regularity of employment, right to refuse work, custom in the trade

SOURCE: Quoted by Newell (2009) based on Burchell, Deakin and Honey (1999)

- creative tendency: able to come up with novel solutions to problems, to see things in a new way;
- propensity to take risks: calculating the chances then taking the gamble;
- an internal locus of control – see below.

Most of these are self-explanatory but 'internal locus of control' may deserve explanation. Someone with that quality can be expected to possess self-belief and self-confidence, to be opportunistic, proactive and determined.

The General Enterprising Tendency test is online and free to take at **http:// get2test.net/test/index.htm**; on the same website is a comprehensive explanation of the entire scoring system.

First, as self-employed people, entrepreneurs need to be distinguished from employees. Table 2.1 shows differences between the employed and self-employed.

So the self-employed have greater discretion than employees over when and how they work, supply their own tools and lack job security but are free from disciplinary procedures. This belief in standing on their own feet confers a sense of pride that supplies a good deal of their satisfaction.

Women tend to believe less in themselves as potential entrepreneurs than do men:

'In emerging and developing economies, more women start new businesses than manage established ones. This reverses in developed economies where, like their male counterparts, more women are established business owners than entrepreneurs. Similar to men, women are just as likely to see entrepreneurship as attractive, but they are less likely to believe there are a lot of opportunities for starting businesses in their area' *Global Entrepreneurship Monitor* (2011).

There is much anecdotal evidence from professionals associated with business start-ups that, while women – on average – may be more cautious than men, the businesses they start are better researched and more securely founded.

A lucky break?

In business, as in life, luck can play a great part in one's fortunes. To some extent, it depends what you mean by 'luck'. Many entrepreneurs tell of talking to the person in the next seat on a plane, thus meeting their biggest customer, or of their job being made redundant at exactly the moment they'd written their business plan. However, there is a strong case for belief that you make your own luck, summed up in Thomas Jefferson's saying: 'The harder I work the luckier I get.'

Dr Richard Wiseman of the University of Hertfordshire has researched what makes people lucky. His conclusion is that what really counts is your approach to life. He puts forward four principles to ensure good luck:

- Expect good luck: that alone often makes it turn up, not through some mystical force of wishful thinking but by creating a receptive frame of mind.
- Create opportunities, notice them and act on them.
- Trust your gut feelings about people and situations, act on hunches.
- When bad things happen, think about how much worse they could have been and think of ways to tackle them (Wiseman, 2004).

I would suggest a rider to that final point. When bad things happen, analyse what caused them, think of how they could have been avoided and – above all – learn from the situation. With luck, you'll make sure it doesn't happen again.

The Apprentice – *don't be fooled!*

For some years a TV programme has run a competition. The prize used to be the chance to become an assistant to a well-known businessman. Lately it has changed to a straightforward £100,000 reward. There is a danger that some people might imagine that what they see on their screens reflects the realities of business life. It is a game show, not a documentary, so it is important to remember three things:

- The programme's main aim is to entertain, not to inform.
- Game-show contestants are not necessarily selected for their ability: their potential to provide entertainment comes first. In the degenerating world of popular entertainment, the more bizarre their behaviour, the more it is seen as entertaining.
- The vast majority of business operations involve long-term cooperation and collaboration, not trying to knock one's contemporaries off their perches so as to leave you the last one standing.

What is my qualification for saying this? Certainly, I don't have the multimillion-pound fortune of the show's leading character. He is an exceptional individual of great accomplishments, but most people are not, and could not be, like him. Some, myself included, would not want to be.

As a more ordinary individual with less distinguished achievements, I do have a lifetime of experience at levels that most people could identify with. Moreover, I have spent quite a lot of time working with entrepreneurs and studying how they go about things. I cannot think of one who would have excelled on any sort of TV game show – instead, they got on with building what are, in many cases, sound and decent businesses founded on respect for customers, suppliers and staff. That is the sort of business this book proposes.

The entrepreneurial type

Experience shows that it is a major risk for a person to set out on the entrepreneurial path if the individual is unfitted to the challenges it presents. It can lead not just to personal unhappiness, but if the business fails, to the loss of almost all of the entrepreneur's personal assets. This is because banks require the pledging of assets against any lending. Some say this makes them little better than pawnbrokers, but despite any name-calling it remains their policy. This will be explored further in Part 4: Financial management, raising finance, but the central point at this stage is that the only people who should start a business are those who can either afford to lose it without qualm or those who are what true entrepreneurs are made of.

A branch of the UN, the International Labour Organisation, has also studied the characteristics of entrepreneurs and come to broadly similar conclusions. Their model lists characteristics and, alongside, the behavioural traits that manifest each characteristic. These are shown in Table 2.2.

Another angle on what it takes to be an entrepreneur is offered by Peter R Worrell, writing on the website *Positive Psychology News Daily* on 1 January 2007:

> '... a yearlong [sic] research project [was] recently completed on the character
> strengths and grit of seasoned entrepreneurs. We asked, "Do seasoned, successful
> entrepreneurs exhibit a unique blend of signature character strengths and persistence
> compared to the general population? If so, does it matter?" The results of the
> preliminary study support our hypothesis that entrepreneurs do show a unique blend
> of character strengths... The top five character strengths for the entrepreneurs in this
> sample are:
>
> authenticity;
> leadership;
> fairness;
> gratitude;
> zest.'
>
> (Excerpts taken from **http://positivepsychologynews.com/news/peter-worrell/2011060118041**)

While the various authorities do not agree in detail, in general their views cluster around a broadly similar set of beliefs. The US website businesstown.com has published a useful distillation of the main research findings on the characteristics of entrepreneurs. Table 2.3 represents an edited summary of its conclusions.

TABLE 2.2   Profile of an entrepreneur

Characteristic	Traits
Self-confidence	Believes in ability, independence, optimism
Strong willpower	Shows persistence and perseverance, determination
Task or result oriented	Achievement oriented, hard worker, shows initiative
Risk taker	Makes risk assessments and has judicious risk-taking ability
Leadership	Good communicator, responsive to suggestions, develops other people
Originality	Innovative, creative, flexible, resourceful, versatile, knowledgeable
Future oriented	Shows foresight, vision, perceptiveness

SOURCE: International Labour Organisation (1998)

TABLE 2.3   Characteristics of entrepreneurs

Entrepreneurial characteristics
At the end of the eight-hour day, when everyone else leaves for home, the entrepreneur will often continue to work into the evening.
Self-control Entrepreneurs enjoy creating business strategies and thrive on the process of achieving their goals. Once they achieve a goal, they quickly replace it with a greater goal.
Self-confidence Entrepreneurs are self-confident when they are in control of what they're doing and working alone. They tackle problems immediately with confidence and are persistent in their pursuit of their objectives.
Sense of urgency Entrepreneurs have a never-ending sense of urgency: inactivity makes them impatient, tense and uneasy. They have drive and high energy levels, they are achievement oriented, and they are tireless in the pursuit of their goals.

TABLE 2.3 *continued*

Entrepreneurial characteristics

Comprehensive awareness
Successful entrepreneurs can comprehend complex situations that may include planning, making strategic decisions, and working on multiple business ideas simultaneously. They are farsighted and aware of important details, and they will continuously review all possibilities to achieve their business objectives. At the same time, they devote their energy to completing the tasks immediately before them.

Realism
Entrepreneurs accept things as they are and deal with them accordingly. They may or may not be idealistic, but they are seldom unrealistic. They will change their direction when they see that change will improve their prospects for achieving their goals. They want to know the status of a given situation at all times. They will verify any information they receive before they use it in making a decision. Entrepreneurs say what they mean and assume that everyone else does too. They tend to be too trusting and may not be sufficiently suspicious in their business dealings with other people.

Conceptual ability
Entrepreneurs possess the ability to identify relationships quickly in the midst of complex situations. They identify problems and begin working on their solution faster than other people. Entrepreneurs are natural leaders and are usually the first to identify a problem to be overcome. If it is pointed out to them that their solution to a problem will not work for some valid reason, they will quickly identify an alternative problem-solving approach.

Status requirements
Entrepreneurs find satisfaction in symbols of success that are external to themselves. They like the business they have built to be praised, but they are often embarrassed by praise directed at them personally. Their egos do not prevent them from seeking facts, data and guidance. When they need help, they will not hesitate to admit it, especially in areas that are outside of their expertise.

Interpersonal relationships
Entrepreneurs are more concerned with people's accomplishments than with their feelings. During the business-building period, when resources are scarce, they seldom devote time to dealing with satisfying people's feelings beyond what is essential to achieving their goals.

Emotional stability
Entrepreneurs have a considerable amount of self-control and can handle business pressures. They are comfortable in stress situations and are challenged rather than discouraged by setbacks or failures. Entrepreneurs tend to handle people problems with action plans without empathy. Their moderate interpersonal skills are often inadequate to provide for stable relationships.

SOURCE: Adapted from **www.businesstown.com/entrepreneur/article1.asp**

So far the discussion has addressed those individuals who believe themselves fit to take the step into enterprise in order to exploit a compelling business opportunity. There are, of course, others whose motives are defensive and perhaps born of desperation, driven to self-employment because no viable alternative presents itself.

Rates of entrepreneurship vary markedly between economies. In the OECD and EU, about 2 per cent of the economically active are entrepreneurs, in EAP and ECA about 5 per cent and in Latin America 8 per cent (Ardagna and Lusardi, 2010).

The countries in each category are as follows. **OECD:** Australia, Belgium, Canada, Denmark, Finland, France, Germany, Ireland, Italy, Japan, the Netherlands, Norway, New Zealand, Portugal, Spain, Sweden, Switzerland, the UK, the United States. **EU:** Belgium, Denmark, Finland, France, Germany, Ireland, Italy, the Netherlands, Portugal, Spain, Sweden, the UK. **ECA:** Croatia, Hungary, Poland, Russia, Slovenia. **EAP:** China, Hong Kong, Singapore, South Korea, Taiwan, Thailand. **Latin America** includes Argentina, Brazil, Chile, Mexico.

In Latin America, those going into business from necessity were three-quarters as many as those exploiting an opportunity compared with the OECD and EU at about one-fifth. More typical of those in the West is Christian McBride, who is quoted in an article in *Sunday Times Business* on 8 January 2012 as saying: 'I worked for another company that dealt with mobile phones and wanted to move it forward but was restricted. So I started my own.'

Where and how

Once entrepreneurs have decided that enterprise is for them, they need to look around at the environment in which they are to operate. Detailed environmental analysis, necessary for business planning, will be addressed in Part 3, Chapter 7; the discussion here is confined to a general overview.

Despite improvements, there are still some regions to be wary of. For example, a firm with ambitions to work internationally might want to choose a location other than southern Africa: 'In Sub-Saharan Africa 36 of 46 governments improved their economy's regulatory environment for domestic businesses in 2010/11 – a record number since 2005. This is good news for entrepreneurs in the region, **where starting and running a business is still costlier and more complex than in any other region of the world.**' (Emphasis added; The World Bank/International Finance Corporation, 2011: 2)

World Bank tables of international comparisons can only generalize; any specific business will have its own particular fit to the environment in which it operates. Thus an entrepreneur should also apply the model known in various versions as PEST or STEP, STEEP or STEEPLE to the business proposal.

Environmental analysis

The first version of this simple but powerful analytical model was STEP or PEST, the acronym for sociological, technological, economical and political. A later version saw the need to add a further E, for environmental, to make STEEP. Since the business analysis industry has a policy of constant improvement, matters could not be left there so L for legal and E for ethical are sometimes added.

Whichever version is used, the point is to look at the firm's **external environment** and list the relevant issues, both favourable and unfavourable, under each of the headings. That should show where vulnerabilities and opportunities might lie, and so feeds into the SWOT analysis, of which more later.

Task

Undertake an environmental analysis for the business of your choice in the country where it would be likely to operate. Identify the sources of opportunity and the sources of threat. In general terms, what can be done about each of them?

The broad-brush environmental analysis complete, the entrepreneur is ready to make the next move, to start on serious planning. Writing a properly structured business plan, rather than carrying it in the head, is **absolutely essential**. Why? Because:

- The act of writing it forces the entrepreneur to spot and resolve all the contradictions that mental plans contain.
- Following the structure of a business-plan template acts as a reminder of all the things that need to be considered, making the plan thorough, rigorous and complete.
- Running a business is complex: more complex than even a genius can carry in a human brain, so it has to go on paper to be manageable.
- The plan will turn out wrong (plans always do), too optimistic or too pessimistic: having it in writing makes it possible to pinpoint mistakes so as to learn from them.
- Everything in business is connected to everything else: a variation here can cause changes there and there and there – a written plan can recognize that; an unaided brain cannot.

As Drucker says: 'Plans are worthless but planning is invaluable.' Eisenhower said much the same thing.

Writing the plan need not be complicated but it does need several tries. Going over it again and again to recognize new or changed facts is a process known as 'iteration'. **All business planning is dynamic and iterative, so a plan, once written, remains a** living document – it does not disappear into a drawer, never to be seen again but is constantly being worked on, checked on and updated. This point is emphasized as it is of crucial importance.

What sort of firm to start

Success stories include people who stuck to a field they knew, as well as those who broke away into something completely novel. The only really sound advice that applies to everyone is this: take time to investigate every aspect before committing. Never again do I want to meet people like the tragic couple who, having taken early retirement because of the wife's health, took out a big loan and sank their savings into a hotel. Only once they had started did they realize it required from each of them 18 hours a day, seven days a week.

Even so, it is possible to come to a decision. Anyone undecided about what to do can try these as starting points:

- Using your knowledge of an industry, look for unsuspected opportunities in a field you know.
- Using your knowledge of a sport, game or pastime, seek ways to supply others with that interest profitably.
- Using your knowledge of an occupation or profession, supply erstwhile colleagues with some service they need.
- Look at things for sale on auction sites such as eBay to see what strange opportunities exist to sell almost anything.
- If you have contacts in retail or manufacturing, buy ends of ranges and seconds cheaply.
- Get a job in an SME (small or medium-sized enterprise) and learn how the firm works.
- Above all, look for problems that nobody else has bothered to solve.

If you conclude that you have no useful knowledge at all, check that belief with someone used to thinking creatively and laterally. It might be a family member, someone in the pub or a business adviser; the important thing is to free the mental logjam.

Unless there are very good reasons to the contrary, do not just copy on a small scale a former employer. If that was a manufacturer, you might be able to supply the market without making a thing, perhaps by linking up with a subcontractor or even an overseas supplier, relieving you of a great deal of trouble. A talk to the commercial attachés of the newer EU countries or even a trip to them could yield all kinds of opportunities to import or to act as sales agent in the UK.

These thoughts lead on to another, one of general principle. Which do you feel more comfortable with, the idea of dipping a toe in the water at first and building things up if it seems to work, or right from the start committing to doing the full job? In many types of business either is possible. Those are questions of temperament and you need to think out the answer for yourself, best of all with advice from someone who knows you well.

It is worth forming a relationship with a business adviser so as to have someone to bounce your ideas off. This must be someone with a fine balance between imagination and realism as well as experience outside a narrow, professional field.

Buying an existing firm

A ready-made firm that seems to be going well could look like a good short-cut through all the hassle of starting up. And so it may be but, as with used cars, there is a reason for the vendor to sell. That reason might be innocent or it might not. Two thousand years ago the Romans used to say *caveat emptor* (let the buyer beware), still sound advice today.

As with starting a business, buying an existing enterprise calls for deep and thorough investigation. If you are unfamiliar with the type of business concerned, ask to shadow the vendor for a week. That is how you will discover things you would not have suspected. For example, running a village shop might look restful, but how will your back stand up to shifting several tons of stock a week? That is a van-load lifted off the cash-and-carry shelves on to a trolley, off the trolley to the van, out of the van into the store and out of the store on to the shelves. Every week. Fine if you're young and strong, but perhaps not for someone less than fully fit.

Thanks to the supermarkets a large proportion of small shops are under threat – not just the grocers. Look at the growing range of goods they sell and ask yourself: 'How could I compete with this?' If you can think of a way, go ahead, but if not, be careful. Online traders can pose a similar threat. For example, most medium-sized towns are lucky if they have a single photographic shop. The reason is plain: people try out the £300 camera in-store, then buy it online for a little over £200. (This creates a problem for camera manufacturers. People want to look at and handle cameras before they buy. When the last camera shop closes, where will they go? Does this spell a business opportunity for someone – the 'test drive' shop where manufacturers pay to have their goods on display?)

Does the business depend on the involvement of the seller – does it virtually cease to exist without them? What is to stop them selling to you, then opening up again down the street? Your solicitor would ensure that there was a clause in the sale agreement to stop that particular trick, but you are potentially open to every form of human knavery.

When buying a business you are expected to pay for:

- any freehold or unexpired leasehold, which is reasonably easy to value independently;
- any machines, vehicles or equipment, again easily valued independently;
- stock, usually 'at valuation', a major source of trouble since the valuer might in haste not notice that the stack of boxes is hollow or that the liquid stock long ago dried out;
- 'goodwill', which is a payment for expected future profits: since it is based on assumed future earnings it can be highly contentious.

If you think it appropriate, try to get a clause in the sale contract to commit the seller to consultancy for three or six months, so that you have someone to turn to for information over anything puzzling you.

Franchises

The uncertainties of starting your own enterprise and the risks of buying an existing business can cause people to think of franchising. A franchise is a (usually) proven idea that is already running, offering the reassurance of an established model.

In a nutshell, you pay the franchisor a sum of anything from a few thousand to over a million pounds, sign an agreement to buy your supplies from the franchisor and observe certain standards, hire some premises and get to work. In return the franchisor usually offers national publicity and advertising support together with plentiful business advice. There may even be a loan scheme. As far as the public is concerned, you are just the local branch of an (inter-)national concern.

Many highly respectable firms offer franchises. There is an annual fair at which many exhibit.

You might ask:

- Do I need to buy a franchise to get into this business, or could I do it off my own bat?
- Am I the right person for this?
- What is the turnover of franchisees and why is this particular one available?
- Does the franchisor want a high fee up front and low continuing payments? Is this suspicious?
- What is the franchisor's record?
- Can I finance it, especially if sales turn out worse than they project?
- Have I evaluated this as carefully as I would my own business idea?

Talk to the banks (some employ franchising specialists), advisory agencies and (for the UK) the British Franchise Association (**www.thebfa.org**). Get your solicitor to explain the full range of your responsibilities under the agreement.

Green business opportunities

The opportunities for new businesses that take account of environmental concerns are many. Consumers and organizations seem keen to reduce waste and their carbon footprints; governments announce almost weekly new initiatives designed to boost the sector. It is such a new area that it presents both special risks and special opportunities: both are covered at greater length in Appendix 3.

Opportunities crop up almost daily, many offering to relieve society of its unwanted substances and therefore not offering the cleanest of working conditions and processes. At the time of writing, an enormous one has suddenly appeared. It seems that surplus food is at present macerated and flushed away down the drains. This presents water companies with problems so great that the practice is to be banned. What will hospitals, prisons, army bases and other large-scale caterers do with their surpluses? In the bad old days they were sold to local pig farmers to feed animals but waste food is thought to be a source of foot and mouth disease, so that is also banned. Someone will solve the problem and profit from it.

Conclusions

- People who naturally become entrepreneurs behave in special ways dictated by their personal characteristics. Some of those characteristics ensure that the firm is driven forward with the relentlessness essential to it taking its place in the world, but they can also ensure interpersonal strife and thus limit growth, unless they are consciously controlled.

- Women tend to be more cautious than men but often build sounder businesses. Their research tends to be more thorough and they take fewer risks. Consequently, they ought to be welcomed by financiers but that is not always the case.

- The decision to start a business can be driven by necessity or to exploit an opportunity: the state of the local economy is the main deciding factor. In the West it can be conjectured that the high, and increasing, level of regulation may curb entrepreneurial activity either by deterring entrepreneurs from founding firms or by persuading them to avoid employing people.

- The attractiveness of business environments varies greatly between countries and regions, some of the variation being accounted for by official action, but mostly due to the vigour of the local economy.

- Formal, written business plans are essential, otherwise the complexity of interrelationships cannot be recognized. Moreover, the absence of a written plan denies the opportunity for comparison between plan and outcome, and thence for learning.

- The written business plan is a living, dynamic document that is constantly being worked over and updated as time moves forward.

- Buying an existing firm or a franchise may look like a quick way into business but still requires considerable investigation. While much of the uncertainty of the initial launch phase is eliminated, there is usually a price to pay in lower margins and loss of control, and vigilance is essential to avoid possibly calamitous error.

- New business opportunities abound in the newer business sectors. Anywhere that change is taking place may look chaotic and thus to be avoided, but often it spells opportunity.

03
Not-for-profit (NFP) entrepreneurship

In this chapter

LEARNING OUTCOMES

By the end of this chapter you should be able to:

- understand the special situation of NFP organizations;
- see the particular position of the entrepreneur in the NFP sector;
- recognize the range of organizational forms available and their implications.

Entrepreneurship and the NFP sector

Application of the ideas of entrepreneurship has come to the NFP sector only lately. Until quite recently entrepreneurship was thought of as belonging firmly in the private sector, to be deployed solely for the purposes of personal satisfaction and enrichment.

Here there is a danger of terms with similar, but different, meanings being used interchangeably. 'Social entrepreneurs' perceive some need in society and create and run organizations aimed at addressing it. They can act in both the for-profit and the NFP sectors – witness the many organizations that have intentions usually associated with the charitable sector, yet are operating like businesses. It is a term that is so elastic that it can be used to embrace the likes of the great Quaker business-people such as those in the UK behind Rowntree's who, while businesspeople first and foremost, tried to give their employees good working and living conditions and to guide their moral welfare. Social entrepreneurs can take the general principles so far offered in this book and apply them more or less directly.

True NFPs, however, are different. While they, too, seek to address social ills they have traditionally distanced themselves from commercial or quasi-commercial activity. Admittedly, the traditional boundaries are blurring, as registered charities step up the level of activity of their commercial arms that raise funds via profitable trading, but as it is a useful distinction, and it is still possible to tell the NFP from the rest, so the term will be used here.

The NFP heritage

NFPs have existed for a long time. In the Victorian era (1819–1901) many of the huge fortunes made from the growth of industry and empire were ploughed back into society. Christianity may have played its part: the injunction to look after those less fortunate, coupled with the threat that the rich would not get into heaven, may have influenced attitudes to the retention and spreading of wealth. Organizations sprang up everywhere to address all kinds of needs. One example in the UK might be the National Trust, the driving force behind which was Octavia Hill, a serial social entrepreneur who had taken on challenges in providing housing for the poor and protecting London's open spaces. Today the National Trust is a vast organization with over 4 million members. Still today, as new problems emerge, or old problems are reinterpreted, new organizations come into being to deal with them or existing organizations evolve in order to cope.

Arguably the greatest ever writer on organizational management, Peter Drucker, wrote with typical robustness and humanity:

> "The 'non-profit' institution neither supplies goods or services nor controls*. Its 'product' is neither a pair of shoes nor an effective regulation. Its product is a changed human being. The non-profit institutions are human-change agents. Their 'product' is a cured patient, a child that learns, a young man or woman grown into a self-respecting adult; a changed human life altogether" (Drucker, 1990).

(*compared to government, which does control.)

Today's NFP operator's job differs from the commercial entrepreneur's situation in one key respect: the number of stakeholders that needs to be taken into account. (A 'stakeholder' is a person or body that has some sort of interest in the organization plus power or influence. That influence can help to advance the organization's objectives or it can have the potential to block them.) Think of a simple shopkeeping operation. A commercial shop has customers, suppliers, staff, the bank and the landlord to worry about. A charity shop has all of those plus the Charity Commission as well as a variety of supporters upon whose goodwill its success depends. Volunteer staff need different handling from employed staff and can present many more headaches; donors of goods for sale must continuously be courted; cash handling must be above suspicion, yet systems may be antiquated and volunteer staff unaware of the need to observe rigorous disciplines.

As NFP organizations move to embrace the managerial techniques of the for-profit sector, adopting its vocabulary and, in some cases, some of its values, it is possible that the distinctions may blur further. There is in any case a long history of philanthropy by those who have made their pile: without it the universities of the United States would be much poorer. The shining examples among many worthies are perhaps the great US steel magnate, Andrew Carnegie, who declared that it was wicked for a man to die rich and set about giving away his enormous fortune, and Microsoft co-founder Bill Gates who has devoted billions of dollars already to challenge disease. On a smaller scale, but no less worthy, is Genuine Solutions Group's Christian McBride. His UK mobile phone company collects used and surplus accessories from various sources, repairs for reuse where possible and reclaims the materials where not. So far, so normal, except that turnover is £100 million after only six years. He puts that expertise to work to help charities, providing materials and know-how to help them flush out disused phones for which he gives a fair market price, feeding them into his main, commercial, operation. In this example, where does conventional entrepreneurship end and NFP entrepreneurship start?

The social entrepreneur and social enterprise

The term 'social enterprise' is much used for reasons that seem more connected to image and perception than to reality. In general contexts it provides a useful generalization to denote the phenomenon brought into being by the social entrepreneur, but for more serious purposes it has no place. The fact is that there is no legal definition of social enterprise: it is no more than a popular catch-all term for enterprises that reinvest any profits into community welfare (whatever form those profits might take – see Drucker above). Consequently, in any discussion of the form that a community-based organization is to take, the term 'social enterprise' is best left to one side.

A number of recognized forms exist which carry legal force from among which the social entrepreneur will choose. The choice depends on several factors, including:

- the nature of the governing body: paid or voluntary?;
- the certainty that purposes will remain unchanged over time (the 'asset lock');
- likely sources of income;
- likely magnitude of risk;
- attitude to risk.

For any entrepreneur for whom the last two points loom large, some form of limited liability status will appeal – but there can be drawbacks (see below). Some will wish the purpose of the organization to remain constant, others to see it flex with social changes. Consider the Metropolitan Drinking Fountain and Cattle Trough Association, founded in London in 1859 to improve an aspect of animal welfare, it ceased building horse troughs in 1935 (now called the Drinking Fountains Association, it still provides fountains for humans).

Unincorporated associations

The NFP field has its own equivalent of the commercial sole trader or partnership, where one person (or for a partnership, more than one) decides to get on with some needed social intervention, and so forms an unincorporated association. The paperwork is close to zero – there is no need to register with anyone – and the risks are similar – the individual(s) are responsible for all of the organization's liabilities. In these days of no win-no fee lawyers who can pursue the silliest and most frivolous claims at no cost to the supposedly aggrieved person, this is a serious consideration.

The association will usually have a written constitution that lays out how the organization runs itself – such matters as the appointment of officers, frequency of meetings, voting arrangements and so on – and how any spoils are to be divided if it is dissolved.

Unincorporated trusts

An unincorporated trust is more formal than the association. If someone gives a sum of money or some other asset to a group of people (the trustees) and asks them to use it charitably on behalf of some section of the community, a trust exists. The arrangement will be confirmed in a deed of trust which will set out the arrangements for the organization's conduct in the same way as does the constitution of an association. Once more, the trustees are exposed to personal responsibility for the organization's liabilities.

Charitable incorporated organizations

A further problem with the less formal forms of organization is that the original purpose may easily be overturned by disagreements among the founding members or by new members gaining a majority vote. An effective way of insulating the purpose from this threat is to set up as a registered charitable incorporated organization. This is costly, in that charities are regulated rigorously but, to compensate, tax treatment is lenient.

Community interest companies

These have come about as a result of legislation passed in 2005. They confer limited liability (that is, those setting up and running the organization are largely protected from personal liability) but incur heavy regulation and policing to ensure that the purposes are being fulfilled.

Community benefit societies (BenComms)

BenComms are similar to community interest companies from the point of view of their founders, but work under stricter regulation of who might benefit from their activities.

Limited companies

If after due consideration none of the above forms suits the particular need of an entrepreneur, thought may move towards this long-established form. Contrary to the popular view, limited companies are not used solely by the for-profit sector. Such is the flexibility of the form that it can be made to serve almost any purpose in the NFP field as well.

On the topic of limited liability, its attractiveness to the risk-averse social entrepreneur makes it equally unattractive to risk-averse bankers or landlords. Knowing that entrepreneurs can avoid personal liability for loans taken out or leases signed in the name of a limited company, they will probably demand personal guarantees from the principals of the organization, whatever its form, where limited liability exists.

Grasping the differences is made easier by the UK Business Link website, where a tabular analysis shows the main features of each of the available forms at:

www.businesslink.gov.uk/Taxes_and_Returns_files/LegalStructures.doc

Conclusions

- Just as private-sector managerialism has been embraced by the NFP sector with the aim of increasing efficiency, so general ideas of entrepreneurship can be applied successfully in the NFP sector in order to respond to new social challenges and provide answers to needs.

- NFP entrepreneurs are driven by the same vision of introducing improvements as are those in the private sector, but their rewards lie more in social rather than in private gain.

- NFP entrepreneurs need to take account of a much wider range of stakeholders than those in the private sector.

- The range of formal options available to the social entrepreneur is wide, each offering benefits and posing difficulties. The decision on which form to adopt is complex and multifaceted.

PART 2:
Evaluations

04
Business ideas – creation and evaluation

In this chapter

LEARNING OUTCOMES

By the end of this chapter you should be able to:

- create business ideas;
- understand general points about creativity;
- evaluate business ideas.

Creativity and innovation

This topic is important. Drucker (1974) wrote: 'Business has only two functions – marketing and innovation' and again: 'Innovation is the specific instrument of entrepreneurship... the act that endows resources with a new capacity to create wealth' (Drucker, 2007).

So innovating and being creative is half of the entrepreneur's core function. We'll come to marketing later, but for the present we'll examine aspects of the vital topic of innovation.

Creating business ideas

Where do ideas come from? How does creativity really work? Anyone with the definitive answer could sell very expensive consultancy to the biggest corporations and governments on earth. Mere mortals have to make do with a mixture of common sense, experience handed down and the signposts given us by the psychologists.

First, we'll start with definitions of 'ideas' and 'creativity': not the dictionary ones, but the way that these words actually work in real businesses.

Business and the big idea

Every successful business – even if it's only a small firm – is powered by a big idea. It comes before the product, the market, the premises, the staff, the money or anything else. (Those things are vitally important, of course, and we'll come to them later in great detail, but it helps a lot if you first develop a big idea to drive your company.)

Consider a religious or political movement; the whole point of a religion or a political party is that it puts forward a big idea, in these cases a picture of future bliss, either in an afterlife or here on earth. In the case of Germany's Christian Democrats, perhaps both. The human need to believe in some meaning beyond mundane daily existence makes such ideas the most potent commodity known to man. They are responsible for all the political and social revolutions that have ever taken place, for the way that we live our lives and for the way we bring up our children.

Tap into the strength of the big idea, and you harness a surge of power that can carry a business on to worldwide recognition. Consider what I see as the big ideas behind these great businesses:

- John Lewis Partnership: if the staff own and run the company, they really care.

- Apple: offers powerful IT made relevant and easy, presented in beautiful forms.

- Mercedes-Benz: utmost performance and reliability is enjoyed in comfort.

Two of these firms started some generations ago, one more recently. What drives them, and drives their public appeal, is not the product itself, but the big idea behind it.

There is no government control on ideas, no exam to pass, no licence to buy – to power a business with a big idea all you have to do is to think, to project your mind into that of the customer, to think what that person really wants. And then you have to put it into action, in every aspect of your operations. Make everything you do, say, write or make fully consistent with that big idea.

That consistency is important. Suppose your big idea is to make the best-engineered kitchens in the world: the finest design, the best materials and made to the closest tolerances; inevitably, dizzyingly expensive. Think of the customer who buys your kitchen, then finds it is installed by ill-mannered people who make a mess and run weeks over schedule. Too expensive to do the installation well? Ask yourself if a footballer earning £100,000 a week cares about the extra £10,000 it costs to have the finest kitchen in Cheshire installed by people so discreet they might as well not be there. It's not enough to do one part of the job well – the whole of the customer's experience has to be consistent with the big idea. That runs well beyond installation, to after-sales service and even a phone call a few weeks before the guarantee expires to see if there are any niggles to be sorted out.

What could be the consequences? For a small firm that intends only ever to service a local market, that business should become a permanent fixture that everyone flocks to, which scares off thoughtful potential competitors who realize that they could never compete, and flattens the foolish ones who dare to try. For a firm with operations that are scalable, it could lead to national or even global standing.

Scalability: is bigger better?

Some firms are limited to being one-person operations, simply because there are few, if any, benefits to be gained from making them grow. Let's take as an example a domestic window cleaner. The costs of entry are low (basic equipment, simple marketing are needed) and the only market resistance comes from people happy with their present arrangements. The service is provided by the business owner, with all that implies for quality, responsiveness and low overheads. What could a multi-employee firm offer instead? It would stand a chance only where there was a shortage of window cleaners. It might get some business, whereupon the staff doing the work would quickly see their chance, resign and offer the service themselves. Thus the multi-employee firm would quickly fail. The only way it could work would be in offering a total glass-cleaning service to firms with large or multiple premises, where a number of staff would be needed because of the size or dispersal of the job.

On the other hand, many businesses are scalable, that is to say they can be built up from one member of staff to several, dozens or far more. Precision engineers might start with a couple of CNC machines that they alone operate, acquiring more and more as they gain more and bigger customers and ending up with an empire in which they wear a suit and tie all day and spend half of their time out of the country.

Many, many types of business are scalable. However, if your ambition is to get big, be sure that you go into the sort of business that can grow, not one that will prove to be a dead end.

What governs scalability? Basically, as the firm grows there must be disproportionate gains from occupying more or bigger premises, buying more materials and supplies, employing more people, shipping greater quantities or having more or bigger customers. If your firm cannot show at least one of those, and preferably more, do not expect to make it grow significantly.

Kelly Hoppen MBE, a designer, handles the problem of scaling-up her business cleverly. Many designers are limited by the amount of work they can take on by their need to do or supervise everything themselves. Ms Hoppen's deepest involvements are at the start and the end of each of her big design projects, but she sets things up to run almost without her between times. She makes the sale and masterminds the design plan, but then assigns members of her team to carry it out. She is available to help and advise, obviously, but while the team are sweating over the current job she is off working on the next, which may be on the other side of the world. Once a project is finished, she inspects it to make sure that the agreed brief has been fully met and delivered to her high standards. Only once she is satisfied is it handed over to the customer. In that way the customer gets the full Kelly Hoppen product but in a way that does not limit the designer to working on a single project at a time.

The big idea doesn't have to be complicated – indeed, it's probably best if it is simple. Think of the example of the shirtmaker T M Lewin, based in London's West End, who had a single shop in the 1970s and grew in 30 years to 85 branches, plus a thriving mail-order and web-based business. Rather than selling an individual shirt for around £30, the firm packaged four together for £100. Customers often felt confused about choosing between a number of attractive styles, and the package gave them permission to spoil themselves and buy several instead of one or two. Due to that simple idea, the average sale rose from something over £30 to close to £100.

The big idea can come about just by observing the constant swirl of events. Outsourcing has created innumerable opportunities for experts in some business process or activity to set up their own outsourcing operations. Again, the move to cloud computing (discussed elsewhere in more detail) means that immense computing power is available to anyone. This change means that where a decade ago only very rich individuals or big corporations could contemplate running an IT-intensive business, now anyone can do it. However, to know what the opportunities might be, one needs to keep up to date with what is going on.

A business idea is almost always the result of someone making an unusual connection, of seeing things in a new light and reasoning things through in a new way. Afterwards everyone says: 'Why didn't I think of that? It's so obvious!', but before the event it was anything but. Yet some people seem to have the gift while others lack it completely.

How can you raise the chances of it being *you* that makes the next breakthrough? In three ways:

- Know more than other people – read, listen, observe; always be 'on duty', looking out for things you did not know; explore how things are done in contexts with which you are unfamiliar (other organizations, other industries, other countries).

- Talk to other people, but make sure always to listen for four times as long as you speak.

- From the storehouse of knowledge that your brain builds up, look for discontinuities, for problems, for frustrations and unnecessary complications. Focus on those problems and design solutions.

What sort of reading should an entrepreneur do? The three main categories are:

- For what's going on and what's new: read serious business newspapers and magazines.

- For inspiration and to avoid reinventing the wheel: read the history of business, especially biographies of great businesspeople and histories of great organizations; science and the history of science, to see the amazing story of how we got to where we are; listen to jokes, look at cartoons, for all humour subverts assumptions.

- For managerial technique: extensions of the reading you will need to do for your course.

A word here about history. Many English people are persuaded at school that history is composed entirely of the Tudors and aspects of both world wars. An older generation learned that it relates to a time-line of monarchs, states and battles. While that was perhaps more complete, it still grossly misrepresents what history can and should mean to the entrepreneur. To the businessperson, history is no less than the distillation of other people's experience – moreover, the experience of people who have gone the same way before. If you were venturing into shark-infested waters you would listen to someone who had been in them earlier that day. Why dismiss the views of someone who did it 50 years earlier? A few things may have changed, but sharks have been around for over 400 million years. Learning by other people's mistakes, and successes, is simply the intelligent thing to do.

Remember, too, that reading need not be the chore that it can sound. Make use of the different qualities of reading, different ways of doing it, each suited to a different need: for any particular document you can go in for:

- skimming – looking only for your main areas of interest, triggered by key words or phrases;

- speed-reading – a bit more thorough than skimming but still not reading and pondering every word;

- reading in depth – consuming and digesting every point made by the writer, reflecting on them and forming your own view by comparing the writer's ideas with your own experience.

Questions

What is the chief source of the ideas reported in this book's mini case studies in the 'Learning resources' section near the end of this book?

Do any of the ideas exploit discontinuities, solve problems, relieve frustrations or simplify?

Where does undercutting competitors on price feature?

Are any of the mini case studies based on any other principle?

Is it possible that someone once said: 'If only they would…' and one of Pasteur's 'prepared minds' was listening (see below)?

Just cutting prices rarely works, as established firms are usually better placed than a newcomer to win any price war. Look around at any successful firm and, I suggest, you'll find it was founded to solve a problem for its customers – getting rid of complexity, frustrations or inefficiencies. Solve a problem and you've struck on a business idea. It's still got to pass other tests, but it's a place to start.

Once you've got one idea, don't stop, but keep on thinking. Keep playing around with the problem, putting the pieces together in a different order and taking out pieces or putting in new ones. As Darwin teaches us, in its extraordinary quest to improve an organism's fit to its environment, nature generates many variations, most of which die off, but the few that survive go on to reproduce. Nature is wasteful of its innovations and it is just as wasteful of entrepreneurs' ideas – the estimate is that fewer than one-tenth make it through the tests of real life.

That fact should not deter if you remember the maxim of that brilliant innovator, Louis Pasteur: 'Fortune favours the prepared mind'. Prepare your mind and risk being lucky.

In passing, another saying on luck is from Sam Goldwyn, one of the three founders of MGM, who echoed the words of Jefferson: 'The harder I work the luckier I get'. Hard work is assumed; what gives the edge is not working harder (and possibly heading for a breakdown) but working more thoughtfully, more inventively and more intelligently than the average.

Creativity

This can be a difficult area for some people, a bit like maths. The fact that they've convinced themselves that they're no good at it becomes a self-fulfilling prophecy. If only they'd contain their fear, recognize that they've nothing to lose and have a go at some of the techniques, they might surprise themselves. We can *all* be creative (just as we can *all* do the maths taught at school – but we need first to believe it's possible and second someone to show us how).

If you enjoy quizzes and want a break from study you could try an online creativity test. Here are two examples. The first is a bit breathless and Californian, the second rather more serious: http://creativityforlife.com/2011/12/28/quiz-are-you-creative/ and www.creax.com/csa/

Whether or not you took a test, whether or not it gave you low marks, the fact is that creative thinking can be learned. In this chapter so far we've already discussed some of the techniques for having ideas – isn't that just what creativity is about? The good news is that there are a few more ideas available to help us (see Table 4.1).

The technique known as brainstorming can be useful. The name has been in use for more than half a century but has recently been criticized as insensitive to people with epilepsy (though one epileptic of my acquaintance, a trainer, used the term quite happily). What it involves is, essentially, allowing the mind to run free along the lines of the predetermined topic. It works best with groups of a dozen or so but can be useful with small numbers of people or even individuals.

TABLE 4.1   Ideas-generation techniques

Technique	Practical illustration
New visions	Seeing the impact of the rise of internet shopping on transport and delivery services
Connecting	Putting IT into an established market to change the game
Visualizing	Asking the 'what if?' questions; asking 'Who else needs to do this sort of thing and how do they do it?'
Information search	Combing data to look for gaps that could be filled, rising and falling sectors
Upending	For example, instead of selling phones then billing for use, selling airtime and giving the phone 'free'
Inquisitiveness	Asking 'How does this work? How do other firms or industries deal with similar problems?'
Observing	Looking at all sorts of industries and businesses to see how they do things
Solving problems	Identifying existing problems (felt anywhere in the industry's supply chain) and solving them

Brainstorming

The idea is to gather as many ideas as possible in a short time, however crazy they may seem, then to sift for the good ones. It depends on the belief that we are usually self-censoring to an extent that inhibits creativity. By eliminating criticism from the stage at which ideas are created, brainstorming claims to produce a richer mass of ideas. Most will eventually be rejected, but none will be strangled at birth.

At the time of idea-generation there is no criticism – the focus is on more and more ideas, all of them written down in full view of the brainstormers as soon as they come up. Ignoring assumptions and introducing apparently unrelated perspectives helps here, as does taking ideas from the list and developing them further. However far-fetched the idea, it is not to be laughed at or commented on.

Once all the ideas are in the focus shifts to evaluation. Here the brainstormers consider the practicality of the ideas, sorting the possibly workable from the probably unworkable. The person or group owning the problem takes them away for further consideration.

There's a simple guide to brainstorming for individuals and groups at: **www.mindtools.com/brainstm.html**. Another website (**www.virtualsalt.com/crebook1.htm**) gives a thorough analysis of creative thinking with 'how to' tips and interesting examples of how changing the frame of reference can cure the problem.

Creative thinking, the British and the Irish

When there was a shortage of oil-based products in the 1970s, UK filling stations enforced a maximum purchase of four gallons (about 18 litres). Result? People went from station to station, queuing for hours to get their four gallons or even less at each station in order to keep their tanks full.

The Irish, as the British might have expected, went the other way. They enforced a *minimum* fill of four gallons, so that a near-empty tank could be filled to the top but there was no point in buying a small quantity. Queues were never seen.

Now, was that difficult?

If you're really stuck – or if you want to get even more creative – take a look at Roger van Oech's *Creative Whack Pack*, a pack of 84 techniques for seeing a situation differently. At the time of writing, as a set of cards it costs $10.88 from Amazon or as an iPhone App it's $US 1.99 (about £1.50) from: **http://itunes.apple.com/us/app/creative-whack-pack/id307306326?mt=8**

Not all situations demand a throbbing intellect: some opportunities are seen as soon as the fact is stated. For example, *The Sunday Times* reported about China on 8 January 2012: '50% of Chinese big spenders say they plan to take up sailing' and 'The number of millionaires is expected to rise from 500,000 to 800,000 within three years.'

'Sailing' can be taken not only in its own right, but also as an example of probably most Western luxury goods. How could the creative entrepreneur benefit from this? Selling direct to the Chinese market is an obvious route, but if you think of how these people will find the products on which to spend their cash, more opportunities emerge. If they are to see the full range of what's on offer they will have to travel, mostly to Europe and the United States. Aside from all the yachting paraphernalia that could be sold, anyone with a telephone, a computer and a driving licence could set up as a specialized driver and fixer to work out an itinerary, book accommodation, set up meetings and conduct buyers to manufacturers' showrooms using a hired car. Do a good job and word-of-mouth could do the rest.

Evaluation

You have now assembled an impressive list of business ideas (well, at least one), and the time has come to pick the winner and discard the losers. If you really have only one idea there's nothing wrong with that, but instead you'll be assessing it for viability.

When it comes to sorting out your new ideas into the good and the bad, you may be confused. How do you decide? The eminent expert on creativity, Dr Edward de Bono, has a trick that could help: his 'six hats' technique. 'The biggest enemy of thinking is complexity, for that leads to confusion. When thinking is clear and simple it becomes more enjoyable and more effective' (De Bono, 1985).

While the six hats are mainly meant to reduce conflict in meetings and ensure better outcomes from them, as an individual you can use them too as a way of exploring your judgements from the points of view of:

- the information you have;
- your emotional responses to it;
- the bad aspects – useful to eternal optimists as it points out the possible problems;
- the benefits – where the eternal optimists come into their own;
- creativity and novel possibilities;
- process control (needed by the chairperson of a meeting).

That all has to do with refining the idea, a very necessary activity. After that come the tests that really matter:

- Does it solve a real problem or are we just imagining things?
- Are we the people to solve it (either using our own resources or by buying in expertise)?
- What is the cost of the solution and will enough people pay what we will have to charge?

At this stage it is unlikely that you can be utterly certain of the answer to any of these questions. But you need more than just gut feeling if you are to create a serious business plan and invest a chunk of your life and money in pursuing the idea. Nonetheless, these tests must be passed.

We have now reached one of the most difficult phases of the launch of a new business, the point at which dreams collide with reality. There is no alternative to going out and speaking to potential customers, presenting the idea and seeing what response it evokes. (**Important note: please read the later section on patents, registered designs and copyright before ever discussing the idea with anyone outside the business**. Why? Do it the wrong way and you could unwittingly destroy your claim that the product is your idea.)

To do a realistic job you may need some idea of the price you will have to charge. Without a lot of research into the costs of utilities, premises, staff, taxes and a lot of other things you simply cannot say. At some point later in the process you will do all of that research, but at this early stage you can simply side-step the matter.

When interviewing potential customers they will ask what you will charge for this new product or service. Your answer can be along the lines that it's too early to do detailed costings, but could the customer tell you what he or she would be prepared to pay, based on the improvements it would bring or the savings it will make? Some customers will answer truthfully but others will craftily try to beat you down to a low price – a price at which it would probably be uneconomic for you to sell. You'll need to evaluate the customers as well as the information they are giving. In any case, this is very much a first run, and any indication at all is an improvement on the complete ignorance which is all you can claim at the moment. Ask, too, about how they made their evaluation – you'll learn a lot about how buyers' minds work as well as getting valuable information on how to pitch your sales presentation when the time comes.

Don't be too downhearted about the figures you are given. When it comes to live selling you will have a far more complete proposition to put (see the chapters in Part 3 on selling and marketing) and will be able to justify pricing possibly quite a lot higher than a buyer's first impression suggests. Once you have developed some idea of the range of likely prices (perhaps with an uplift for the extra sales appeal you will create) you can do the detailed calculations of costs, on the simple principle that you will not set out to sell below cost. Comparing cost with price produces a straightforward go/no go decision.

Conclusions

- Most new business ideas come about through seeing problems to be solved and/or making an unusual connection. Some ideas (such as the iPhone) demand extraordinary levels of technical skill, but the vast majority of ideas on which new businesses are founded involve no more than spotting something straightforward that could be done better (such as Snap-On Tools taking their mobile showroom and warehouse – in the back of a van – round to garages and engineers).

- Ideas may present themselves spontaneously, but the odds improve if the mind is prepared. Preparation does not involve standard formulae but requires being aware of and inquisitive about developments in the world; often great ideas come from transferring an idea from one field to another, so that finding out about apparently irrelevant things can yield benefits.

- While innate creativity varies from person to person, anyone can employ simple tools to raise their own performance. Sometimes collaborative effort works best, sometimes the individual (prepared) mind.

- Once ideas have been generated they need to be evaluated so as to sift out the potentially useful ones and discard the rest: at this point they might be exposed to potential customers to evoke responses, but a well-founded (note only a well-founded) conviction should not give way to unimaginative responses from customers. Equally, only a fool would proceed in the face of massive customer resistance. Telling the difference between the two situations requires judgement, a characteristic that cannot be taught.

- Responses from customers to research activity do no more than indicate – buyers react differently to research questions than to sales presentations, a fact that can be misleading and deeply frustrating.

- If the idea should be protected by design registration or patent, it must never be disclosed outside the company before professional advice is had from a patent agent. Once a provisional patent has been taken out the world may be told, but it is prudent to insure against the risk of copying.

05
Running a business yourself

In this chapter

LEARNING OUTCOMES

By the end of this chapter you should be able to:

- understand the demands that entrepreneurship places on a human being;
- recognize the personal characteristics that help (and those that don't);
- describe the difference between being a boss in a big organization and being an entrepreneur;
- see how advisers might help.

The demands of entrepreneurship

Running a business is, in a word, busy. There is a lot to do and, in the early days, probably only you to do it. If you are to avoid being overwhelmed you need to not jump straight in, but think first.

The key tricks are simply stated:

- Spend your time as if there were only one hour in the day; that is, with great care.
- Choose what to work on; don't let other people dictate your agenda.
- Concentrate on what produces the results; neglect trivia.

Good use of time can be managed, though, and the key word is 'managed'. Most of the really effective managers use three tools:

- Pareto analysis;
- the priority matrix;
- time targets.

All of these tools aim to do one simple thing: ensure that you use your time to best advantage. Take the example of two people of reasonable intelligence and education who live to the same age. Over their lives they get exactly the same allowance of time, yet one may be highly successful, the other not. What makes the difference? The answer is: **how they put their time to use.**

Pareto analysis

The Italian economist Vilfredo Pareto (1848–1923) found that 80 per cent of the wealth in Italy was owned by 20 per cent of the population. From that finding much research was done in many fields, culminating in the '80/20 rule', which states that, in most situations, about 80 per cent of the effects come from about 20 per cent of the causes. In a shop, that means around four-fifths of the sales come from one-fifth of the stock; in a sales force, four-fifths of the business comes from one-fifth of the customers; and in a firm like yours, **four-fifths of your profit will come from one-fifth of your effort.**

It is perfectly obvious where to focus your time: on the few things that will achieve a lot. Conversely, you will avoid or postpone the majority of things that earn relatively little.

The message becomes even more stark if you apply the 80/20 rule to the rule itself: 80 per cent of 80 per cent is 64 per cent; 20 per cent of 20 per cent is 4 per cent. This suggests that 64 per cent of your results will come from a mere 4 per cent of your work. Just think what that means: in a couple of hours you could earn two-thirds of a week's income.

FIGURE 5.1   Pareto analysis

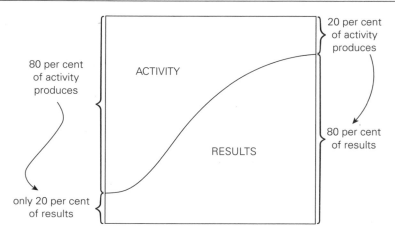

The priority matrix

Everything you do, or don't do, can be put into one of the four boxes on Figure 5.2.

FIGURE 5.2   The priority matrix

	IMPORTANCE	
	High	Low
High	Urgent and important	Urgent but unimportant
Low	Important but not urgent	Neither urgent nor important

The entrepreneur is faced with a challenge in which there is never enough time to do everything, and so is faced with a stark choice: either to try to do everything, fail to do so and probably become ill, or to be highly selective about where time is spent. Pareto showed us why; here we look at how. Train yourself to:

- look at each e-mail, letter, phone call or visitor;
- stop for a split second to place it in the correct box on the matrix;
- deal with them accordingly.

This way you get all the important things done. You may even do nothing at all from the bottom right-hand box, at least until tasks there have migrated to another box, but a lot will just sit there and fade away. No problem: deal with them once they migrate, but not before. You will save a lot of time.

Above all, do not aim for perfection. If you do, you will waste time on trivia – time that is better spent on important things.

Time targets

For each task that you elect to do, set a target time or date for completion – and stick to it. If you are falling behind, look at the task list and see if some reordering is needed. Learn from where and why you went wrong and don't make the same mistake next time. Be as unforgiving of yourself as you would be of an employee who persistently failed to deliver what was promised.

What do you do with the rest of the time? You can, of course, take it too far.

If Tesco offered little more than pet food, washing powder, cornflakes and wine, some people with eccentric lifestyles might still shop there, but most would go away.

Just as Tesco has to carry lots of slow-moving products, so you will have to do a certain amount of low-profit work. Nonetheless, it is vital to minimize it and ask yourself two questions: from minute to minute ask, 'Am I, at this moment, doing the right thing?'; at the start of each day ask, 'Am I planning to do the right things today?'

Family matters

Family does matter: businesspeople need understanding and support from their nearest and dearest. An absent mother, father, spouse or sweetheart tries the patience and dumps responsibilities on others, yet you will still want to be looked after following your difficult day. Moreover, there may be times when money is tight – think what that could do to cherished relationships. So keep others in the picture, listen to their viewpoints and keep them on board. You, personally, may at first find it hard to come to grips with your new situation. If you are used to long hours, hard work, uncertainty and stress, you have some idea of what is in store. You may need to pick up all sorts of new skills quickly. Ideally you are a person who:

- takes responsibility for your actions;
- has a go, but assesses risks first;
- is disciplined, sticking to the task even when things get tough;
- understands most of the jobs that will be done in the new firm;
- picks up information quickly;
- has reasonable intelligence and a good memory;
- is imaginative, seeing problems before they crop up and getting round them;
- looks for better ways to do things;
- leads, rather than being led;
- keeps clear records;
- can make yourself understood easily;
- gets your own way, pleasantly;
- has good general health and bags of energy;
- really, really wants to succeed.

Don't get depressed – it says 'ideally'. Few people get 100 per cent on all of those measures and, in any case, there are short cuts. If your memory is poor, you have probably found ways of keeping notes and filing them. If you are unimaginative, you can use other people to have bright ideas (there are all sorts of sources of help – see later). If you don't naturally keep records, you can either employ someone who does or discipline yourself to do it. And so on. If you are inclined to doubt yourself, think of the generations of immigrants over the past century who moved to foreign countries with nothing, yet built great business empires. Don't you have a head start already?

If you are worried about failure, reflect on what many tycoons say: that their failures taught them what they needed to know in order to succeed. Failure is a permanent state only if you make it so.

Personal characteristics

Many people who start businesses fall into one of these categories: craft or technical specialists, managers, salespeople or administrators. Each has strengths and weaknesses.

The craft or technical specialist

Strengths are:

- practicality;
- know-how;
- curiosity about how things work;
- creativity;
- high standards;
- concern for detail.

Weaknesses are:

- being more interested in things than people;
- undervaluing their work;
- missing the big picture;
- making things better and more expensively than the market wants;
- being obsessed with the product rather than customers;
- spurning sales skills, believing that good things should speak for themselves.

The key challenge for craft and technical specialists is getting on top of the people skills. If they team up with someone, that person should have a big vision, perhaps a salesperson.

The manager

Strengths are:

- getting things done to deadlines;
- planning;
- dealing with and managing people (some managers, that is);
- vision;
- understanding complexity;
- language and numeracy (some managers).

Weaknesses are:

- being used to an institutional setting where many essential things are done by others;

- being unused to doing the detailed dirty work;
- sometimes having an inflated sense of personal importance;
- belief that the small firm is just a microcosm of the big firm (whereas it is qualitatively different);
- difficulty in switching from institutional to entrepreneurial life.

The key challenge for managers is making the transition from narrow to total responsibility.

The salesperson

Strengths are:

- vision;
- optimism;
- drive;
- persistence;
- people skills.

Weaknesses are:

- misplaced self-confidence;
- being unused to doing the detailed dirty work;
- over-optimism;
- inexperience of the complexity of other commercial functions;
- making commitments incautiously;
- believing paperwork unnecessary;
- spending heavily on 'front';
- overriding colleagues through force of personality, even when others are right.

The key challenge for salespeople is to grasp the complexity of the whole while still using sales skills effectively. A good partner would be a strong-minded administrator.

The administrator

Strengths are:

- getting things done to deadlines;
- planning;
- understanding complexity;
- numeracy;
- organization;
- meticulousness;

- keeping records and being able to access them;
- caution.

Weaknesses are:

- being over-cautious;
- being indecisive;
- having narrow vision;
- lack of social confidence;
- lack of people skills.

The key challenge for administrators is broadening their vision and developing people skills. An ideal partner would be a salesperson.

Women entrepreneurs

Compared to most men entering business, most women are:

- harder working;
- more careful;
- more accurate;
- more serious;
- more enquiring;
- more likely to admit to inability;
- more likely to seek and listen to advice;
- quieter and less flamboyant;
- less inclined to push themselves forward;
- better at dealing with people;
- more likely to worry;
- more likely to underestimate themselves;
- more likely to blame themselves when things go wrong.

This list generalizes, and people vary, but on the whole I believe it to be true. Lacking confidence, women tend to do more research and seek advice more readily. Being worriers they will think round a situation before committing themselves. Consequently, they tend to set their firms up on good foundations. They also tend to keep records and to be good at dealing with customers, suppliers and staff.

My hope is that sharing these views and reflections will encourage more women to develop the confidence that their ideas and abilities deserve. I write it hoping I have avoided being patronizing.

Male entrepreneurs

Although the gap is closing, men still start more companies than women. In comparison, their firms tend to:

- grow faster;
- get bigger;
- be more ambitious;
- be technically based;
- be faster-moving;
- be better at self-promotion;
- have trouble keeping staff;
- go bust more frequently;
- have more crises on the way.

I leave it to anthropologists and social psychologists to explain why. The sheer fact of numbers means that male-run firms continue, for the moment, to be the backbone of the small business movement. At a time when some aspects of masculinity are under attack, it may help to know that we chaps can claim to be useful in one field at least. More seriously, any man starting in business would do well to pause in the headlong rush to get going and ponder the comments above on his female counterpart. A more thoughtful approach can pay off, handsomely.

Personal finances – spring-clean while you can

As a new entrepreneur you will be close to a financial untouchable. Until there are three years' accounts to show, nobody will want to lend you money. When raising finance for the firm this need not be a problem, but as a citizen it could be.

Do the following straight away. Build into the business plan a reasonable and rising personal income. If you are currently in work and plan to buy a house at some time, do it now or postpone the idea for five to seven years (when your accounts will show you have the income to pay the mortgage).

Table 5.1 gives only a selection of some of the main differences between running a small firm and working for a big one. Not all companies have the somewhat muddled attitudes suggested but, despite the shakeout of recent years, many still do. Nevertheless, a major challenge that the big-firm manager must undergo is to adjust successfully, build on strengths and survive.

TABLE 5.1   Main differences: big business employee versus small business owner

Activity	Big company	Small business
Collecting money from customers	Someone else's job (unless you are the credit manager)	Your job, and crucial to survival
Monitoring return on investment	Often expect to postpone profit for a year or two, as long as there will be a return eventually	Has to be more or less immediate
Overall management of the firm	The job of some remote figure	Your main job
Attention to a narrow specialism	You are paid to be a specialist	You are a *general* manager now, so keep the specialism in its place
Monitoring break-even point	Break-even point is often at a high level of sales	Needs to be kept as low as possible
Monitoring profit margins	Profit margins are preferably fat, but volume makes up for thin ones	Must be high, because there is little opportunity to go for volume
Raising money	Usually the job of someone else, on behalf of a firm that carries real weight	Your job, backed up by little or no clout
Attention to detail	It pays to have three people working on something affecting 1 per cent of £100 million sales	Deal only with important things; 1 per cent of your sales in year one is less than £1,000, most likely
Spending 'small' sums of money	£1,000, £2,000 or even £10,000	Spend nothing, if possible; if not, spend little
Using specialist advisers	Specialist advisers are on the staff, available free and more or less on demand	Select good ones, be prepared to pay, use wisely and get value for money

TABLE 5.1   *continued*

Activity	Big company	Small business
Prestige and appearances	Big offices and cars, good furniture and location are vital	Get nothing that doesn't really work hard for you
Delegation and help	People are on hand to take on tasks	You do it or it doesn't get done
Complete understanding of objectives	Held by only a few people at the top, with big problems of communicating the objectives more widely	Possible for every employee to have it
Responsibility for going broke	Shareholders and directors	Yours

Pay and rations

There are some other adjustments to make as well. An employee may be used to deductions for income tax, National Insurance (NI) and pension contributions. In addition, employers supply hidden subsidies, including:

- employer's NI contribution, about one-tenth of pay;
- employer's pension contribution, up to one-quarter of pay;
- paid holidays and bank holidays, another one-tenth of pay;
- private use of a company vehicle;
- private health insurance;
- life insurance;
- lunch allowances;
- free use of phone, PC, photocopier, unmetered supply of pens, paper, envelopes, other stationery.

Alone, the first three items on the list total up to 45 per cent of pay. Just because you do not see them does not mean they do not need to be made up in income from your firm. To ignore this point is to fool yourself. The practical implication is clear. When planning your finances, require the business to pay what you need to live on, plus half as much again.

Using advisers

Running your own firm can be lonely and exposed. Even when you have staff, you will be unable to know for certain whether agreement signifies an attempt to ingratiate or a genuine opinion. Nobody is above human motivation, but advisers of integrity who are genuinely independent can offer a perspective of immense value.

There can be an issue of 'horses for courses' as some specialists come to believe that they are competent beyond their own area. Equally, some generalists develop the conviction that they know a number of areas in depth. The only answer is to make your own assessment of the individuals and, as ever, to follow your instincts and take up references when you can.

Finding a generalist consultant or adviser

A good place to start is Business Link: its predecessor organizations employed mainly retired business people to give advice, some of them of the highest quality. There is also a wide range of local initiatives which, by their nature, cannot be covered in a book like this. Check with the following:

- Local authorities (county, city and borough councils), some of which employ or fund business support activities.
- National governments in Northern Ireland, Wales and Scotland.
- Chambers of Commerce, which are often involved directly with Business Links, but also offer their own services (they are strong in help for exporting).
- Business Link itself: ask about all the services available to you, not just the ones it provides.
- The local reference library: the staff there know, or know where to look for, everything.

Operations launched by the Prince of Wales often address the needs of youth, but he has also created PRIME (the Prince's Initiative for Mature Entrepreneurs, **www. prime.org.uk**).

The Business Link equivalents in Scotland are Business Gateway (**www.business. scotland.gov.uk**) and Scottish Enterprise (**www.scottish-enterprise.com**). Highlands and Islands Enterprise (**www.hie.co.uk**) operates through a number of Local Enterprise Companies. In Wales, **www.wales.gov.uk** offers similar support. Invest Northern Ireland (**www.detini.gov.uk**) appears to operate under the full-service model, with advisers and consultants as well as a website.

The two national organizations that have never wavered are the Prince's Trust (in Scotland, The Business Programme) and Shell LiveWIRE. Both for entrepreneurs aged up to 30, the Trust gives advice, loans and grants (**www.princes-trust.org.uk**) and LiveWIRE runs training and a national competition (**www.shell-livewire.org**).

Specialist advisers

The main advisers a new business needs are a chartered accountant and a solicitor (both in private practice) and an insurance broker. In all cases they should specialize in, or at least be well versed in, small business. The best sources are from your local contacts, especially other small firms, who can recommend people.

Colleges and universities can yield surprising types of help, but it depends on local commitment, often on particular individuals with an interest in small firms. Technical and scientific advice is an obvious field, but there are also academics who study management, some specializing in small business. For the price of a phone call they are worth investigating.

Conclusions

- Sound working methods, consistently applied, can make the difference between success and failure. One of the most important decisions an entrepreneur makes is how to spend time. The most effective people identify the few matters that will get the most results and direct their time in that direction.

- Simple tools exist to demonstrate how important good working methods are and how to impose them on the chaos of events. No such intention will be carried out flawlessly, but even faulty execution is better than no direction at all, resulting in being thrown about by whatever winds should blow.

- Family issues need to be planned in to business life. The entrepreneurial personality can take family members for granted, assuming they are in position, self-sustaining and requiring no maintenance, existing solely for its own support. That personality can get rude shocks: it is better to plan the family and its needs into life and thus retain the support on which the entrepreneur depends.

- Differences exist in the entrepreneurial challenges facing different characters and genders. In general, many men would benefit from less boldness and more forethought; many women would be better off acting more and thinking a little less.

- The level of pay to be planned for is much higher than that which appears on an employer's payslip. Employees' wages need to be increased by up to double to account for the extra on-costs arising from the obligations on employers.

- The use of advisers can confer benefits throughout the firm's life, from long before launch and right through to maturity. Most advisers will be technical specialists (eg accountants, lawyers) and others generalists (eg strategy specialists). The former category is widely recognized as valuable whereas the latter is capable of making at least as great a contribution.

06
IT strategy

In this chapter

LEARNING OUTCOMES

By the end of this chapter you should be able to:

- decide what to do about IT;
- see how to trade on the web;
- start an internet business;
- keep internet customers happy.

Every firm needs to record data, analyse it to create information and communicate. In all but the very smallest, IT is needed.

The minimum that most businesses have is:

- accounting software (approved by HM Revenue & Customs, or your VAT submissions might be suspected);
- a spreadsheet for budgeting, costing and 'what if?' exercises;
- word processing, for correspondence and documentation;
- internet access;
- e-mail;
- a printer, copier and/or scanner.

Some firms will also have specialized software suitable for a specific type of business.

Getting equipped ought not to be haphazard, but planned along organized lines:

- Specify your current and likely future requirements (not the equipment, just what you want it to do).

- Select the operating systems and software.
- Decide if you will ever need a LAN (local area network, to link more than one terminal).
- Specify costings and the programme for implementation.
- Consider the impact of implementation on the main business and have contingency plans ready in case of delay or failure.

You may need advice from an adviser skilled in this area. It is best if he or she is independent of suppliers. Use of IT for web marketing applications is discussed elsewhere, but it has a further role in keeping suppliers, staff and associates in touch.

There is an alternative to owning your own IT system, by using 'the cloud'. Under the traditional arrangement, the firm owns, leases or rents its computing power and applications software and takes responsibility for network security and maintenance. Under cloud computing (CC), the firm buys or creates the software applications it needs, but then places them on a server that sits somewhere else on the globe, with a simple terminal connecting to it via the telephone line. All the complexity of maintaining IT hardware is removed at one sweep; instead of owning the means of IT, the firm rents an all-in service. At the same time it is not using some centrally provided software but creating its own, which it then places on the CC server. A major advantage is said to be the ease of recovery from some catastrophe: a small firm that has its PCs stolen and that has not done its data backup is crippled, probably to the point of collapse. Conversely, if the data are held not locally but somewhere else, the loss of terminals is a small matter as the data themselves are still safe and untouched. A new terminal and a telephone socket put the firm back in business. All that is true, of course, unless the catastrophe takes place at the server farm used by the CC contractor – then everything may still be lost. However, one has the right to expect that a properly organized contractor operating in a developed country will have not only the most sophisticated means of preventing catastrophe but also back-up arrangements for immediate recovery, should one occur.

Superficially it may seem that CC is ideal for the smaller user, and such may prove to be the case. The big firm can justify having in-house arrangements as the costs are spread over so many PCs, laptops, notebooks and other items of equipment. Yet even there, as firms pare back their operations to the core activity, outsourcing what they do not strictly need to do themselves, CC is growing in popularity. Whether it is right for the new firm, where start-up requirements may amount to no more than a PC and a laptop, is likely to depend on its likely rate of growth. It may be worth paying over the odds at first, secure in the belief that the basic systems are in place so that growth can take place smoothly. Possessing its own equipment implies occasional upheavals imposed by the need for leaps forward in systems development. As the CC market develops and competition intensifies we could quite possibly see packages aimed at one-person firms and even individuals.

All this is fine, so long as the internet and the CC provider remain viable. What happens if some disaster, natural or man-made, overtakes the internet or the remote server farm is not entirely clear.

Beshpande (2011) argues that to look to CC for savings in standardized computing activity is to look in the wrong area: '... if any of the SMBs [small and medium-sized businesses] were using cloud to get covered on basic productivity suites and expecting a big saving, they would naturally be disappointed. But this is not how one must look for benefits from cloud computing.'

He goes on to argue that the real benefit for the smaller enterprise lies in its access to highly sophisticated analytical software which would otherwise be unaffordable. The message is clear – if the business would gain greatly from clever ways of analysing the data it generates, CC could be worthwhile; but for bread-and-butter operations it will not save money. Some would see this as a one-way bet: go on to CC, spend much the same, but have access to analytics if you need them.

Trading on the web

The fundamentals of web trading are identical to those of any other form of selling. There must be a proposition relevant to the customer, at a suitable price and available on the right timescale. The business must generate cash faster than it absorbs it, and preferably make a profit. But such a firm ought to have one enormous advantage over its conventional competitor: it saves money on promotion (a good website need not be expensive) and on premises (nobody needs a fancy shop to sell top-end watches on the web).

Typing almost anything into a search engine produces enormous numbers of links to websites that want to sell something. Should you follow their example of how to go about it, or not? There are so many that this is an impossible question to answer. What I can do is to commend two companies with which I have had dealings and for which I have great admiration. For the record, I know nothing of them apart from as a customer, they are not paying me for this and I have not even sought their permission to mention them.

MailOrderBatteries.com: The high street shop wanted £18 for a replacement camera battery. The web threw up several promising-looking contacts. All except one needed further information before committing to supply me, so I ordered from the one that simply gave me a price, £10. It came two days later and MailOrderBatteries is now my first port of call for batteries. I hope that my purchases never make them rich, but I think they have the right formula.

The Map Shop: I wanted Netherlands maps that showed cycle paths. Again, more than one supplier turned up but the online information was not quite what I needed. I rang the name I knew, a big firm, but they put me in a queue. Then I dialled The Map Shop. They answered after two rings, the woman I spoke to immediately recognized my problem, knew the answers and told me what I needed. The maps even arrived the next day.

In both cases the firms have the web-trading fundamentals right, but back them up with authoritative phone support. They understand the customer, know their field and deliver satisfaction. The web is not propping up a fundamentally weak business model; rather, it is projecting a sound model widely.

The lessons I draw are:

- Any niche is worth exploring, even if it looks crowded already.
- Add extra value for the customer and you can brush even large competitors aside.
- Dissatisfaction with an existing service can spark off ideas for a new business.
- The total service is what matters, not just the website.

Starting an internet business

The phenomenal rise in internet trading, with plenty more potential yet to come, must put this option on everyone's list. While adding an internet dimension to a conventional business (a 'clicks-and-mortar' operation) is discussed on page 92, here we look at a purely web-based business.

For the time being, all projections for web-based sales continue strongly upward. People are increasingly short of time, and those most time-poor are often cash-rich – by working long hours they earn well, and so can pay to have things delivered, which is just as well as they do not have the time to visit the shops themselves. The extraordinary spread of Ocado and other home-delivery retailers is testament to that. Yet it is not a new idea – 50 years ago every small grocer had a delivery boy, who collected orders from customers' homes and delivered the merchandise (and the bill) later that day or the next.

One barrier to entry has been swept away by recent developments. No longer is there a need for an intimate understanding of web-page programming: contractors have always been available, but, since many now specialize in the small-business market, costs are now affordable at a few hundred pounds upwards. Alternatively, it can be done really cheaply, using the various free tools that the internet offers. A website that gives both an excellent overview of the process, and detailed instructions on how to do the entire thing free, is **www.setup-website.co.uk**. Free hosting and a guide to doing the whole thing yourself are offered by Google at: **www.google.com/sites/help/intl/en/overview.html**. These are just examples – there are many more.

Another model is to sell via eBay, which offers a range of packages to would-be traders. It is not for everyone, but many an individual has developed a lucrative sideline or even a full-time business by selling (and sometimes buying) there. A word of warning: even though each component in eBay's charging structure costs mere pence or a tiny percentage, taken overall the charges do mount up. Their in-house payment method, PayPal, has attracted criticism, which might be worth investigating too. That is not to argue against the model, but to counsel caution, research and calculation before plunging in headlong.

Attracting the customer

Only a few years ago it looked as if internet trading might be no more than a useful adjunct to conventional selling, perhaps adding a further way of getting to the market similar to mail order. Things have developed so quickly that it is now quite normal to deal with a business that has no physical presence, being represented solely by a website. That, in turn, has brought a number of new concerns for customers. Some websites act as if a low price is the sole consideration driving buying decisions. That may be true for a proportion of customers, just as there are people who will happily buy goods from a stranger in a pub car park, sight unseen, for cash. Sometimes everything is all right, but for many people's taste such a transaction leaves too much to chance: the more cautious will prefer to pay a little more in order to get some assurance of service if there should be a problem.

A customer who finds a website that admits to no physical address is immediately on guard. Some forms list under 'contact us' their physical address, telephone and e-mail contacts; others omit all of this, using just a form to enable the customer to speak to them. In the latter case, if the seller declines to respond, there is no possibility of the customer taking a problem up. Not all customers are stupid enough not to realize this, so the website that overlooks it appears suspect and puts itself at a disadvantage.

Web-page and website design

What the homepage looks like obviously matters; especially to be avoided is too much text. It is important not to go too far the other way, with all kinds of bells and whistles that slow down loading (customers are impatient, and a slow load will have them going off elsewhere). Things to watch out for are:

- over-elaborate content;
- automatic video (optional is fine);
- visual effects (flashing effects, animations, etc).

Typeface for text should recognize that not everyone's eyesight is perfect. Navigation needs to be straightforward.

The FAQs (frequently asked questions) should be comprehensive, covering all conceivable problems and thus cutting down on the number of queries that come in for personal attention. 'Contact us' should incorporate an enquiry form, rather than just an e-mail address hyperlink. On most Windows PCs that will open Outlook Express, which is not everyone's preferred e-mail editor, and takes time to load.

Where there is a lot of information to cover, break it up under separate headings and devote a page to each. This is better than creating one or more pages of dense text.

'About us' on many websites is sometimes boastful, saying too much, sometimes bashful, telling too little. The happy medium is to tell the story of the business briefly but with enough detail to make its founders and other key staff seem human.

Happy customers

Customers, and the satisfaction of their needs, lie at the heart of any proper business, so it is worth spending a moment considering some of the relevant issues. Anyone who has bought from the internet will be familiar with the trader who offers low prices and quick delivery, takes your money and then reports that they are briefly out of stock.

Only after a week or two, when it dawns on you that they had no stock in the first place, do you start to chase them in earnest. If you have spent £100 or more and have bought with a credit card, you will get your money back if the delivery never turns up, but for lesser purchases the customer is unprotected.

To pontificate, it should not be part of any business plan to behave so shoddily. Quite apart from morality and the law – the seller has no right to take money for goods they cannot supply – there is the practical matter of reputation. Satisfied customers are said to tell five people; dissatisfied customers, 20. But wrong is not always on the part of the seller, so wise vendors protect themselves from unjustified claims of non-delivery by use of one of the signed-for services.

Part of the FAQs section should be answers to questions about what to do if things go wrong, either with the delivery or after the sale is complete.

It must always be remembered that, although a web-based firm may have many characteristics different from those of its conventional equivalent, it is identical in one simple respect: it makes its living only by pleasing its customers. On the assumption that those customers are happy, their e-mail addresses should be harvested and used for periodic mail-outs of news and special offers.

Consequently, it is also well-advised to follow the guidance elsewhere in this book. Using the internet does not confer immunity from the eternal truths of business.

Back-office systems

As has already been hinted at, designing and operating the website and getting the order is only part of the job. Processing of payments and fulfilment of those orders accurately and in the time promised is crucially important. Systems should be set up to ensure that all this takes place, and they should be tested (even if only on paper) to see if they can cope with extreme conditions.

If your product has a physical presence, storage, handling and delivery need to be planned for. The performance of subcontractors should be carefully monitored and feedback scrutinised for any sign of poor service. Most firms will use a parcel company to deliver their goods. Since keeping to delivery promises is a key part of any business proposition, this means that a vital part of your reputation is in someone else's hands. There are excellent delivery companies; their quality costs a little more. There is certainly one national organization in the UK that is infamous for its inefficiency, yet it is cheaper. Every firm has a choice over which carrier to place its business with.

Finally, like running a pub, operating a web-based business is a 365-day-a-year commitment. How will it run while you are sick or on holiday?

Conclusions

- Doing business over the internet expands the universe available to a firm, enabling even the most obscure operation in a distant place to achieve global reach. This overturns many previous beliefs about location and, as with any change, throws up opportunities. Those opportunities will often be unpredictable and visible only to the prepared mind that revels in peering into odd places.

- The basic truths and imperatives of business apply everywhere that business is done, including on the internet. Customers must be located, attracted and satisfied, and cost must not exceed price in the long term.

- Thorough organization is essential. It may appear that an internet-based operation can muddle through and learn 'on the hoof', but preparation for a range of scenarios is wise: since its reach is so great, demand could be far greater than at first expected. Equally, an expectation of great demand could be disappointed.

PART 3:
Customers and profits

07
Markets, market research and forecasting

In this chapter

LEARNING OUTCOMES

By the end of this chapter you should be able to:

- see what markets are and source information on them;
- understand the roles of customers and consumers;
- segment the market for maximum impact;
- do or avoid market research;
- forecast sales;
- forecast the factors of production.

Markets, customers and consumers

First, some definitions. Markets are made up of customers and consumers. Customers have a direct commercial relationship with the supplier: the supplier supplies the customers and the customers pay the supplier.

Consumers are those who use the product but do not necessarily have a trading relationship with the firm. They might buy from a distributor who is the firm's customer (for example as patrons of a shop which sells the firm's products), or they might have the product bought for them (such as a child eating a branded sweet which the child asked his or her grandmother to buy).

To a conventional business (that is, not those engaged in City trading activities) 'the market' is used to identify or describe:

- a place ('the Singaporean market');
- value ('the market is worth US $3 billion');
- a group of people with characteristics in common that influence their spending patterns ('the market among mothers of pre-school children').

Deciding on the market the firm is in is a useful first step, but a more specific definition needs to be made before it can settle on its exact product and its specific appeal. It is no good a firm – any firm, no matter what its size – deciding it will sell to, for example, the Chilean market, the brake-pads market or the over-60s market. Those terms are too general. This is where 'segmentation' comes in.

Segmentation – picking your customers

Segmentation comprises looking at the total market, working out each of the possible ways in which it can be sliced up and selecting the slices that are of interest. This confers three major benefits:

- It creates the possibility of products and services being as near as possibly tailor-made to consumers within the selected segment(s).
- It ensures exclusive concentration on the needs of those consumers.
- It ensures that all other segments are intentionally ignored, so as to maximize focus where it is needed.

Every business needs to segment its markets, select the segment(s) of interest and concentrate solely on it or them. By doing that it becomes of maximum relevance to its customers and consumers; by not doing it, it risks its offer being diffuse and the proposition apparently not standing for anything.

Segmentation can be conducted in as many ways as the imagination will allow. The most frequent bases are:

- geographical ('within a 20-mile radius of Johannesburg');
- socio-economic ('retired people with family incomes of at least £50,000 annually');
- gender ('women');
- age ('aged between 25 and 45');
- by activity ('arable farmers specializing in grain');
- by size ('operating at least 10 aircraft');
- by spend ('spending less than £3,000 a year on travel');
- by value of purchase ('buyers of wines retailing for between £10 and £20 a bottle');

... and so on: whatever split makes most sense to the business in question.

Different bases for segmentation can be stitched together, and probably need to be to ensure the greatest possible specificity ('women living in the suburbs of Chennai who supervise their own gardening on plots of at least 0.5 hectares').

Once the segment has been defined it should be put through tests for soundness:

- It must be clearly distinguished from other segments.
- It has to be big enough to be commercially viable.
- You must be able to contact its members to be able to sell to them.
- You must be able to deliver to them in a timely way.
- Your message needs to be tailored in such a way as to beat competition for that segment.

Thus there is a tension, between making the segment small enough for your message to be so distinctive that it makes you the only realistic supplier, yet big enough for a living to be made off it.

A little more theory and generalization is in order before we proceed to the practicalities.

The supplier's job is to sell what customers want. If it is an innovation, they may not know they want it – yet. But even within the realm of what they know, different customers want different things. Think of reasons why people might buy clothes:

- warmth;
- weatherproofing;
- lightness;
- fashion;
- allure;
- long life;
- versatility;
- good service;
- quick delivery;
- ... and so on.

No clothing supplier could satisfy all those needs, which is why different suppliers address different segments of the market. One of your first jobs is to identify the segment(s) you are aiming at, then sell to it or them.

Sometimes the buyer is buying for himself or herself, sometimes not; sometimes the decision is influenced by others. You may need to reach those others, too. Think about who takes the decision to buy from these suppliers:

- building contractor – householder or architect?;
- toymaker – child, parent, grandparent, other relative or friend?;
- subcontract precision engineer – engineering designer or engineering buyer?

Do those different audiences want to hear the same message from the supplier? How is it in your chosen trade? Look carefully at your market, ask around, investigate; find out how people buy where you plan to operate and gear your proposition accordingly.

Now you are in a position to begin transforming your idea into a more concrete form. Before you can do so, your assumptions about what people want should be tested. If that leads to changing the idea, or even disposing of it altogether, so be it.

Although that would undoubtedly be a nuisance, it is cheaper to dump it now than to wait until further time and resources have been invested.

Researching the market

Market information sources

So far we have assumed that you either know what you need to know or can easily lay hands on it. Even if you do, the time will come when you need to do research. But where to look?

Internet searches are an obvious starting point. One good place is **www.rba.co.uk**, which provides a number of lists, many useful to business. They have so much that it can seem confusing at first, but perseverance and following lines that might make sense, can bring real rewards.

If you are a business-to-business (B2B) seller, you may at first need little more than **www.yell.com**. It lists all the 1.6 million *Yellow Pages* entries and enables searches by geographical area as well as business type. So if you want to sell to accident investigators (there are 90 entries), fencing contractors in Bradford (152), right through to zoos (46), you can list your sales prospects instantly and free of charge.

Information on the web is not always reliable, though, and some that is, is costly. At some point you may wish to visit your local public library. The commercial and reference section (all the bigger libraries have one) is staffed by people who know their way around the information scene. They also subscribe to the important directories, so that you have free access.

Often, the challenge lies in knowing where to look (another area in which professional librarians can be surprisingly helpful). Ask yourself who else has contact with the people you want to talk to. For example, to sell B2B locally, try asking for lists from:

- local authority estates department – information about tenants;
- local authority promotion units – lists of businesses that exist in the area;
- Chamber of Commerce – membership directory;
- Chamber of Trade – ditto;
- trade associations – membership lists;
- business clubs – membership lists;
- colleges – local employers.

Not all will help, but some will, so ask. More widely, there are government development agencies, government websites, national trade associations, industry directories and web-based lists.

The more specialized your target group, the more likely there are to be societies, websites and magazines to serve it. Some even commission research among their members which may tell you exactly what you want to know.

The research scene

If you were to brief one of the well-known commercial market research firms to investigate your market for you, the firm would do so but at an eye-watering cost – not because these firms are greedy, but because they have to have the international coverage and full professional analytics that their multinational clients demand. Smaller firms that operate more locally do exist and can do a thoroughly decent job, but again at some considerable cost. In some cases cost is less important than quality of results, but in market research that is often, but not always, so.

In most start-up situations, the research questions to be asked and the analysis of the answers are likely to be on a small scale, straightforward and easily understood: the major contractors' computers would spit the analyses out in a split second, so a simple human should be able to get on top of them in a few hours, at most.

As can be seen, the argument is moving towards do-it-yourself research. Not only will it be cheaper, it will also:

- be designed to meet your needs exactly;
- be capable of amendment 'on the hoof' if new questions crop up;
- give a far better insight into what customers and consumers really think than would reading someone else's report.

There are dangers in this, of course. First, the research needs to be designed and executed in a particular way; second, the interpretation of results might be richer if someone else had been involved. The latter point can be addressed by calling in a small business adviser with marketing experience. The first point will be covered if a few simple rules are followed.

The research brief

While the entrepreneur knows what he or she wants the research to do, it is useful to write it down as if briefing an outside research contractor. To start with the basics. Whenever you don't know quite where to start, your best friends can be Kipling's 'honest serving men, who taught me all I know', the questions:

- Who?
- What?
- Why?
- When?
- Where?
- How?

More specifically, you will be asking these questions:

- Who buys, specifies and uses the product?
- What price do buyers pay at present?
- Why do they buy it? Why would they switch if asked?
- When do they buy, how often and in what quantities?

- Where do they get their supplies at present?
- How do they order? How do they get delivery? How do they use the product?

A further question to ask is: what problems do they experience in buying, storing and using the product?

CASE STUDY Problems, wonderful problems!

A case study

Jim wants to break into a market that is already well supplied. Asking potential customers how his product could perform better than the competitors', he meets with a wall of resistance. All the present suppliers make superb equipment that is completely reliable and cannot be faulted. Quite naturally, Jim is getting despondent. Then one of the friendlier types – who had said exactly the same as all the others – let drop that the waiting time for new equipment was three months and spares took even longer, meaning that, in the rare event of a breakdown, equipment was useless for ages.

Suddenly Jim realized he had been asking the wrong question. He had been looking solely at the core product whereas, as well as that, customers buy all sorts of ancillaries that go to make up the complete package. He knew he could turn out equipment in 10 days, so with an efficient production operation he could promise delivery within... well, three weeks would be on the safe side, one-quarter of the time the others took. Instantly, he know he had his sales proposition – it was nothing to do with the performance of the equipment itself, and had everything to do with his production control system. If his equipment worked as well as the others' and he could keep his delivery promises, he should succeed.

The moral is: obvious. Problems are the source of more business opportunities than even new technology but, unlike technology, exploiting them rarely requires specialist, technical knowledge.

Now we know what we want to know. The next task is to design the questions that will get the answers.

Questionnaire design

In writing research questions – and also in putting them to the respondent – remember that this is not a sales exercise, but a research contact. Writing them down ensures that you don't forget any and that you ask the question in the same way every time. If you don't, the answers from different people cannot be compared and you will have wasted your time. (Strictly speaking, a questionnaire is a form sent out for self-completion and return; there are names for other research instruments but since 'questionnaire' is well understood by everyone we stick to it here.)

First, decide the method by which the research is to be conducted. The most popular options include:

- Personal visit – this is time-consuming and it is difficult to get interviews but they can yield rich results.
- Telephone – this is less time-consuming and less effective, but better than using the post.
- Post – there may possibly be a very low rate of return, perhaps so low as to invalidate the survey (the answers from only 5 per cent of respondents may not reflect the views of the other 95 per cent).
- The internet – if you have a stock of e-mail addresses of potential customers it would be sensible to use it: mailing-out costs nothing and if it gets past firewalls and junk filters it could be useful.

The choice of method is usually governed by the number of people you need to hear from to get a good picture of the scene in general. Suppose there are 127 aeronautical engineers in the whole of Europe to whom you would hope to sell. Suppose you decide that a sample of 10 per cent might give a good general indication: you therefore need to hear from 13 of them. Those 13 need to be spread around among the companies that employ them, rather than all being from BAE Systems, just because you can get to their Hatfield HQ easily. You get their names and titles from company websites, trade directories and professional associations' membership lists.

Equally, if you need responses from large numbers of people, personal contact will not work. One of the other methods will come into play.

Start the questionnaire with the minimum of identity information; the answers need to be tied to a particular source, but asking lots of detailed questions about general aspects, before getting to the nub of things, can irritate a respondent. Remember, you will have the interviewee's attention for only a short time and only as long as that person's patience lasts.

Leave plenty of space to write in answers.

If you are mailing out questionnaires, the wording and appearance of the covering letter are crucial. The letter needs to be brief but to get your message across clearly, and addressed personally to a named individual. Your personal signature should be written at the end. A stamped, addressed envelope should be attached for the reply.

Make out a form for every respondent, with a couple of spares, just in case of accidents.

Research in action

Some of our hypothetical aeronautical engineers you try to visit, by setting up appointments on the telephone or, if that doesn't work, by e-mail. Some (in Toulouse, maybe) you telephone and interview down the line. Do not underestimate the time it will take to get hold of people: some days you can be calling all day and get not a single appointment. It might help if you send out personal letters to say that you would appreciate their help for 10 minutes with a few short research questions and will ring at a given time on a particular day.

Analysis

After sweating some blood, you've got the answers in. What do you do with them? In the case of a simple questionnaire of the type envisaged here, the conclusions will probably jump out at you – analysis will involve little more than some simple sums and some reading of answers.

An unintelligent but possibly correct response

There may be a radical way of avoiding all this palaver and getting more reliable results as well. That is to launch the product or service and see what happens. Offers that have the following characteristics may be suitable for this treatment:

- low-cost and high-margin, so that a high level of returns would not be financially ruinous;
- trivial outcomes from broken contracts (eg you didn't start the promised milk-round);
- a highly dispersed customer base, so that in case of dissatisfaction word of mouth does not operate;
- trivial implications of faulty design or manufacture, so that lawsuits are unlikely;
- easy and cheap to redesign and alter manufacture.

Even in these cases, a little prior probing of customers' preferences would be highly rewarding.

Forecasting

The sales forecast

At the outset, there are three possible approaches to forecasting:

- Don't bother, just do your best and see what happens.
- Make a forecast based on cautious realism arising from research, then try hard to beat it.
- Forecast at a level that will at least pay the bills, then try hard to make it come true.

Either of the second two is fine, depending on your character and circumstances. The first is not. All of the planning – financial and otherwise – for a firm starts from its sales forecast, so one is really necessary.

Objections to forecasting

Many people refuse to make a forecast on the grounds that it is bound to be wrong. They are right, it is: all forecasts are wrong. But that is no reason not to make one.

So why spend time and trouble on something that will be wrong? Because accuracy isn't the point. You try to get it as right as you can, of course, but being 5 or even 10 per cent adrift does not matter a jot, as long as you spot the deviation early and correct for it.

The case for forecasting is compelling. Running a firm is a complex game, with many variables having an impact on each other. The owner needs to keep on top of the game, and the best way so far devised is to make a forecast, then see how things turn out. If the forecast is wrong, you change it. In changing it you also change all the variables that depend on it, which provides a new set of benchmarks against which to measure progress.

It is a bit like riding a bicycle: you proceed in a series of swerves, never a straight line, but always in the general direction of the objective. Remember the wisdom of Drucker and Eisenhower, quoted earlier as saying that plans are valueless but planning is invaluable. Forecasting sales is the very start of the planning process.

From the sales forecast you will know:

- how big the production facility needs to be;
- the production capacity required;
- how many staff to take on;
- what transport capacity is necessary;
- your cash needs;
- how much material to order;
- seasonal peaks and troughs;

... and so on.

Think about running a business without knowing anything from that list. It would be impossible.

Practical forecasting

Understandably, the new business founder can feel intimidated by this task. Uncertainty and ignorance are the problems. If the topic of purchase quantities was not covered in the earlier programme of research visits, do some investigation now. Cut down on the unknowns by visiting some potential customers and simply ask what you need to know. Explain it is a research visit and avoid all temptation to sell, but listen, really listen, to what is said.

Even then you may lack the knowledge to have sufficient confidence to take the plunge full time. Could you start up part time? Could someone else make what you supply until you are confident enough to go in for the big investment yourself? This discussion is closely linked to the 'Break through to profit' section (in Chapter 13), which looks at the minimum level of sales needed to pay the costs, which is the point where you start to earn profits.

One mistake that people new to forecasting sometimes make is to assume that sales will take off in a straight line. They can do, of course, but more often a lag is built in, with things being slow to start but then gathering momentum. This can lead to terrible problems. The entrepreneur, seeing sales in the early stage lower than expected, cuts the forecast, reduces forward commitments and lowers the volume bought in or made. Usually this creates much bad feeling with suppliers and staff, to whom promises have been made. Since we humans are only the playthings of the gods, usually this happens immediately before the sales graph starts to shoot skywards. No doubt the sight of someone cutting a sales forecast then reversing the cut causes much merriment on Olympus, the home of the ancient Greek gods (whose capriciousness is what really runs the world), but it can play havoc with the nerves of mortals.

Forecasting other factors

Once the sales forecast has been formed other aspects of the business can be more clearly foreseen.

The main factors of production – the things necessary for production to come about – include:

- premises;
- equipment;
- materials;
- people;
- distribution;
- finance.

The quantity of each of these depends on the level of sales and will vary with seasonal ups and downs. In some cases the need can be answered only by making a major commitment, a course of action it may be desirable to avoid in the early stages of the firm's development. Instead of the fixed commitment, variable means may be found that solve the problem, though these may cost more. In that case there is a simple calculation of risk to be made: of whether to exchange the possibility of being stuck with an unwanted resource with the certainty of a little higher cost. Variability could be introduced as shown in Table 7.1.

In most cases a black-and-white choice is neither desirable nor required. Often a firm will cover the normal level of demand from its own fixed resources, using the variable type to boost capacity when needed. Equally, in the early stages, it can make

TABLE 7.1   Fixed and variable solutions to business factors

Factor	Fixed solution	Variable solution
Premises	Buy, or rent long term	Use storage contractor
Equipment	Buy	Hire equipment or subcontract activity
Materials	Buy to a set pattern	Vary purchases with need
People	Employ staff	Use temporary staff from an agency
Distribution	Own the vehicles	Hire the vehicles or subcontract
Finance	Sink your own savings	Use a bank loan

sense to use variable resources exclusively, allowing a cheap and easy escape if things do not go as planned.

Conclusions

- Markets are complex, consisting of consumers (who use the product or service), specifiers (who influence the purchase) and customers (who buy).

- As there is a great variety of customers within any given market, it is important to concentrate effort on those most likely to buy. To do this, the firm identifies segments with common characteristics and formulates a specific sales proposition for each.

- Those segments should be the sole focus of attention and promotion in the short to medium term. That concentration of effort ensures efficiency of operation, but it also implies a rigidity which could lead to missing new opportunities. Since markets are constantly evolving, as well as short-term concentration, sensing mechanisms should also be in place to spot attractive, newly emerging segments.

- There is a large amount of information to be had free of charge; the problem is knowing where to look. Self-guided internet searches can yield a great deal but are often patchy in their results. Professional librarians, skilled in seeking out information and often with access to specialized databases, can help.

- Most markets should be researched before entry is attempted. Even what is apparently the most obvious situation can conceal useful information, some of it potentially damaging and expensive.

- Much market research can be conducted effectively by the layperson as the levels of certainty required to guide a SME, which can change course and flex so easily, are much lower than those demanded by a large corporation which must have a high level of certainty about, for instance, the level to which the capacity of some vast investment is likely to be occupied.

- The chief problem in research may lie in reaching respondents. Such people are themselves busy and may be disinclined to be available on the telephone or to casual visitors. Persistence, ingenuity and perhaps cheek may be required.

- In some markets research can safely be avoided, with learning on the job taking its place, but only where the cost of error is low and immediate changes of direction to correct errors are possible.

- A forecast of sales is the basis for most operational planning, since what is to be sold dictates requirements for staffing, premises, finance and distribution.

- Once sales have been forecast, forecasts for demand for the factors of production (that is, all the things that go into the production process) can be made.

- During the early stages, minimizing fixed commitments and using instead variable resources confers a flexibility that could be valuable, even if it costs more. Once things have settled down post-launch, thought can be given to continuing the original arrangement or switching to a different approach.

08
Your proposition and pricing

In this chapter

LEARNING OUTCOMES

By the end of this chapter you should be able to:

- define exactly what the sales proposition is to be;
- express it clearly;
- create a pricing strategy.

Following the work done in previous chapters, you should now be able to use at least one of these words somewhere in your claim:

- faster;
- more thorough;
- bigger;
- smaller;
- cheaper;
- more;
- lighter;
- less;
- tougher;
- easier;
- safer;
- prettier;
- more economical;
- greener.

And you may be able to use others, as long as they set your product clearly apart from competitors. Note that the word 'better' does not appear here, not because it should not be used, but because, even more than the words in the list, it absolutely must be used alongside another word, like 'performance' or 'economy' – just saying your product is 'better' than its competitors is meaningless.

Take a butcher's knife to verbiage

Using words meaninglessly is a waste of time and space, yet people do it all the time. All meat shops in the UK seem to call themselves 'high-class butchers' – as opposed to what? Could they be confused with low-class butchers if they didn't make that claim? What does a high-class butcher do to distinguish himself from the lower-class butchers? It's just a waste of words, getting in the way of communication rather than aiding it.

'Greener' comes fairly close but still retains some meaning. Greener in what way? Uses fewer resources in manufacture? Shorter delivery distance? Better fuel economy? In the case of electric cars, the claim is close to specious: the pollution from petroleum products is being replaced by the pollution from power stations, which it is difficult to see as an advance. Moreover, electric cars depend on batteries, which last for only three years and then need a £3,000 replacement.

Any time a claim is made it should be as specific as possible. Rather than 'greener' say, for example, 'uses 10 per cent less electricity' or 'incorporates 80 per cent recycled materials – more than any competitor'.

Being specific means being clear. (That cannot be why politicians avoid it, can it?)

The customer proposition

The whole of intelligent marketing is based on one simple assertion: **customers do not buy products or services. Customers buy propositions.**

The product is, of course, a key component of the proposition, but the total proposition is much more than just the product or service. If that were not true, Marks & Spencer (M&S) would never sell another shirt, for shirts are available from market stalls at a third of M&S prices.

Why does the M&S proposition work better than that of the firm selling shirts much cheaper? Compared to the market trader, M&S offers:

- a quality-controlled product;
- self-selection;
- protective packaging;

- authoritative advice if needed;
- a guarantee of performance;
- instant, no-quibble exchange or refund;
- payment by credit card;
- a pleasant, clean, indoor environment.

The shirt itself, plus all of that list, comprises the M&S proposition to its customers. Yet, probably to the company's dissatisfaction, M&S does not have a monopoly. Why?

M&S aims at the middle 60 per cent, leaving 20 per cent at either end for others to pick up. Those two lots of 20 per cent are the people who want either something much fancier or much cheaper, or easier parking out of town, or the convenience of a retailer near their workplace, or to buy at home by mail order or on the web. Those other suppliers have their place, providing what *their* customers want, at a profit. As time passes it may be that the M&S proposition will lose its power, as consumer tastes change in favour of one of the other propositions. It is one of the M&S management team's tasks to sense which way the wind is blowing and adjust the M&S appeal accordingly.

Work up your proposition, looking at every aspect of the way the customer might view it. Above all, remember that not all the people who make it big invent a better mousetrap. Many attach other benefits to perfectly ordinary mousetraps, which is a lot easier than inventing improvements to a design that already works perfectly well. With that in mind, whether or not your product truly is a revolutionary leap forward, look at all the variables that you can change: response to enquiry, order size, delivery speed, guarantee, servicing, spares, after-sales follow-up and others. If you can be better at any of those in ways that matter to your customer, you should win the business.

Whenever you are in doubt about a course of action, it helps to draw up a table showing the pros and cons. Here I have made one to help you assess how different patterns of delivery could affect your competitiveness against the opposition.

Making this sort of examination of every aspect of your plans against what the competitors do helps you to:

- see how high your competitors have set the bar;
- carve out a specification for exactly how you run your firm;
- once you have been running for a time, review why you do it that way.

Every other aspect of service could be treated in the same way, with an analysis of how you could be different and its effects on you and the customer (see Table 8.1 for an example).

The importance of doing this is that most customers assume that what is on offer now from existing sources is all that will ever be on offer. You do not want to fall into the same trap. You want to lead, not follow, if at all possible. Probably the most important aspect of your proposition is the benefits that your products and services offer. There are two kinds of benefits: those arising from something built into the thing itself (such as a self-sharpening feature on a knife) or those separate

TABLE 8.1   Delivery competitiveness matrix

Factor	Competitor does it	What we could do	Extra benefits to customer	Our costs
Deliveries	monthly	monthly	none	same as competition
		weekly	lower stocks, more responsive	higher?
		daily	lower stocks, much more responsive	higher?
	weekly	daily	as above	higher?
		two-hourly	as above	much higher?
		monthly	lower prices	lower

TABLE 8.2   Benefits analysis

Examples of built-in benefit	Examples of outside benefit
Better-looking materials	Faster delivery
More resistant finish	Longer guarantee
Better performance	No-quibble replacement
Needs less maintenance, more reliable	Free replacement while servicing done
Lasts longer	Easy payment terms

from it but still part of the proposition (such as a warranty). Table 8.2 shows some of the possibilities (the two sides of the table are not meant to correspond with each other).

You can ring the changes on the second part far more easily than on the first. Thus this is the area on which you concentrate when planning promotional support to give customers reasons for buying now, not next month or next year.

Don't overlook the importance of this. Because the outside benefits are easier to see, they are more real to the customer. That is why an inferior mousetrap in a beautiful package will often outsell its superior competitor in a paper bag.

The customer and your proposition

Customers buy from you because your marketing is better, meaning that you have put together a proposition that is more relevant to their needs than anything else on offer; and your selling is effective. And that's it. Get this right, and you could be on the way to a fortune. Get it wrong, and there is no point in going any further. Instead, keep working on the proposition until it **is** right.

But the job does not end there. Competitors could copy your approach and neutralize your advantage. If they do, you need to know. So keep your eyes and ears open and, best of all, have your next two moves up your sleeve ready for immediate use when needed – but don't deploy them until you need to.

Saving it up

In the 1960s a new business started, selling specialized consumables to the healthcare industry. The firm thought there was a window of up to two years before it was copied by one of the multinationals that dominated this business. Accordingly, it set its margins very high, ready to reduce them when necessary, and thought out the phase two and phase three versions of its proposition, fully expecting to have to deploy them, at great cost, in a life-and-death struggle for survival. To its amazement, nobody copied it. Today it is still making those high margins and has become something of a giant itself, albeit a smallish one.

Following the same general strategy, a company founded in the 1980s to make diagnostic electronics had its Mk 2 and Mk 3 versions almost ready when it launched Mk 1. Expecting the same two-year period of grace it was surprised to find that all three models had to go on the market within the first year.

The moral: look beyond the immediate horizon, anticipate the competition's reaction to your launch and have your counter-blow ready.

Take a look at your firm from the point of view of a customer. What sort of image does it present? Since, in the early days, you and the firm are one, much of the answer will revolve around your personal appearance and presentation. However, there is more to it than that.

Unless you are a skilled designer, don't try to mock up your logo, letterhead and other documents on the PC. Give the job to a professional who will take what you are trying to put across to your customer and translate it into graphic design. He or she will also ensure that the design is carried over into all aspects of your contacts: business cards, website, letterhead, invoices, quotations, compliments slips, vehicle livery, company uniforms, sales presentation materials, advertising and even the typeface used for correspondence. It all matters. It will cost a few hundred pounds, but could lift you above the crowd.

Once won, customers will keep on coming back provided you keep your promises (some people under-promise so as to be able to over-deliver) for as long as your proposition remains relevant. Their needs will change, so you need to change with them. To allow for the fact that some will stop buying through a change of policy or, indeed, closing down, you need to keep on recruiting new customers all the time.

Pricing your proposition

Pricing for marketability

The first thing to get clear is the distinction between **price** and **cost**. Price is what you can sell for. Cost is (not surprisingly) what the product or service costs you.

The obvious point is that price has to be at least equal to cost, and preferably it will be higher. Chapters 11 and 13 deal with costing.

Prices are determined by the market – in a simple example, suppose that onions sell at £1 a kilogram on the five other stalls in my local market, but if I sell at that price I make no money. I need to raise the price to £1.20, but then I will sell nothing. Alternatively, I need to get the cost down. (This all assumes that the onions on offer are identical and the stallholders equally charming, efficient and helpful.)

If mine is the sixth stall, how can I compete? First, I could try to get my standard onions cheaper, perhaps bypassing the local wholesaler and going direct to the grower, or by buying in bulk from the wholesaler, but then I would have a storage problem. Alternatively I could look at Table 8.2 above and seek some way of differentiating my onions from the others. Switching the built-in properties of onions could be done by buying a different variety – maybe one that is bigger and looks more luscious, or getting supplies that have been better cleaned, or milder ones that affect the eyes less when cutting them up. The outside benefits could come through pre-packing in an attractive net for convenient handling, or offering a free cabbage with every 10 kg bought.

Competition will limit the extra you can charge over and above cost. That is not to say you have to be cheaper than others. As discussed, what customers buy is the total proposition, not just the product, and if your proposition looks worth more, you can charge for it.

To put it another way, what customers want is value, not low prices. In some markets, commodity markets in particular, low price matters. Petrol is a case in point. Most people assume supermarket petrol to be good enough, and will shop around for the best offer, thinking all petrol to be the same. However, those in the know believe it worth paying the premium for Shell or BP. They think that the extra price is more than worth it in terms of economy, performance and engine life. However, some objective testing organizations disagree.

Where, despite all your efforts to avoid it, you feel you have to compete on price, try setting prices a little higher than the rest. That makes your product look better than theirs. Spend the extra you make on sales promotion activity. This is a trick played in some parts of the motor accessories market. Car wax might have a high list price, which is then reduced by promotional offers. Consumers are invited to think they are getting a superior product for the price of something ordinary. The trade buys the offer, knowing that the customers will buy it in turn.

It is hard to over-emphasize the psychological role of price, in both directions. Something priced higher than the generality must be better, people assume. Something priced lower must be worse. The price that people actually pay can be quite different from the label on the pack, made affordable via promotional offers. In that case, customers feel they are winning, getting a high-priced item almost as cheaply as an ordinary one. The seller, in turn, is happy because the margin is better than it would otherwise be.

Shops' and distributors' margins

This is dealt with here since everyone selling via a third party needs to set their pricing in the light of what that party expects to sell for and hence expects to pay.

Some people become incensed when they learn how much retailers add to their cost prices to produce their selling price. It is a waste of energy, akin to complaining about the weather. My advice is just to accept it and get on with the important things.

Most trades have conventions on what margin they add, based on the speed of turnover, perishability (physical or of style), cost of premises and other overheads and risk. They vary widely. A small grocer might take 7p out of a tin of beans retailing for 69p, or 10 per cent; a greengrocer, 30p in every pound; a Bond Street fashion shop 70p in every pound or even more.

When discussing the profit the distributor takes one needs to be aware of the specific terms and how they are sometimes misunderstood and misused. The terms 'gross margin', 'gross profit', 'margin' and 'mark-up' are used interchangeably, but they mean quite different things. Table 8.3 shows how.

To avoid the potential for confusion, ask each person you discuss this with to take you through the simple calculation of a selling-price, starting with a cost-price to them of £1, £10 or £100. You will quickly see what each of them means by the terms they use.

On a point of detail, the product in the table would be unlikely to be priced at £18.00. Instead, the shop will think of either £17.95 or £17.99. They will want to keep their existing margins, so what difference does that make to the supplier's price? Obviously it cannot remain at £10.00. Taking £17.95 as the example, it drops to £9.97, as shown in Table 8.4.

TABLE 8.3 How shops calculate their selling price 1

Cost to the shop	£10.00	
The shop adds 50 per cent of its cost	£5.00	This is a 'mark-up' of 50 per cent on cost; 'margin' or 'gross margin' of 33⅓ per cent on selling price excluding VAT. It is also a 'margin', 'gross margin', 'gross profit' or 'mark-up' of £5
The shop's selling price excluding VAT	£15.00	Usually worked out separately as VAT doesn't give profit to the shop
VAT at 20 per cent	£3.00	
Price to the public	£18.00	The price tag in the window

TABLE 8.4 How shops calculate their selling price 2

Cost to the shop	£9.97	(e)
Shop adds 50 per cent of its cost	£4.99	(d)
Shop's selling price excluding VAT	£14.96	(c)
VAT at 20 per cent	£2.99	(b)
Price to the public	£17.95	(a)

Once you know the way the retailer calculates prices, you can work out what was paid for anything in the shop. Using the example in Table 8.3, this is how you do it:

$c = a \div 1.2$ (or divide by 1.15 if VAT is at 15 per cent and so on)

$b = a - c$

$ = c \times 0.2$ (or multiply by 0.15 if VAT is at 15 per cent and so on)

$d = c \times \dfrac{50}{150}$ (or $c \times \dfrac{m}{100 + m}$, where m = the percentage mark-up on cost price)

$e = c - d$

Conclusions

- The proposition to be put to buyers includes, but is much more than, the product and what it does. Ancillary factors can even be more important than the core product. An understanding of the product mix for a given market can come about only from rigorous enquiry.

- It is essential to tailor the proposition exactly to the needs of the market segment. The entire point of segmentation is to ensure that the product exactly meets the needs of the specified group, so to fail to do so is to become vulnerable to some other, sharper-eyed, supplier.

- Pricing should be based on what the market will bear, a calculation that is far from easy and involves taking into account all aspects of the marketing mix. As a matter of commercial survival, costs should be lower than price.

- Where distributors are involved, pricing must recognize their imperatives and suppliers must not overtly compete directly with them, or they put the relationship at risk.

09
Channels of distribution

Getting it to the consumer

At the two extremes, a firm can deal either direct with the consumer, the end-user, or through a chain of distribution that ends with the consumer. There are different routes from you to them, each with its own benefits and drawbacks. Selling direct gets you the full sales price but takes time, costs money and involves a good deal of administration. On the other hand, selling through distributors relieves you of a lot of administration but at the price of giving a lower income per unit. Which is best? It depends on you, your market and the strategy you are putting together. Among the issues are these:

- Who has the whip hand, the salesperson or the producer? (Ask who wins: the salesperson who withholds the order or the maker who withholds delivery?)
- Who would be best at selling for you – you or someone else?
- Which makes more money – selling or making?

- If you dropped selling or making, what would it cost to get someone else to fill the gap?
- If you dropped selling, how would you maintain an independent view of what was happening among customers?

In asking some of these questions, we are assuming that there is a realistic option of finding a sales agent, which might not be the case.

These are the channels available:

- Retailers are the shops we are all familiar with, of course.
- Wholesalers or distributors buy from suppliers and sell to independent shops. Occasionally they sell some specialized goods to larger retailers. They usually specialize in a particular sector – hardware, pet goods, giftware, etc. They may operate cash-and-carry outlets or make deliveries.
- Sales representatives (reps) draw salary and expenses and are employed to sell to customers.
- Sales agents are independent, self-employed sales representatives working on commission only, usually between 10 and 20 per cent of sales. They meet their own expenses. See **www.themaa.co.uk**.
- Multiples or chains are shops with several, or more, branches, often with regional or national coverage. They may have a central warehouse or take deliveries direct to branches.
- Mail-order catalogues are big catalogues, such as that of Argos. Other than Argos, their main consumer proposition is that goods are available on credit. (Many specialists operate mail-order catalogues to sell their own merchandise. It is a route open to any firm, but here we deal solely with the large, general catalogue operators. Running one's own catalogue is dealt with separately.)

If you choose to use a channel of distribution external to your firm do the maximum amount of research possible before going ahead. You may decide to do the selling yourself after all. If so, make sure you learn from each encounter, whether you get an order or not. Keep records and analyse them, as you would if you were employing someone.

If you get more than about one order from each of four pitches your proposition is being received well, and you might be able to cut back on some expensive element of it, or to raise prices. You can try out different propositions, to see what effect it has on the number of orders you take as well as on profits. Like a good scientist, change only one variable at a time. If it turns out to be a mistake, it's easier to decide where the error lies than if three things have been changed.

Dealing direct with the public

The usual methods of reaching the public direct are:

- Selling in the home, as with Avon. To reduce the customer's right to cancel, make sure you are invited in other than on a first visit. Drop a leaflet for the customer to ring you and make an appointment from that.

- Mail order: in response to either an advert or a catalogue that you send.
- Direct mail: leaflets through letter boxes or letters through the mail. Newsagents will deliver leaflets in small areas, Royal Mail anywhere you like (and cheaply).
- Website: see later sections.
- Stalls: in markets, at fairs, shows and car boot sales.
- Party plan: as used by Tupperware and others.
- Showroom or shop.
- Mobile showroom: a converted trailer or caravan, taken to the customer.
- Piggyback leaflets: eg a catalogue for seat covers placed in every new car.

There are more. Just look around and every time you see someone trying to sell, ask: how could that be made to work for me?

If you want to sell direct as well as through the shops, be aware that retailers will resist. Use another trading name and address for your direct sales. If you want to advertise before many shops have taken on stock, say in the advert 'Available from good chemists (or whoever) or from the manufacturer'. That gives you a let-out for selling direct.

This applies to all sectors of business and works best where a clearly defined segment is addressed, such as anglers, plumbers or local authority planning officers. All have their own trade press and specialist websites. There are also in some national newspapers' pages devoted to adverts for mail order. Those adverts can be for 'off the page' sales (where the customer orders from the advert) or can invite people to ring for a catalogue. If you sell off the page, look at **www.shops-uk.org.uk** to see if you have to conform to SHOPS, the Safe Home Ordering Protection Scheme, before your advert will be accepted.

TABLE 9.1   A website or mail-order advert: advantages and disadvantages

For	Against
Direct communication with user	Pay for adverts with no guarantee of results
No dealer to pay	At mercy of press circulations
Usually cash with order	At mercy of Royal Mail prices
Can reach many consumers	At mercy of Royal Mail and press unions
Fast, even in minority-interest markets	Results sometimes unpredictable
Can turn demand on or off by adjusting advertising expenditure	
Reaches consumers that other methods miss	
Can operate from home	
Over time, builds up a mailing list	

Display adverts average about 1 to 2 per cent response from the readership (reader-ships are available from newspapers' and magazines' websites). A display advert is where you pay for space, rather than a lineage (pronounced line-age) advert which is charged per line. Equally, a small advert can aim to do no more than stimulate enquiries for catalogues or brochures.

Check whether your business falls within the requirements of the Consumer Protection (Distance Selling) Amendment Regulations, 2005. Information on that, and other regulations, is on **www.oft.gov.uk**.

Direct mail is another route direct to the customer. Lists of people with almost any interest under the sun can be bought, or, if you operate only locally, *Yellow Pages* or **www.yell.com** may yield all you need, free. To buy lists, go to the big magazine publishers' websites or search for Mailing List Brokers. The Royal Mail publishes a lot of advice to would-be direct mailers.

Designing direct-mail materials is a specialized skill. One of the masters is Laithwaite's, the wine merchant. To see what good mailings look like, get on their mailing list. That should persuade most people that they would benefit from using a specialist copywriter. Be careful, or it might also sell you some wine.

Before sending any mailing, check with the Mailing Preference Service (**www.mpsonline.org.uk**) as it is unlawful to send unsolicited mail to anyone who has registered not to receive it. The same organization covers the Telephone Preference Scheme, should you wish to sell by telephone.

Party plan works best for businesses with items to sell at up to £100. You need to recruit hostesses (they usually are women) who invite their friends to their homes using invitations that you provide. You demonstrate and sell, paying the hostess a commission on sales. People already running party plan may tell you the names of hostesses, as they are keen to see good hostesses kept fresh by running parties for a variety of goods. The Direct Sales Association (**www.dsa.org.uk**) might be able to help. Everyone who attends gets a free gift and it is usual to supply the hostess with wine for her guests. Guests order at the party and either pay there and then for later delivery or place a deposit, paying the balance on delivery.

You get the full retail price, in cash, with only a small promotional outlay. You build up a mailing list for future business (include a tick-box on the order form to allow you to mail people) and may find that some customers are happy to become hostesses. You will need to operate in pairs so that one person deals with the customers and the other with necessary to-ing and fro-ing.

Attracting the distributor

Distributors, shopkeepers included, would like everything they stock to be:

- demanded by customers without prompting;
- exclusive to them, at least in the immediate area;
- not affected by season or fashion;
- unlikely to spoil in storage;
- difficult to steal;
- compact and easy to handle;

- faultlessly reliable;
- cheaper than competitive goods.

Shopkeepers would also like the company supplying them to:

- keep plenty of stock of all varieties, colours, sizes, etc;
- have an instant delivery system;
- offer high profit margins;
- give plenty of support through free display material, display stands, heavy advertising that mentions them by name, contribution to advertising costs, and incentive bonuses that require little effort to win;
- offer unlimited credit;
- be entirely dependable and honest in all its dealings;

... and a lot more besides.

Most retailers are not fools. They know that there is something wrong with things that are too cheap. So, unless you have a real advantage that enables you to undercut competitors, do not try. Especially, do not start a price war, for the longer-established firm is usually better placed to win. What the distributor truly seeks is merchandise that is easy to sell and keeps customers happy.

If your product needs a lot of selling by the distributor, see if you can get packaging and display material to do that job, for shop staff rarely sell anything. Nonetheless, ask the buyer if you might take a few moments of the sales staff's time to explain the product and answer any questions. Take a look round the shops, builders' merchants and other distributors to pick up ideas and see how other firms tackle the problems of selling through display. Marketing advisers from advisory agencies might be useful here, and elsewhere, too.

If your distributor has a sales force, as most wholesalers do, try to get a slot to present to its next sales force meeting. Stick strictly to the time it allows and you may stand a chance of being noticed among its 4,000 or so other lines. You may want to discuss with the buyer a temporary sales force incentive scheme to get the product going.

Some may ask for sale or return (SOR). This means you placing the goods with them and being paid only if they sell. Ask yourself: which will be sold first, goods the shop has paid for or those it has not? Which goods will be kept in good condition, those paid for or those on SOR? Even if you agree to SOR, expect disputes and damage when you come back weeks or months later to collect the unsold goods. If SOR is mentioned, make it clear that your policies do not offer it and get back to selling.

As with any other type of customer, attracting the distributor is only part of the job – holding on to it is important too, accomplished by good service, never being a problem and always listening and looking for new ways to help the distributor to sell your product.

Visiting the customer

Previously you have reviewed the information and illustrations you need to take with you and browsed the shelves of a commercial stationer to find attractive binders to hold and display it. You do not visit at the busiest times: Friday afternoons, market days and weekends.

You have done the research, now you are about to walk in and try to make a sale. You are dressed appropriately, with clean clothes, hands and fingernails, and some attention to personal grooming, including avoiding the use of aftershave and embracing that of antiperspirant-deodorant. (It may seem patronizing to mention these matters, but you must meet the buyer's expectations of cleanliness, which may be stratospheric, for all you know.) In your (smart) briefcase you have:

- a note of the absolute lowest price you can afford to sell for, just in case;
- price lists;
- terms and conditions of sale (see Appendix 2);
- order form (or enquiry form if yours is the sort of product that is specially made and quoted for);
- calculator;
- pencils (two, sharpened – one always breaks);
- pens (two – one always runs out);
- notepad;
- business cards;
- diary;
- worked illustrations of selling prices, savings, incentive bonuses, etc;
- photographs;
- samples;
- comparisons with competitors' performance;
- advertising plans and layouts;
- press cuttings;
- display material.

All this should be clean and neatly arranged. One good thing to buy is a loose-leaf ring-binder-cum-clipboard. In the ring binder you can put clear plastic sleeves in which to keep your documents and photographs in the right order, and the clipboard holds order forms and a notepad. There will usually be pockets for spare price lists, customer record cards and so on. If video demonstrations are important, your laptop will be set up with DVD, CD or a link to your website.

If a sales rep is already with the buyer, withdraw unobtrusively. Either wait until that person's interview is over, or leave and return later.

If the buyer is unavailable, make a note of your proposition on the back of a business card and ask for it to be given to the buyer. Something like: 'Mrs Edwards (are you sure that is the spelling?) – small, low-cost swarf-compactor for machine shops. May I demonstrate, please (3 mins)? John Jones.'

Be pleasant to everyone you meet; you do not yet know who is important. Smile.

If you find yourself in a waiting room with other salespeople, get them to talk about customers you might call on. They are gregarious and often helpful. Beware of joining in gossip about any customer.

Plan the interview itself along the lines of AIDA (see below).

Smile. Use the person's name – Mr, Mrs or Ms until invited otherwise. In your circle first names may be usual. In the buyer's they might seem over-familiar, so play safe.

The sales interview – AIDA

AIDA is the initial letters of attention, interest, desire, action. Those are the stages you take the sales interview through. Questions will feature heavily:

- **Attention** may best be gained by a question: 'If I could show you how to reduce waste by 10 per cent, would you be interested?' That displaces any other thoughts from the person's mind.
- **Interest** is built by demonstration and description of benefits.
- **Desire** may be difficult. We can all think of things that seem interesting but we do not actually want. It can be developed by showing potential customers how much better things would be if they bought. 'From next week you could be enjoying reduced staff absenteeism. How would that feel?'
- **Action** involves placing the order. Do not shrink from asking for the order. If you get a refusal, don't give up. Seek agreement that your basic proposition is attractive, then ask what the problem is. 'What do I have to do to earn your business?' The answer could be anything from a misunderstanding about the proposition to the need to get someone else's approval. Whatever it is, get back into selling. And keep on selling.

Part of your prior planning will be the sales promotion package: the killer reason you give for buying now rather than later. Promises to buy later are rarely kept. Change the sales promotion package every time you call, to keep the offer fresh.

Ideas you could try include:

- a free item (perhaps a first aid kit) that you can buy at wholesale price;
- a voucher worth 20 per cent off essential maintenance items;
- £25 rebate for a purchase of two;
- the maintenance contract at half price;
- a free product with every five bought;
- promotional materials to help their sales;

... and so on. It costs money, of course, but it is all built into your pricing, so there isn't a problem.

Selling via the big catalogues: big orders, quick payment

In most respects these catalogues are much the same as any other customer. They are open to smaller suppliers but operate in specialized ways.

The buying process runs like this:

- preliminary selection by committee nine months before catalogue launch;
- final selection three months later;
- notification of suppliers and orders for further samples from the successful;
- launch of catalogue;
- repeat orders to suppliers.

This demands completion of many forms and the prediction of prices for the life of the catalogue. All samples you submit for the selections they should expect to return or pay for. The quotation expects transit packaging (be advised by the buyer whether a padded bag or mailing box is needed), but you can take out your normal retail packaging. Guarantees of rapid replenishment will be expected. They will usually pay 50 per cent of their retail price. In return you get fast payment, straight dealing and sometimes big orders.

There is a large number of smaller, specialized catalogues offering all kinds of merchandise, some aimed at the public, others at business. Watch out for them and see if your product could fit in.

Conclusions

- A wide variety of channels of distribution is available, some suiting the firm that knows its specific end-users, others best for firms that need to rely on distributors to find customers for them.
- Each channel has its peculiarities and imperatives which it is important for the entrepreneur to understand and live by. Retailers, for example, do not like to be undercut by their suppliers selling direct more cheaply.
- Use of one channel does not preclude use of another, but the appearance of direct competition for the same customer should be avoided.
- The sales visit to the potential customer is a complex affair and demands good preparation. In particular, rebuttals should be anticipated and prepared for.

10
Marketing communications

In this chapter

LEARNING OUTCOMES

By the end of this chapter you should be able to:

- advertise, knowing why and how;
- write news releases for free publicity;
- understand uses of the web;
- make sales via the internet;
- decide on your use of newer media.

Dealing with customers one by one, speaking directly with the decision makers, is possible for some firms. For many it is not, and this group needs to find ways of addressing its market without making individual contact with every potential customer. In addition, the first category will benefit from speaking to its customers in ways that differ from its usual contacts.

Variety in marketing communications is important because:

- Customers do not always cotton-on to a message delivered in one way: they might pick it up, or pick it up better, if it is delivered in more than one way.
- Different methods of communication allow the use of a different 'tone of voice' to get messages across more effectively: in a sales letter or an advert, one can speak more stridently and more to the point than in a face-to-face meeting.
- Delivering messages by varied means gives a sense of a greater presence in the market.

- Customers who have already bought inevitably experience some doubt about whether they took the right decision. Seeing the message again (and again) after they have bought can give post-purchase reassurance, making them less likely to find fault and complain and helping them to turn their attention to other things.

Knowing what you want to say

Before starting to speak it is best to know what you want to say. Thus, before deciding on a communications strategy, listing the aims of the communication is the first task. Once the communication has been written or otherwise prepared, it should be compared to the statement of aims – it is surprising how easy it is to drift off the point once one gets immersed in the process.

Effective advertising

The magazine market is so highly segmented that it is easy to find a suitable advertising medium for almost any proposition. The best source of information on advertising media is BRAD (*British Rate and Data*), which operates by subscription online. *Willings Press Guide* is next best and all public libraries carry it.

Once you have shortlisted a few titles, look at actual copies in detail. Check that they look like the right setting, and that they do not hide adverts like yours away.

Costs of adverts can be very negotiable, especially as the copy date approaches and the publication has empty spaces left to sell. If you can afford to take it or leave it, try a silly offer at the last minute and see what happens.

When designing adverts, make the benefits the most prominent part of the message. Always have artwork produced under your own control rather than by the helpful people at the magazine or newspaper. When you get the proofs, check them in fine detail and pick up even the smallest fault, like a spot or a broken letter. Once you have signed them as passed there is no going back.

Once you have become a substantial advertiser (spending £200,000 a year, say) you should look at small local advertising agencies. You could find that they introduce a level of professionalism and give much valuable advice to make the expense worthwhile. In any case, some of their cost will be met by the discount on space given to agencies but not available to you. As always with important suppliers, see more than one and buy only if you feel sure.

Having bought advertising, you will want to know how well it is working for you. To do that you need to know what your aims were before you took this course – exactly what objectives did you have for the adverts? If that is clear, and your objectives were SMART (specific, measurable, achievable, relevant and timed), all you have to do is note the results and compare.

Beware, though, of expecting too much. A manufacturer of equipment for local authorities once told me that advertising doesn't work in his industry. The evidence was that he had placed one advert but no enquirers said they had seen it. Advertising does not work like that. What it can do in that market is deliver messages about you that ensure a warmer reception next time you call. Who can recall which adverts they have seen today? Yet be sure, you have been influenced by some of them.

Some advertising terms

Some commonly used terms are:

rate card: advertising price list;

rop: run of paper, ie we put it where we like;

facing matter: opposite editorial text, not other adverts;

ifc/irc or ibc: inside front cover/inside rear cover or inside back cover, plum sites;

scc: single column centimetre, ie one centimetre deep and one column wide; advertising costs are often quoted per scc;

litho: lithography, a printing method which makes printing plates photographically, requiring the advertiser to supply 'camera-ready artwork', which most small design studios can accomplish;

copy date: deadline for receipt of artwork for adverts;

proofs or **pulls**: single sheets printed from the plates for final checking by the advertiser;

publicity: this is nearly free and better than advertising.

It is a myth that the papers are full of news garnered by energetic journalists. Much of the media's content is supplied by organizations keen to get their latest news read. Even the smallest organization can get in on this free(ish) ride.

The mechanism is the news release. In essence it is a news story, ready written in journalistic style, which the medium has only to tidy up to match its own policies. If it is too long, the medium cuts it by chopping off the end, so it pays to get the key message across early on. Almost any event in the firm's life can form the basis of a news release; some will be printed, others not, but as it involves no more expense than a stamp or e-mail plus a little time in writing it, most people regard a press release as value for money.

Publicity is better than advertising in one way: since readers think it has been written by journalists they trust it more. On the other hand, the story can be changed from the interpretation you wanted to one you dislike.

Matters that might trigger a news release could include:

- a new firm being formed;
- new premises being opened;
- business expanding – more jobs being provided;

- a new trainee being taken on;
- a trainee passing exams, getting an award;
- a big order;
- new products being taken on or developed;
- the first, hundredth or thousandth order;
- overtime or weekend working in order to get a job out;
- the opportunity to show at an exhibition;
- the results of showing at an exhibition;
- a first, second (etc) anniversary;
- securing a government grant;
- hiring a new executive;
- acquiring a new machine;
- holding an open day.

Media addresses appear in BRAD and *Willings Press Guide*. Don't overlook local radio and TV, both BBC and independent.

To write a news release jot down the key points of the story using the journalist's six prompts: who, what, why, when, where and how? Write the story, or get someone to do it for you, with key messages early on. Double-space and print at 10 words per line on one side only. Head it 'News release' with the date, then the headline and the story. At the end, write 'Ends' and put a contact address to show it is genuine, and give a number for further information. The result might look something like the example shown in Figure 10.1.

In the example the author wants the press release not to be published immediately, but 'embargoed' (delayed) until a date in April. It is no good sending it out months in advance with an embargo, but it should work if it is sent a week or two before the date selected. For immediate publication, insert the word 'immediate' and the date of issue.

The usual reason for an embargo is a risk that the magazines on a long copy date (that is, their next issue is some way off) might send it to the dailies under the same roof, blowing the story prematurely. That would be important if, for example, you wanted no publicity until a particular event such as an open day.

The web and your market

It is a cliché to say that business has been transformed by the internet. Clichés are clichés because they are true.

A small guest house on a remote Hebridean island used to rely on referrals from tourist information centres and advertising. Demand was uncertain and often arose from people stranded by ferry failure. Demand was limited by consumer assumptions that there would be no accommodation on the island, so it was not worth visiting.

FIGURE 10.1 Example of a news release

Unit 16

Hurley Road

Faraday Industrial Estate

Portsmouth

PO 1 1lI

0239 12345678

NEWS RELEASE: EMBARGOED TO APRIL 22ND

A new range of classical urns and other garden decorations is launched by newcomers to the Pompey business scene, McKenzie Enterprises. Run by Jim McKenzie and his wife Mary, the firm spotted a gap in the market for reasonably priced reproductions of the classic designs seen in the gardens of any stately home.

'We were giving our garden a makeover,' said Jim, 49, 'and wanted something classic, but the only things we could find were either beautiful but impossibly expensive, or cheap and not very nice.' Deciding that the only way the couple could get what they wanted was to make their own, Jim researched the casting of imitation stone and found that the technology was not all that complicated. 'I'd worked in civil engineering, so I was familiar with different types of concrete,' he said, 'so when I lost my job it wasn't hard to see which way to go.'

Taking up the story, Mary, 43, said she was delighted that Jim would now be at home instead of working on contracts all over the country. 'Our shared love of the way the great gardeners of the past put together hard designs with soft landscaping made it easy to design a range that would reflect the spirit of the past yet sit well in the smaller, modern garden.'

The range is illustrated on the website www.mckenzie.biz and is on show at the studio-workshop at 16, Hurley Road, Faraday Industrial Estate. The firm plans to sell direct to the public and also to distribute through a number of the better garden centres in the south of England.

[ENDS]

Further details from Jim or Mary McKenzie on 0239 12345678

Proprietors: JG McKenzie, MA McKenzie. e-mail: enq@mckenzie.biz www. mckenzie.biz

Since launching its website it attracts advance bookings from all over the world. The romantic description of the island, its bird-watching opportunities, the chance of real peace and quiet plus good food and accommodation have led to a wealth of enquiries and bookings. There are click-throughs to ferry timetables and reservations, so that visitors can plan the entire trip from their keyboards.

A children's clothing designer produces colourful clothes but her sales were limited to the area she could cover physically. They are expensive and so only a few could afford them. To become more widely known she needed colour brochures, which would have to be renewed every season, but was prevented from reaching the wider market by her inability to afford them.

After investing in her website an amount that would have paid for a single brochure printing, she updates it now with photographs she takes herself. Click-throughs, on which she earns a royalty, take visitors to websites of associated products. Orders are coming in from around the world and she is working on extending the range to sell footwear, accessories and toys so as to provide a total 'look'. She sees her biggest problem now as managing to retain the personal design vision that inspired the company while expanding it to exploit the opportunities on offer. In one role she is a designer, in the other a manager.

The web is also a research resource, especially into marketing matters. Competitors and customers helpfully disclose what they are up to and the chance to look for new ideas, worldwide, is unlimited. Governments and trade bodies publish statistics. Research organizations offer the results of their work on different markets.

The sheer quantity of information presents its own challenges, for when the monthly trade magazine was the main source of information keeping up to date was not a problem. Now the alert business has to set up a regular schedule of site visits to stay on the ball.

Sales via the internet

The main options open to a firm are to:

- set up a shop within an existing web business – eBay and Amazon offer this facility;
- run its own website, confining it to pre-sales information and after-sales queries but offering no means of immediate contact;
- offer a full service covering enquiries, orders and payments.

The cheapest to set up is the first: conversely, it is also the route with the highest running costs per sale. There is no bar to running simultaneously an eBay shop, say, and your own website, so a cautious strategy would be to start off in Amazon or eBay and later launch your own site.

Search-engine optimization: more hits for your site

When a web search is performed, for example by Google, the search engine examines billions of pages of web content and gives its results in a second or two. Partly that is achieved through awesome computing power, partly through the cybernetic equivalent of a quick glance at each page.

That quick glance can be hindered by the type of software used to create the page (easy-to-use page-creation software is nice for the designer but creates tons of code for the engine to search through), by the structure of the site (frames slow things down a lot) and by the text used (which might give meagre clues to the search software).

The first two of these should be checked with the web designer, who should demonstrate familiarity with the issues and say how he or she avoids them. The last item is related to the text the website owner puts on the screen. It should not only tell the story, but every page or so the story should contain a keyword phrase, of the kind that searchers will type into Google.

Sites will need at least several keyword phrases. They should be generated by creative thinking as well as reading competitors' websites to identify the keyword phrases they are using. Software is available that, after the event, will analyse hits to see which keyword phrases are working and which not.

Keyword phrases will be of two to four words each in the vocabulary and structure used by the desired enquirers. For example, a heating engineer may talk of thermal efficiency, where a member of the public speaks of fuel saving. Test the list of keyword phrases for relevance by searching on Google to see what they turn up. Get them right and they will put your site in the top few results every time.

The process for starting a website is straightforward:

- Specify exactly what the site is to do.
- Design the site to meet the specification.
- Check legalities (mainly the Data Protection Act and electronic contracts rules).
- Select a domain name (eg **www.yourname.co.uk**).
- Check on **www.nominet.org.uk** that the name is available.
- Select an agent to register that name to you.
- Select a host internet service provider (ISP) or decide to host the site yourself.
- Create policies and documentation both for internal use and to appear on the site.
- Set up arrangements for handling incoming queries and fulfilling orders.
- Set up payment handling (if relevant): if you take cards, banks have tough rules on CNP (customer not present) transactions.
- Test and debug.
- Go live.

Look carefully at how your preferred domain name could be read and avoid the problems of the Italian branch of electricity supplier, Powergen, the directory of therapists and the list of experts who are said to have come up with powergenitalia. com, therapistfinder.com and expertsexchange.com.

Design of your website is obviously critical. It must look right, expressing visually what you want to put across. A professional web designer will cost money, but ought to get you into business quickly and reliably. Not all designers are the same; some use software that actively slows a web search, so when selecting a supplier, run a three-stage test:

- Trawl a number of the sites the supplier has already designed to see how fast they open.

- Perform a web search on those sites using the key phrases you might expect an enquirer to use (for a Portsmouth estate agent try 'houses for sale in Portsmouth' and see if they come up in the first 10).

- Ask what the designer does about search-engine optimization (SEO) and how the designer takes it into account. The results might be surprising and, if so, give you a warning.

The main features of the site should be speed of loading and ease of use, as people switch elsewhere after only a few seconds' wait. Speed up loading by avoiding fancy graphics, sound and video.

Before operations start you will obviously plan for levels of e-mail and phone contact that seem reasonable. You should also have a contingency plan. What will you do if you get five times that level? Could you get the necessary terminals, phone lines and staff quickly? Do you have the space and insurances?

When customers contact you, put a tick-box to permit you to e-mail them with future special offers. Spamming them (sending them promotional e-mails) without permission is bad behaviour and will lose customers. Never sell your address list to other firms: it is a breach of the trust implicit in the relationship.

Getting this process going is easy. Many website designers advertise locally and firms like BT offer fixed-price packages (at the time of writing six of them, from £199 to £1,999 plus VAT). Some advisory agencies will set you up. Costs for a reasonably sophisticated custom-built site should be no more than £2,500 to set up plus £250 a year for maintenance fees.

Here we can give only an outline of a complex topic. Go to **www.businesslink. gov.uk** for a more thorough treatment.

Other new media

Would you benefit from a Facebook page? Could you demonstrate your product or service on YouTube?

Lauren Luke did, demonstrating make-up tips. After getting 70,000,000 hits, she launched her own range. Twitter now operates in 22 languages worldwide, from Bahasa Melayu to Russian and hosts daily enquiries now measured in billions. A presence there could be worthwhile.

Conclusions

- Varied communications usually achieve goals better than a single medium because not all people are hooked by the same approach. In any case, customers need to see the same message several times before they can spontaneously recall having seen it.

- Clarity of aim is essential – both in what to say and in whom to say it to. This starts with knowing with complete certainty what you want to say, no more and no less, and to whom you want to say it.

- The wide range of communications media now available should be looked at carefully and used where possible and meaningful. Electronic media have produced extraordinary phenomena whereby apparently unremarkable video clips have achieved millions of hits. The low cost of distribution (though not necessarily of production) can create worldwide recognition almost instantaneously, a fact which it is tempting to exploit.

PART 4:
Financial management, raising finance

11
Costing

In classical economics, the market determines the price of a product or service, the seller (in that very inadequate description) being powerless to affect the price one way or another. In fact, we know that there are all sorts of ways in which a firm can enhance the price that a buyer will pay. However, accepting for a moment the classical economist's rather restricted view, if the firm is to sell at a profit it needs to know the cost of what it sells. In a perfect world, price will always exceed cost – but as the world is at present less than ideal, businesses need to know their costs.

To take a really basic service, such as window cleaning: what is the cost of providing the window cleaner's service? Vehicle, ladders, wash-leathers and so on are easy to identify. But what share of those and how much of the window cleaner's phone bill should go to each customer? Or the insurance premiums (which can be sizeable) or pension contributions?

Questions like those have prompted the writing of large textbooks. Here we shall use a single, simple method that serves many firms well in their early stages, and for much longer than that if they do not grow. It is the 'absorption' method: in summary, it says that for any one job:

cost of materials + overhead expenses + labour cost = total cost.

Simple, as I said.

TABLE 11.1   Absorption costing systems: general principles

To price a product, service or job, you first need to know what it costs. The simpler the costing system, the quicker and easier it is to use. Absorption costing is ideal for the small operation as it is the simplest of all the systems available.

To use it, there are three easy steps:	Find out what hourly rate ought to be charged for labour and overheads.
	Multiply that hourly rate by the actual number of hours used on the job in hand.
	Add on the cost of materials.

The answer is the total cost of that job. Once you've got that, you can move on to deciding what to charge. The system depends on making assumptions and judgements (so it is not precise), but it is close enough for practical purposes. In summary it works like this (further detail appears later, but it is important to get the general idea first):

Labour:	Annual payroll costs for yourself and any staff, including NI, pension contributions, health insurance, etc.
Overheads: two main sources:	Annual total of all day-to-day running costs (eg rent, rates, insurance, fuel, energy, hire, phones, consumables, etc.
	A year's depreciation of buildings you own, plus vehicles, tools and equipment owned but not hired. (Calculate these by dividing what they cost to buy by their likely life in years.)
Hourly rate:	Total the above. Divide the total by the number of productive hours you are likely to work in a year. The answer is your hourly charge-out rate in £s.
Total cost of job:	(number of hours taken × £ per hour charge-out rate) + materials

Shortly we'll look at how much to charge per hour for labour and overheads. In essence, a firm needs to charge enough to pay running costs plus an income for the owner. For example, the cost of that imaginary manufactured product, a widget might be:

Materials	£24
Overheads and wages:	
2 hours × £40 per hour	£80 +
Total cost:	£104

If all the hours worked on that product are counted, and the hourly rate is right, and they make the number of widgets they forecast, all of their costs will be covered. Simple.

However, there may be a problem. The cost of something to you is not necessarily what you can sell it for. Rather, **cost is the lowest price for which you can afford to sell** it.

There is an important distinction between types of cost: those that go up and down with the level of sales (eg the cost of materials consumed) and those that do not (eg the rent for premises). They are known as fixed costs (which are mostly overheads) and variable costs (which are mostly built into the product or service you sell).

In the early days, at least, it pays to commit to as few fixed costs as possible and to keep as much as you can variable. It might cost more, but it gives more flexibility as the business evolves. As you gain experience, your confidence in fixing some costs may grow. Examples of keeping costs variable include buying-in rather than making things yourself, renting or taking out a loan rather than buying outright, and using subcontractors rather than employed staff.

Working out an hourly rate

First, work out the costs of running your business. At first, several of the figures will be guesses. Include:

- rent and rates;
- fuel, light and heat;
- consumables (but not the materials built into each job);
- vehicle running costs (but not purchase cost);
- staff costs;
- the pay you will draw from the firm;
- depreciation.

Exclude the cost of buying things you will keep and use: tools, vehicles, PCs, software, etc. These are capital costs, accounted for via depreciation.

Depreciation is a charge to your costs that reflects the fact that, little by little, you are wearing out capital items (this is how our window cleaner gets the cost of his or her ladders back). If you buy a machine for £1,000 that will last for four years, you use up £250-worth of it each year until, after four years, it is in your books as valueless. You charge that £250 to each year's accounts as depreciation, and you include it in the current calculation as a cost. (Ignore the fact that in the real world you can probably sell it for something, or may even continue to use it, after the four years.)

Now we move to calculating how many productive hours you work. In new firms people often work 60 or 70 hours a week, but their productive time, the time when they are doing something that a customer will pay for, rarely exceeds 20 or 25 hours.

TABLE 11.2   Working out an hourly charge-out rate 1

Productive hours

25 hours a week × 48 weeks a year = **1,200 productive hours a year**

Overheads to be recovered

Family income (gross)	£35,000
Business overheads	£20,000
Total	**£55,000**

Hourly rate to be charged

£55,000 ÷ 1,200 hours = £45.83 per hour

The rest goes on all sorts of ancillary activity, necessary but unpaid for. So you work out your costs on just the productive hours. Taking out holidays, Christmas and sickness, 48 weeks' work a year creates 48 weeks × 25 hours = 1,200 productive hours.

Finally, we can now calculate the cost per hour. Suppose you need £35,000 gross (that is, before income tax and NI deductions) to feed and clothe the family and the firm incurs running costs of £20,000, it has to earn £55,000 a year. Look at Table 11.2 to see how it comes out.

A caution: do not be tempted to round Table 11.2's hourly rate down from £45.83 to £45, for 1,200 × 83 pence comes to £996 over the year. This is nearly £19 a week, all out of your personal pocket.

If your figure looks high, don't reject it. 'High' does not mean high by comparison with the figures used here – they are only an example – but by comparison with what others in your market charge. Find ways to justify the prices it results in, by being reliable and doing good work. Anyone charging less, yourself included, will fail. Make sure you minimize the effects on your prices by:

- controlling interruptions, so as to increase productive time;
- working intensively, turning out more in an hour than others;
- using modern equipment wisely, for the same reason.

Keeping an eye on costings

Given that the figures used in your costing are estimates and predictions, the one certainty about them is that they will be wrong. That is fine, as long as you keep the error to a minimum through constant review.

To make your predicted costs come about in real life, monitor all the assumptions you made and get early warning of things going wrong. If you manage only 20 productive

TABLE 11.3 Keeping track of performance

| Invoiced sales, Year 1 | | Target £ | | Actual £ | |
Month	Week no	Week	Running	Week	Running
Jan	1	–	–		
	2	100	100		
	3	200	300		
	4	200	500		
Feb	5	100	600		
	6	100	700		
	7	150	850		
	8	150	1,000		
Mar	9	400	1,400		
	10	400	1,800		
	11	400	2,200		
	12	400	2,600		
	13	400	3,000		

hours and get 45 weeks' work, there are only 900 hours to recover costs from. Either the hourly rate (using the figures above) rises to over £61 or your income has to fall by £13,600. Nasty, and therefore very important that you keep track of the key factors:

- invoiced sales;
- overhead expenses;
- productive hours worked.

For each of them, set up a simple table showing your weekly plan and running total, against which you can write the actual outcome and running total. Table 11.3 shows an example for invoiced sales.

It shows at a glance whether you are on target, ahead of the game or falling behind. You then have a chance to take corrective action before the warning becomes a crisis.

Taking on an employee reduces the hourly rate, which does not mean you reduce your price, of course. Table 11.4 shows how.

If the simplicities of absorption costing leave you uneasy, another system is discussed later.

TABLE 11.4   Working out an hourly charge-out rate 2

Productive hours

17 hours from owner (less than before because supervision takes time, and selling the extra output takes longer)

33 hours from employee (44-hour week, 75% productive)

50 hours a week × 48 weeks a year = **2,400 productive hours a year**

Overheads to be recovered

Family income	£35,000
Business overheads	£20,000
Employee's cost to you	£20,000
Total	**£75,000**

Hourly rate that could now be charged

£75,000 ÷ 2,400 hours = £31.25 per hour
This means that hourly costs have fallen by nearly one-third – a saving that need not be passed on to customers.

Conclusions

- Conceptually, the idea of costing is not difficult to grasp, but the practicalities can be complex. However tiresome it may be, costing is central to business activity.

- At the planning stage systems need to be set up for all costs to be monitored, as the assumptions made at the outset might not be fulfilled. It is easy for a cost to drift off course and if proper monitoring is not in place the first that the entrepreneur knows about it may be when losses appear instead of profits in the accounts. If those accounts are produced no more than annually, a serious situation may have developed.

- One way of coping with complexity is to reduce it to simplicity, in the certain knowledge that a simple system will be used, but at the same time it can be misleading. For this reason many firms can use a simple absorption costing system, at least in the early stages, but with a full understanding of its shortcomings.

- Staff can lower costs appreciably – if you can keep them busy. Again, there is a place for monitoring outcomes against the assumptions made initially.

12
Controlling cash

In this chapter

LEARNING OUTCOMES

By the end of this chapter you should be able to:

- understand the vital importance of controlling cash flow;
- predict the cash situation;
- make the distinction between cash and profit.

Cash matters more than anything else in a business

'Cash' is loose banknotes or money in a current account. It is the only thing that can be used to pay bills. If bills are not paid, creditors foreclose and the business usually shuts. Consequently, **cash is the single most important thing in any business**; it is the one thing a business owner watches constantly.

Running out of cash is easy. The best ways of doing it are:

- delaying sending out invoices for work done;
- losing notes recording work done;
- mislaying delivery notes for work sold;
- not chasing customers for payment;
- avoiding opening credit accounts with suppliers;

- paying bills in cash as quickly as possible;
- buying large quantities to get discounts;
- buying equipment and vehicles for cash instead of via loans;
- taking on inefficient or ineffective staff;
- keeping on staff for whom there will be no work;
- never checking what you sign for;
- never getting a signature (and printed name) for goods you deliver;
- being open to theft or fraud;
- taking on unnecessarily expensive offices or vehicles;
- buying expensive but unnecessary insurance policies;
- not cultivating the bank manager;
- never planning ahead to foresee cash needs;
- never recording performance and comparing it with plan;
- taking on a really big order, especially from a slow-paying customer.

Inexperienced people can have problems with that last item, assuming that taking a big order is a matter for celebration. So it should be, but only if it does not bankrupt the firm. The problem is that you pay out your cash for materials, labour and overheads – lots of it for a big order – but don't get cash back from the customer for maybe several months. Too often, when the cheque arrives, it is the liquidator who pays it into the bank.

Keeping on top of the cash

Shrewd businesspeople follow some basic principles:

- Orders agree payment terms as well as price, delivery, etc.
- A sale is complete only when payment has been made.
- Bills are paid only when due, never before.
- Credit accounts are opened with suppliers wherever possible.
- Supplies are bought only for immediate needs, even if that means paying more per item.
- Borrowing is for property and equipment, the easy borrowing; working capital is harder to borrow, so hold back your own funds to finance that, if you can.
- Only productive staff who are currently needed are kept: you are responsible for the business as a whole, not for each individual employee.
- When staff are at work they are working all the time, and for you.
- The firm is run frugally.
- Good anti-fraud systems are in place, including an iron grip on the accounting system.

Foreseeing the cash position

Some people see this as a nuisance, to be avoided if possible. True, just as it is a nuisance to look both ways before crossing a busy road. Remember: cash is the single most important thing in any business; it is the one thing a business owner needs to watch constantly.

Watching cash involves predicting how much there will be and monitoring that forecast. Any serious divergence and you pounce, not resting until you can say why it happened. It is too important to neglect.

You need to know four things to create a cash-flow forecast:

- what points in time the forecast is for;
- expected flows of cash into the firm;
- expected flows of cash out of the firm;
- the timings of each inflow and outflow.

Looking at each of those in turn:

- Points in time are usually month-ends, though more often when things are tight.
- Flows in are your investment, borrowings, sales of goods and services, and occasional disposals of capital items, old vehicles for example.
- Flows out are purchases, overheads, wages, with occasional payments of taxes. Depreciation is ignored, as no cash moves.
- Timings relate to when the sales and purchase invoices are settled, not when they go out or arrive.

Why cash-flow forecasting matters

A practical example is of Tom, a busy teacher with great woodworking skills, who makes mahogany boxes which are highly prized as Christmas gifts. It is now November and he is puzzling over his cash-flow and profit-and-loss (P&L) budgets.

Last month, October, he paid cash for £400-worth of timber, screws and other materials. Half of the boxes will sell for cash to colleagues from school, and a local gift shop will take the rest this month but pay in February. He expects to make 200, and to sell them at £20 each. Fortunately his accountant sister-in-law calls in, and quickly sorts out the puzzle by working out a P&L budget and a cash-flow forecast.

What Tables 12.1 and 12.2 show is that Tom's profit does turn into cash eventually, but only in February. The bottom line of the cash-flow table gives the position month by month. Before he gets his money back he is quite badly out of pocket.

TABLE 12.1   Tom's P&L budget

P&L budget: end December	
Invoiced sales: 200 × £20	£4,000
Materials	£400
Value added	£3,600
Overheads: trivial	–
Net profit	£3,600

TABLE 12.2   Tom's cash-flow forecast

Cash-flow forecast: October–February (£)					
	Oct	Nov	Dec	Jan	Feb
Income					
Cash sales	–	200	1,800	–	–
Sales to shop	–	–	–	–	2,000
Total income	–	200	1,800		2,000
Outgoings					
Materials	400	–	–	–	–
Cash flow for month	(400)	200	1,800	–	2,000
Cumulative	(400)	(200)	1,600	1,600	3,600

NOTE: Brackets signify minus quantities.

For anyone operating on a larger scale the warning is clear: forecast only your profit and you can easily run out of cash. Forecast your cash as well as your profit and you should survive (see Table 12.3). Appendix 1 shows how to create a cash-flow forecast.

TABLE 12.3   What to include in P&L budgets and cash-flow forecasts

	P&L	Cash flow
Sales invoices	all issued, whether or not paid	only shown when payment is expected
Materials	the value used to make the goods sold	shows value when payment is due
Overheads	the share for the period, whether or not invoiced or paid	shown when payment is expected to be made
Depreciation	the share for the period	not shown – no cash moves
VAT	ignore it if you are VAT-registered	show it

Conclusions

- Controlling cash flow is of the greatest importance as, without cash, the firm cannot pay its bills and will not survive. The technique of forecasting cash flow is not complex yet can save the life of the firm.
- Forecasting must be undertaken, as must recording of actual outcomes, followed by thoughtful consideration of any variation to distinguish temporary or trivial factors from established and important ones, so that suitable action can be taken.
- While profit is important, cash is supreme.

13
Further financial planning

In this chapter

LEARNING OUTCOMES

By the end of this chapter you should be able to:

- plan for profit;
- create a P&L budget and account;
- describe common ways of losing money;
- undertake break-even analysis;
- use contribution costing.

Profit planning

So far in the financial field we have looked at costings and cash flow. Profit is the next topic to be examined. Like all other aspects of business, it is better to plan for it than hope for it.

In planning for profits, the main tool is the P&L budget. In principle it is extremely simple (the numbers shown in Table 13.1 are just to show how it works).

P&L accounting answers the vital question: 'How much do I sell, what are my costs and so how much money do I make?'

TABLE 13.1 P&L (£000s)

Sales invoiced			100
	Cost of sales (ie cost of the items invoiced)	just labour plus materials	40 –
Gross margin			60
Overheads			
	Staff	9	
	Premises	5	
	Transport	3	
	Insurance	1	
	Depreciation	1	
	Other overheads	1	20 –
Operating profit			40
	Finance costs	1	
	Tax	2	
			3 –
Net profit			37

NOTE: If it is hard to say how much labour goes into each item sold, it is difficult to specify the cost of sales. The easy solution is to put labour into the overheads, leaving only materials in the second line down and substituting for gross margin the term 'value added'. That simply means the amount of value added to materials by your efforts. This is quite acceptable.

Accounting terms

A **budget** is a forecast that you are working to. When (*not* if) events overtake it and it becomes out of date, you re-budget.

Control is the process of recording alongside the budget what actually happened, to alert you to dangerous deviations.

An **account** is a record of what actually happened over a period of time.

So you start off with predictions in a budget, or a series of budgets, then you report what really happened in an account. These terms can be applied to P&L, cash flow, capital expenditure, sales, staff costs or any other financial matter you want to keep track of.

By now you may feel the need for a summary of what the three main accounting documents do; these are shown in Table 13.2.

TABLE 13.2   Differences between P&L accounts, balance sheets and cash-flow forecasts

P&L account	Balance sheet	Cash-flow forecast
Shows **sales** invoiced in the period, whether or not the customer has paid.	Shows **how much** money is tied up in the firm. **Where** it is tied up.	**Income** – shows how much, and when, cash is expected to arrive.
Shows **expenses** incurred in the period, irrespective of whether the bill has been paid.	Shows **what** were the sources of that money.	**Expenses** – shows how much cash is expected to be paid out, and when.
Depreciation is shown.	**Depreciation** is shown.	**Ignores** anything that is not an actual movement of cash, such as depreciation.
Refers to a PAST PERIOD	Refers to a MOMENT IN TIME	Refers to a PERIOD IN THE FUTURE

How to trade unprofitably

The large number of ways that traders have devised in order to trade unprofitably might suggest that much human ingenuity has been spent on seeking out new methods. That is not the case: mostly it is inattention or, sometimes, bad luck.

According to *The Times 100 Business Case Studies* (**http://businesscasestudies. co.uk/business-theory/strategy/business-failure.html**) the main reasons for early-stage failure of businesses include:

- Poor marketing – this usually arises from poor market research.
- Cash-flow problems – especially from growing too fast.
- Poor business planning – failing to undertake detailed planning across the board.
- Lack of finance – this results in inability to exploit opportunities to the full.
- Failure to embrace new technologies and new developments – and so being left behind in the cost-control race.
- Poor choice of location – for example being invisible to customers or spending too much.

- Poor management – lack of understanding of customers and their business and/or lack of hard work.
- Poor human resource (HR) relations – failure to manage and motivate expensive employees suitably.
- Lack of clear objectives – as they say, 'If you don't know where you're going, any road will do.'

This list is notable for two things: only two of the items on it relate directly to the management of finances, yet every one has an impact on cash flow and profit. In business, as in life, everything is connected to everything else. Gluttons for punishment may go to a website that lists, as it puts it 'the 65 most common reasons for business failure' (**www.bankruptcy-insolvency.co.uk/ltd-companies/common-reasons-for-business-failure.php**). This makes sobering reading, but the time to scrutinize the list carefully is before the business is started, rather than after it has failed and you are trying to pick the reasons for your own demise.

Breakthrough to profit

Once the P&L budget is complete, you are ready for the next stage of understanding how your firm works. The question you address here is this: 'How much do I have to sell before I make a clear profit?'

The answer lies in another simple piece of arithmetic, to calculate your break-even point. That is the level of sales that produces enough profit to meet all the costs. Once you have passed it, all the extra profit is yours... and the taxman's. Equally, if things go wrong, you will want to know the level that sales can fall to before you start to make losses. Table 13.3 makes the point (the budgeted numbers are, as always, just examples).

TABLE 13.3 Working out a break-even point

	Budget £		Break-even (figures rounded) £
Sales	90,000		69,000
Materials	30,000	(33% of sales)	23,000
Value added	60,000	(67% of sales)	46,000
Overheads	46,000	(remains the same)	46,000
Net profit	14,000		–

Divide the annual break-even sales figure into weekly numbers and make a note of them on your weekly and monthly sales budgets. That way you get early warning of profit trends, whether good or bad.

Budgeted value added ÷ budgeted sales = z per cent.

Overheads ÷ z × 100 = break-even sales.

Break-even value added = overheads.

Break-even materials = break-even sales – break-even value-added.

Alternatively, if you prefer charts to tables, you can adopt the break-even chart model shown in Figure 13.1.

FIGURE 13.1   Break-even chart

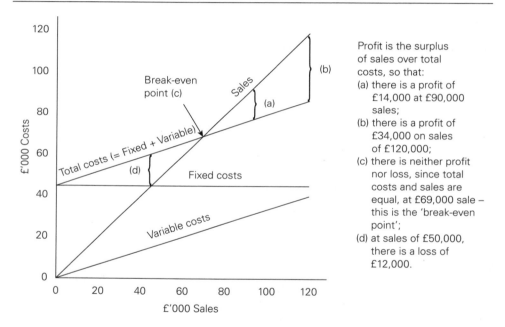

Profit is the surplus of sales over total costs, so that:
(a) there is a profit of £14,000 at £90,000 sales;
(b) there is a profit of £34,000 on sales of £120,000;
(c) there is neither profit nor loss, since total costs and sales are equal, at £69,000 sale – this is the 'break-even point';
(d) at sales of £50,000, there is a loss of £12,000.

One major benefit of using a chart is that it shows how important it is to keep costs variable, rather than fixing them. This is truest at times of greatest uncertainty, such as when the firm is new. Visualize pulling the fixed-cost line downwards and think how sharply the break-even point would move to the left, that is, to a lower level of sales.

Clever costing: the contribution method

Once you are selling a range of products, simple absorption costing may no longer be adequate. You may wish to move to contribution costing. Once again, it is simple in concept, saying: 'We can't allocate every item of cost to each product; it's just too complicated. Instead we'll allocate just those things that clearly belong to each product. The rest we'll put into overheads, and they'll get paid from the general pool of profit.'

Table 13.4 shows how it works in a situation where a firm has three products with very different mixes of labour and materials selling at £30, £40 and £55.

Direct materials and labour are those used directly in the product. For example, for a firm that presses DVDs, these would be the disk, case, notes, outer box and labour for making and packing the product. Indirect costs are those you are unable to allocate easily, such as rent, insurance, cleaning materials and machine maintenance, which go into overheads.

One further calculation reveals the amount of money the firm plans to make. Taking the contribution that a single unit of the product yields (from the last line of Table 13.5), then multiplying it by the number you plan to sell, reveals the total contribution to overheads and profit that you expect. This feeds straight into your P&L budget, providing its first two lines. Table 13.5 shows how.

TABLE 13.4   Costing example using contribution costing

Product	X	Y	Z
Direct materials (£)	10.00	15.00	25.00
Direct labour (£)	2.00	18.00	5.00
Total direct costs (£)	12.00	33.00	30.00
Average sales value (£)	30.00	55.00	40.00
Contribution to overhead, and profit, per item (£)	18.00	22.00	10.00

TABLE 13.5   The total contribution under contribution costing

Product	X	Y	Z	Total
Contribution to overheads and profit, per item (a) (£)	18.00	22.00	10.00	
Sales forecast (units) (b) (£)	2,000	3,000	500	
Total contribution (a) × (b) (£)	36,000	66,000	5,000	£107,000

Looking at the relatively small contribution that only 500 units of Z make, you might be tempted to discontinue it. That might be the right decision, but be aware that you will need to make up its £5,000 contribution from savings or price rises elsewhere.

Doing this investigation on a spreadsheet enables 'what if?' planning (What if I raise the price of Z by 5 per cent? What if I cut the price of X by £1? etc) to see what combination of pricing and volume produces the greatest total contribution.

Conclusions

- Planning for profitability is essential if the entrepreneur is to have any control over the firm's progress. Without proper planning there will be no basis for comparison with actual outcomes, so that those outcomes cannot be judged as satisfactory or otherwise.

- Progress against the profit plan needs to be monitored and the plan changed as circumstances overtake it. This requires disciplined, accurate and timely routines for the recording of facts and the production of reports.

- Everything done or not done in the business will affect profits.

- The only sure way of staying in business is through constant vigilance, a demanding and perhaps intimidating fact. Nonetheless 'doing the job' is not enough – you must also know all the facts associated with its execution.

- Knowing the point at which the firm breaks even allows more flexible decisions to be taken about less-profitable opportunities. While that is useful, it should not tempt firms into selling at marginal costs once break-even has been reached.

- If the firm outgrows simple absorption costing, contribution costing offers benefits. In more complex situations it may be the system to adopt from the outset.

14
Credit control

In this chapter

LEARNING OUTCOMES

By the end of this chapter you should be able to:

- recognize the importance of credit control;
- minimize the credit given;
- minimize the risks from credit granted;
- chase the late payer.

The topic of financial management is a large one, studded with areas said to be vital to business survival. Credit control is yet another such matter. Why? Consider what the granting of credit involves:

- You pass your property over to a stranger.
- The stranger promises he or she will pay you at some point in the future.
- You hope the stranger will keep this promise.

Anyone not frightened by such a proposition ought to be. The things that can go wrong are obvious:

- The person doesn't pay at all.
- He or she pays only part of the bill, claiming that the goods were unsatisfactory.
- He or she does pay, but only so far into the future that it hardly matters.
- The person disappears.

- The person goes out of business, leaving you as an unsecured creditor of a failed limited company.
- The person claims never to have heard of you and certainly never to have bought from you.
- The person says the goods were no use and returns them to you, somewhat soiled.

Control of credit is therefore an important matter and effort should be spent on minimizing credit risks.

In descending order of desirability, the best approaches to credit are:

1 Give no credit – get paid in advance.
2 Get part-payment in advance.
3 Get paid on delivery.
4 Get paid as soon as possible after delivery.
5 Don't get paid at all.

Many firms successfully pull off the trick of getting payment in full in advance; usually they are dealing direct with the public. Many members of the public will fall in with the idea if no alternative is offered, if after the specification has been sorted out the vendor simply says: 'Right, that'll be £500: will that be a credit or a debit card?' and reaches for the terminal. Some will not be browbeaten, in which case part-payment might be acceptable: one-half or one-third of the price, paid now, with the balance on completion, is still very acceptable to the vendor.

However, for the majority of firms, the task comes down to eliminating (5) and shortening the time under (4), both of them laborious. A further penalty of giving credit is the administrative load of keeping on top of who owes you what.

Credit control in practice

Once you start to give credit it is difficult to withdraw, so it is worth seeing if you can develop a strategy for avoidance. When dealing direct with the public things are simplest. People expect to pay on delivery, even to place a deposit with order. In business-to-business (B2B) transactions, the assumption is that credit must be offered. Is that true? Probably not if your business has any of these characteristics:

- Small outlay – nobody really minds paying the window cleaner £20 from the petty cash.
- Emergency – if the only way the big problem can be solved quickly is to pay cash.
- Scarcity – the only person providing something that everyone needs can demand and get cash payment.
- Uniqueness – if the complete package you offer really has outstandingly attractive features, people might swap their desire for credit for their desire for those features.

Credit cards remove bad debt if you follow their rules. As well as the public, many firms use them for small purchases. They cost you up to about 5 per cent of the sale value.

When dealing with firms you can argue that if they pay cash they save your costs, which you pass on to them. Don't be tempted instead to make a charge for credit or you may fall under the rules governing banking, a grim prospect.

Positive strategies

If you conclude that you have to give credit, these are the things to do:

- When selling, be suspicious if the order comes too easily – maybe the customer cannot get credit elsewhere.
- Carry out credit checks and before processing the order ask your customer about any court orders that are disclosed.
  For private limited companies, check on them and their directors via **www.companieshouse.gov.uk**.
- When negotiating an order, make the payment terms an integral part of the deal.
- When dealing with anyone but the owner, and especially if it is a big firm, ask what the accounts settlement policy is. You may find that they always take three months' credit (many do, which might make you think again about accepting the business).
- Depending on what the person says and on your attitudes, either stand your ground and risk losing the order or modify the terms, including price, accordingly.
- Always know exactly who your firm is dealing with (see below).
- Get a specific undertaking about when you will be paid (eg seven days after delivery) and include it in your confirmation of the order.
- Get a signature on a delivery note plus, if relevant, a satisfaction note.
- Invoice immediately on delivery, preferably handing the invoice over with the goods.

Knowing who is placing the order may become very important, especially if disputes arise later. Create a simple form that you keep with order forms, and once the order is in the bag, say that you need one or two details to open the account. The form requires you to ask:

- the exact name of the organization placing the order;
- the customer's constitution – sole trader, partnership, limited company, company limited by guarantee, limited liability partnership, plc, public body, etc;
- names and home addresses of sole trader or partners;
- names of directors, authorized and issued capital, registered office, country of registration and registered number of limited company (some of this you may

be able to get from Companies House, **www.companieshouse.gov.uk**, and some should be on their letterhead, which you may already have);

- names of two trade referees;
- bank name and branch address.

It is perfectly normal for a buyer opening a credit account to be asked for this information. To simplify the task, and to make it look routine, create a simple form that captures the information. Another precaution may be to divide a large order into a number of deliveries, with agreement that you will be paid after each one and before the next is due.

Should the boot eventually be on the other foot and you are asked to provide a reference for one of your customers, be careful. If you give unjustified positive information you can be sued for any damages that may arise. If you are unjustly negative, a suit for slander (if spoken) or libel (if written) may arise.

When you invoice, be sure that your invoices carry the following information:

- the information required by law (see Chapter 16 for disclosure requirements);
- the charge and how it is arrived at;
- the date of issue, which is also the tax point for VAT-registered traders;
- any information that the customer requires, such as an order number or stock number;
- payment terms, shown prominently.

Statements are required by some customers. They are summaries of the transactions with the customer over an appropriate period of time, say three to six months. They are usually sent monthly, and show:

- all invoices issued during the period that the statement covers, those due (or overdue) for payment being marked accordingly;
- payments received during the period;
- the outstanding balance on the account.

See Figure 14.1 for an example invoice and statement.

In view of the rising costs of administration and postage, many businesses now send statements only to those customers who insist on them. They can be a help to customers in checking that their idea of what they owe you coincides with yours, and that you have registered the payments they have made. The statements can also help you, by drawing to their attention overdue invoices. But you can chase overdue invoices just as effectively without issuing statements, so that alone is not sufficient reason for instituting them.

Dealing with the bad payer

Whatever they may have promised, some customers will not pay on time. This affects your cash flow and so threatens your survival. Thus immediate, robust and effective action is called for.

FIGURE 14.1   Example of an invoice and statement

This is an invoice.
It is simply a bill for
goods supplied or
services rendered.

ABCD Ltd

700 High Street
Anytown AN1 1AN

Invoice

No. 217/13

Smith & Co
698 Cook St
Anytown

Date and
Tax Point: 11/3/13
Your Order: 92/2709/pr

Quantity	Description	Each	Value
8 cases X 24	Widgets 10 2050	£12.50	£100.00
	Goods		£100.00
	VAT @ 20%		£20.00
	Total payable		£120.00

PAYMENT DUE 30 DAYS FROM INVOICE DATE
Registered in England no 123456
VAT no 111222233
Directors: A Allen, B Brooks, C Cliff, D Davis

ABCD Ltd

To
Smith & Co
698 Cook St
Anytown

700 High Street
Anytown AN1 1AN
Date: 31/3/13

Date	Invoice	Value	Payment	Balance
Brought forward				120.00
18/1/13	103	55.00		235.00
27/1/13	118	123.00		358.00
3/2/13	124	81.00*		439.00
5/2/13			180.00	259.00
28/2/13	183	97.00*		356.00
7/3/13			55.00	301.00
10/3/13	217	120.00		421.00
26/3/13			123.00	298.00
Balance carried forward				298.00

Items marked* are overdue – please pay now
Registered in England no 123456
Directors: A Allen, B Brooks, C Cliff, D Davis

This is a statement.
It summarizes the
activity on this
customer's account.
The invoice shown
above (no 217 for
£120.00) is the last
one on it. The
information it gives
is taken from the
firm's books, and
enables the
customer to see if
his books agree with
yours. Most people
get something
similar every
month – a bank
statement.

Keep a daily check on outstanding accounts. When an invoice falls due for which payment has not arrived, telephone to see if there is a problem. If there is one, sort it out. If none, extract a promise that the cheque will either go off that day or will be available for collection when you visit at 10 o'clock tomorrow.

Explain that no more deliveries will be made until outstanding accounts are settled. Write or e-mail to confirm.

Know your right to claim interest at Bank Rate (strictly speaking, the Bank's 'reference rate') plus 8 per cent, and fees, for late payment from business customers (see **www.payontime.co.uk**), but never claim interest from the public unless you are registered under the Consumer Credit Act, which no SME should even consider.

Usually a firm but friendly approach will ensure that you get paid this time, and that in future the customer might smarten up, knowing that you mean business. It is not easy to swap roles from the salesperson to the account collector, but your survival depends on it. Put yourself in the other person's shoes for a moment: the person knows he or she has done wrong and that you are in the right. This gives you moral authority.

A hardened few will still not pay. Try a final visit, armed with a copy of the invoice and delivery note to neutralize stories that they have got lost. Explain that you sold to the customer in good faith, he or she promised to pay but has not done so and that it is causing you cash-flow problems and difficulties with the bank. Ask for the money, there and then. If it is not forthcoming, explain that you will need to sue for the debt. That should produce results, for once you start the court process the costs climb sharply and a losing defendant usually has to pay them.

If you can show written orders, conditions of sale and your confirmation of order, plus a signed delivery and/or satisfaction note, a County Court case should be straightforward. The Small Claims procedure is simple and applies to claims of up to £5,000 (£2,000 in Northern Ireland).

Be aware that a judgment does not always mean you get paid, but it is the first step. Despite that, always pursue rogues via the law, not by way of threats, or the tables will turn on you.

Should you receive a solicitor's letter from the defendant, ignore any bluster and look only at the substance of the defence. If they have a case for not paying, or getting a reduction, try to settle out of court and, next time, don't let it get this far but make your case watertight from the start.

It may be worth trying a debt collector; perhaps you should meet one and see what they can offer, as part of your pre-start research. They might be cheaper and more effective than automatically steering everything towards a solicitor.

Conclusions

- Credit control can be an issue of survival since it can govern the rate at which the chief source of cash – debtors settling their accounts – flows into the firm.

- Steps should be taken to minimize the credit given and to minimize the risks from credit granted. Not all will be acceptable to all customers, so a clear policy on the granting of credit needs to be established from the outset, and followed.

- Late payers should be chased promptly. Fears about the possibility of losing future business should be set alongside the possible failure of the firm through non-collection or late collection of its dues.

15
Sources of finance

In this chapter

LEARNING OUTCOMES

By the end of this chapter you should be able to:

- describe the reasons for financing a firm;
- describe types of finance;
- name financial providers;
- understand bank policies;
- recognize types of bank lending;
- present a case for borrowing;
- understand equity investment and its difference from bank borrowing;
- accept the scarcity of grants, but that it is worth enquiring;
- know of the Prince's Trust, which can help people under 30 and those over 50.

The need for finance

It is a rare entrepreneur who has enough money to finance his or her own business without regard to external sources of finance. Consequently, the vast majority have not only to devise and plan their own business model, but then have to go to others – the people with the money – and convince them to risk it on this proposition, rather than some other. For there is no shortage of people wanting to borrow money, although bankers often claim that there is a great shortage of *credible people* with *convincing propositions* wanting to borrow it.

Much of this book is given over to advice and know-how on thinking the proposition through until it is completely sound, and presenting it persuasively. That still leaves the matter of individual credibility over which the writer has no control. Still, it is a fair bet that most of the propositions presented to lenders or investors will not have been formulated along the lines advocated here, so the entrepreneur who does it this way boosts the chances of success immeasurably.

The hard work done by an entrepreneur who has to justify the business to an investor or lender is worth it, however demanding it may seem at the time. Most of the people whom the would-be borrower will apply to have seen many a business dream bite the dust and have grown sceptical – and maybe a little wise – in the process. Their views are worth having. Contrast the position of the self-funding individual, who is free to make whatever basic errors they choose, with nobody to point out that perhaps, the emperor's clothes are, in places, somewhat ragged if not absent altogether. It is a source of sadness to any business adviser to see the proceeds of a legacy, possibly assembled painstakingly by a loving relative, blown in a few months on some scheme that it was clear from the start could not work.

Businesses need two forms of finance. They need short-term finance to cover ebbs and flows of cash in and out of the firm, and long-term finance to cover major purchases of the sort that enable it to earn its living.

Long-term finance is the core finance at the heart of the business. All businesses experience fluctuations day to day or from season to season and have to be able to meet instantaneously the demands that places on their cash flow.

It would be wasteful to hold finance for an entire year in order to meet a peak in demand for cash that occurred for only a month or so, so short-term needs are usually covered by a separate arrangement, an 'overdraft'. The overdraft confers the right on the firm to write cheques for money it has not got, thus taking its bank account into the red, up to a certain figure, the 'overdraft limit'. Equally, it would be foolish to finance the entire firm by overdraft (even if any bank would allow it), since the firm needs a stock of dependable finance that it can use year in, year out, and which will not desert the firm except under the most dire of circumstances.

Any lender is keen to see that would-be borrowers have their own money at risk otherwise, the lender will ask, should I be the only one exposed? Thus lenders have to raise as much money as they can from savings, potential loans against assets and promises of loans from friends and family before approaching a lender. Once the lender can see real commitment, the conversation can start in earnest. That may, and indeed should, sound daunting, but it is that preparedness to put everything on the line that marks out the entrepreneur from others.

Long-term finance

We have discussed resources from the entrepreneur's own sources: even if they are apparently sufficient to fund the operation a discussion with a lender may be worthwhile, in case extra money is needed in an emergency. If the relationship has already begun, especially if periodic reports have been put through about the progress of the business, the lender will be more on-side and thus less prepared to turn the application down out of hand than if the conversation were starting from cold.

Long-term finance from banks takes the form of loans over periods of up to 20 years. However, hire purchase is also available to businesses as it is to individuals.

In most cases the entrepreneur's own funds plus some loans and an overdraft will cover start-up needs. If the business does not expand rapidly and has good margins, those sources may be all it needs for its entire life, although the amounts borrowed may vary with time. But not all start-ups are like that.

Equity finance

Equity finance – the selling of shares to raise funds for business – is typically for the bigger and more ambitious start-up or for the firm that is expanding to a considerable size. Chapter 16 describes the legal status of the kind of company that may sell shares in its operations.

Equity finance is money provided in exchange for a share of the firm. Preferable from the entrepreneur's point of view is a minority stake – that is, the investor takes less than 49 per cent of the shares in the company, leaving the entrepreneur with the 51 per cent that can outvote the investor on any board decision.

Dealing with banks

Borrowing in hard times

Raising money for business is never easy, and at the time of writing it is much harder than it has been at times in the past. Nevertheless the banks – the main source of external capital for UK start-ups – under pressure from government, claim that they are lending colossal amounts. In 2011, in an article published in *The Independent* on 4 November, James Grierson reported:

'Barclays, Royal Bank of Scotland, Lloyds Banking Group, HSBC and Santander UK lent £56.1 billion to small and medium enterprises (SMEs) in the first nine months of the year, the Bank of England said.

Under the Project Merlin agreement the banks said they would increase lending to SMEs to £76 billion this year, which equates to £19 billion in the first quarter, or £57 billion by the end of the third quarter'.

(**www.independent.co.uk/news/business/news/banks-behind-on-sme-lending-target-6262099.html**)

The Financial Times's Sharlene Goff was less optimistic at that time, yet in an article entitled 'Kick-start to lending for SMEs under fire', published on 4 December 2011, she reported that: '...banks and the government are rushing to provide new commitments to small and medium-sized enterprises...' (**www.ft.com/cms/s/0/629fce66-1cf1-11e1-a134-00144feabdc0.html#axzz1jdnxY5Y9**)

The sceptical reader will discern a distinction between 'rushing to provide new commitments' and – what is not reported – rushing to provide lending. The problem the banks seem to have is that the government and regulatory authorities require them to strengthen their balance sheets by writing-down or writing-off altogether some of their less reliable investments – which requires them to retain cash – at the same time as demanding that they lend more. Not a few people have spotted the paradox.

The messages to take away are perhaps that:

- The banks do vary in their policies (James Grierson, in the same article quoted above, reported that the buyout team at Norton Motorcycles tried 10 banks before Santander agreed to back them).
- To get finance is to win a competition, so the best-prepared case will probably win.
- The banks are not the sole sources of finance, even though they are likely to be important to any SME.
- Forming a sound plan and communicating it clearly and with persistence are essential.

Borrowing from banks

The principles behind bank borrowing are simple. For lenders, it offers a profit by hiring the money out for less than they have to pay to hire it in. Their back-up is that they will rarely lend unless they have some security or collateral, usually by taking a charge over some valuable asset. Then, if the borrower doesn't pay, the lender sells the asset – usually the borrower's house – and dips into the proceeds to clear the debt. If you do not have collateral, see the Enterprise Finance Guarantee Scheme later in this section. For the borrower, if it costs £10,000 a year to borrow £100,000 and he or she can make £30,000 by doing so, the motive is obvious.

Before assuming that borrowing is essential, see if you can devise a business model that avoids or minimizes it. Try considering these ideas:

- Buy goods on credit, then take cash with order. This way you pay for purchases only after you have been paid.
- Sell any personal asset (perhaps a caravan or boat) that you will have no time to use.
- Look into releasing capital by moving to a cheaper house.
- Stay put in the house but remortgage. (Housing loans are cheaper than business loans – but recognize that business failure could mean homelessness.)

If none of those is possible or to your taste, the high street banks will be the next port of call. They offer three types of loan finance:

- overdrafts, suitable to cover the day-to-day fluctuations in your cash position;
- medium-term loans over up to five or seven years, for equipment;
- long-term loans from 7 to 20 years, for property purchases.

An important point is never to use overdrafts for longer-term finance. Overdrafts can be called in at a moment's notice, and are quite unsuitable for anything but day-to-day needs.

Many other lenders exist, but extreme caution must be exercised. We used to say that at least one of the usual banks could be expected to lend for any viable, well-presented proposition. More recently, the pressures on the banks to rebuild their damaged balance sheets means they are less reliable, so more shopping around may be needed. Nevertheless, if they do turn you down, look at yourself rather than blaming them; take a good look at the proposition and the reasons given for refusal, perhaps with an experienced business adviser.

So-called secondary banks and moneylenders should always be avoided. If matters are so dire that resort to them is the only hope, liquidation now is usually preferable to liquidation at some point in the future with huge debts and unsavoury characters making insinuations about your personal safety and that of your family. As someone once said, if they are the answer it is a very silly question.

It ought not to be easy to borrow. Banks are putting shareholders' funds at risk when they lend and should conduct searching enquiries into the destination of their money. They should analyse and criticize your business plan, giving you a hard time and lending only when they are satisfied.

That may seem perverse, but ask yourself this: who will put you in the best position, the lenders who hand money out recklessly, knowing they can bankrupt you to get repaid, or those who use their experience to help you foresee pitfalls and develop your business plan, seeking to be repaid out of a healthy cash flow?

It follows that your approach to the bank must be well prepared and thought through. As they say, you get one chance to make a first impression.

Banks charge interest and fees, which they may present as inevitable but which can be negotiable. Ask about fees as part of every discussion and ask for their reduction or removal. Try to get a reduction in the interest charged: even one-quarter of 1 per cent is worth having – on £100,000 it is £250 a year.

Local bank officials are given lending limits above which they have to seek permission to lend. It is worth enquiring what your business manager's limit is, or their boss's limit. If the local limit is £100,000, you will not want to put in a proposal for a loan of £100,200, thus ensuring that the request has to go up the line to someone who has never met you.

Government guarantees

The government offers the Enterprise Finance Guarantee Scheme (EFGS), aimed at removing the bar to growth that lack of collateral imposes on a small business. Its main features are:

- 75 per cent of the loan is guaranteed.
- The borrower pays 2 per cent extra interest on the outstanding balance.
- Loans up to a 10-year term and £1,000 to £1 million are covered.
- The borrowing firm must have a turnover of less than £25 million.

Most of the main banks offer this scheme. Most sectors and activities are eligible, but some are not. The detail is on the Department for Business, Innovation and Skills website, **www.bis.gov.uk**.

In addition to the banks, finance houses offer loans to business. The basis is similar to the hire-purchase agreement the public is familiar with, but the term can extend up to 10 years. Security cover will be a primary concern. Alternatively, they offer long-term leasing arrangements.

Other banking sources

Merchant banks are not interested in the minor league of business, but in the present climate of change a web search may throw up opportunities to attract institutional equity investors. Equity (a shareholding) is quite different from a loan, as the section on limited companies (in Chapter 16) will show.

Factoring may be of more use once your firm is established, but if you start off with blue-chip customers and substantial orders, factors could be interested immediately. A factor buys your debts from you for less than face value, then collects all of the money due from your customer. It is a useful way to minimize the requirements for working capital.

Banks are not identical

Really, they are not – it certainly is worth shopping around to decide where to do your business banking. Popping into two neighbouring branches on the local High Street recently revealed quite different offers for start-ups. Taking the core offer as payments processing and loans, they seek to differentiate themselves via the extras.

One gives:

- credit-management software;
- legal, marketing and accountancy advice and a legal helpline;
- seminars and online training;
- online data back-up.

The other provides:

- planning software;
- an online start-up course;
- marketing support;
- no fee on a business credit card and a free overdraft of £500.

How to choose? It depends on what is important to you, but it does seem sensible to look at what is on offer and pick the one you like most.

Many entrepreneurs find that their first choice of bank does not agree to fund them, or will do so but on disadvantageous terms. Consequently, they may not be able to get the free extras that appeal most, but are forced to go elsewhere. No matter: the main thing is to fund the firm; relative to that the free extras are candy-floss.

Putting the case to the bank

An existing business seeking to borrow can present a record of achievement but even then has to persuade the bank to lend it the money. The new business finds the bar set higher and so must try harder.

The presentation revolves around a written business plan. Do not worry about your secrets: bankers understand confidentiality. The plan should cover the following headings with no more than two pages, preferably less, on each:

- the service or product you plan to offer;
- markets, competitors, customers and why customers should buy from you;
- experience and background of key individuals, with personal bank details for the principals;
- premises and equipment, with costings;
- a monthly cash-flow forecast for year 1 together with a detailed P&L budget, plus outline plans for years 2 and 3;
- how much you want to borrow, what for, for how long and how you will repay;
- security, if any, that you can offer.

Do not doctor figures to make them look good but show what you can reasonably expect to achieve, for getting the money is only part of the job; once you have landed the loan you will be expected to fulfil your forecast.

Let the bank have all this information a couple of days before the meeting. If you do not feel confident about compiling it all yourself, get advice and help from either a business adviser or your accountant.

Finally, remember that some banks still think in terms of lending a pound for every pound you put in. This leads to the accusation that they are prepared to lend only to those who have. The banks reply that financial standing is not all; they are judging competence and character as well.

Investors and others

Equity investors

The equity investor from outside the firm (an indulgent relative buying shares might take a different view) will usually look for two things: a sound proposition, managed well, and the prospect of getting the investment back as soon as possible by selling out. Such investors are not necessarily easy to find, for most of them believe in getting involved only in a business they feel they understand. That does not mean that, for example, experts on fashion will back only fashion companies; their interest may extend to quasi-fashion items such as home decorations that follow much the same rules as their primary industry.

Few equity investors are in it for life, though exceptions do exist. Thus, taking on an apparently benign investor could mean discovering one day that those shares have been sold on to someone with a different, more abrasive, attitude altogether.

Even if the ideal of less than a 50 per cent share in the business has been sold, that situation may not persist for ever. Suppose a firm sells 30 per cent of its shares, leaving 70 per cent in the control of the founder. The firm does well and expands rapidly, to the point where it is demanding more and more overdraft funding for longer and longer. By then it will be obvious to the bank that core funding is no longer adequate and it requires it to be raised. The outside shareholder has the funds, but wants another 30 per cent for the shares he or she is to buy, bringing that holding to 60 per cent. If that went through, the founder would see his or her share of the equity fall from the comfortable majority of 70 per cent to only 40 per cent, a position in which he or she becomes virtually the employee of the other person, though with all of his or her fortune on the line. That would not be comfortable. While some of the issues have been simplified here in the interests of clarity, the general point is made: ownership of shares of a business does not necessarily remain static.

Business angels are rich individuals who may invest in the shares of promising businesses as well as providing managerial guidance. Under the Enterprise Allowance Scheme they can get tax relief on their investment. HM Revenue & Customs' website, **www.hmrc.gov.uk**, gives details.

One source of finance used to be local authorities, but the squeeze on their expenditure has dried that up. It is worth approaching the Local Enterprise Partnership for your area (most county authorities are in one) to see if it is prioritizing SMEs and start-ups in its plans.

Government start-up loans for young people

In May, 2012, the government announced a scheme to lend sums of 'typically in the order of £2,500' over up to five years to young people aged 18–24 who live in England. In addition they will get 'expert and personal support to help develop a business plan and access training'. The interest rate will be 3 per cent plus RPI inflation, which at the time of the announcement stood at 3.5 per cent.

http://businessinyou.bis.gov.uk/start-up-loans/

Grants

There is not much free money around, but given that it is free, it is worth looking for. Business Link (**www.businesslink.gov.uk**) offers a free search of its database ('online grants finder') for any money you might qualify for.

Generally speaking, money is available for projects that look likely to increase employment directly, or indirectly by developing a commercial proposition. The main sources are:

- central government (some of it originating in the EU);
- local authorities or bodies they support;
- national bodies, such as the Welsh Development Agency, Scottish Enterprise and Invest Northern Ireland;
- Chambers of Commerce;
- The Prince's Trust.

Here we discuss the situation in England. Information on other parts of the UK is available from the websites of bodies listed above.

The Work Programme, a government scheme aimed at the unemployed and introduced in 2011, purports to support trainees and employers financially. Provision is designed to meet localized needs, so it varies from place to place; details are available from Jobcentres. The Department for Business, Innovation and Skills (BIS) R&D Tax Credits can help small firms with technological projects via grants to develop and prove them. The Prince's Trust offers loans and grants to people aged up to 30 starting a business, plus the support of a volunteer mentor. There are other schemes, mostly from the BIS and the EU, designed to increase cooperation between researchers and industry. If you might find this useful, use the Business Link site to find out more.

Conclusions

- The financing of a firm needs planning as carefully as any other key aspect. It may be easy to borrow from some sources but then find oneself in an uncomfortable relationship with people who do not observe the rules of polite society.

- Three basic forms of finance are available – short-term and long-term lending (usually from banks) and equity investments. Each has its special place and each is suitable for different aspects of the financing need.

- Equity investors have their own agenda, which may not coincide with that of the entrepreneur. While they may start off as a minority interest, as the firm expands its need for further financing may make one of them into the majority shareholder. It is not easy to have a minority shareholder demanding better performance, but it is much less comfortable if that person holds a majority of the shares.

- The present climate makes it difficult to raise funds, but money is out there and is being lent. Emphasis should therefore fall on trading methods that minimize the requirement to borrow, by such stratagems as renting equipment, rather than buying it, and not giving credit to customers.

- Bank lending would, in normal times, probably represent the core of funding after the entrepreneur's own funds. The return of those conditions is unlikely to be postponed indefinitely.

- The chances of success depend largely on the quality of the proposition and its presentation (that is, the way it is put across, not the quality of binders used). This has always been the case, but extra emphasis falls on it now.

- Equity investment is probably needed by the highly ambitious firm. Only in truly exceptional cases can firms finance expansion solely through retained earnings.

- Equity investment should be entered into with great care as an initially sympathetic and cooperative investor can easily change to something else.

- All other financial sources, except banks, are likely to play a minor role, if any, except in specialized cases.

PART 5:
The law and the firm

16
Business legal entities and business names

In this chapter

LEARNING OUTCOMES

By the end of this chapter you should be able to:

- make a suitable choice of business name;
- understand the implications and regulations affecting it and the alternatives;
- understand the range of business legal entities available to the entrepreneur;
- understand the implications of each.

Business legal entities

The choices available

The main options are:

- sole trader;
- partnership;
- limited company;
- cooperative.

We shall address all of these except cooperatives. There are special organizations devoted to their development, and the best way into the system is via Co-operative and Community Finance, **www.coopfinance.coop**. The situation described is true for England and Wales but there may be variations elsewhere.

Sole trader

By far the most popular way of getting into business, sole tradership is also the simplest. You simply notify HM Revenue & Customs so that it can change your income tax and NI status to self-employed. You will now pay NI contributions in Class 2 and Class 4.

Legally, you and the business are one. Anything the business does is your responsibility. If the firm fails owing money, **the debts are yours personally**.

It is wise to review all your insurances, particularly those for the house and car, to be sure that you are covered for using them for business. Cover for the car, especially, will almost certainly require changes. Apart from following any regulations and acquiring licences that apply to the activity you plan to undertake, you are free to operate.

Partnership

In a partnership, two or more individual people are involved as principals of the firm. On the whole, partnership is much like sole tradership, with one important difference. In a partnership **each partner is responsible for all of the liabilities of the firm**. Common sense says it should be only for a share, but the law says otherwise.

It is clearly important to select partners with care. If one runs off with the money, those left behind are saddled with all of the debts.

Like a marriage, partnership can be subject to many strains, so just as celebrities arrange through a pre-nuptial agreement how their assets will be split on divorce, wise business partners have their solicitor draw up a partnership agreement before going into business together. If they do then fall out, at least the separation can be orderly. Limited liability partnerships (LLPs) are a recent innovation, limiting partners' responsibility for commercial debts – see the Companies House website. LLPs must be registered at Companies House.

Limited liability company

A limited company is very different from the other forms of constitution. Where partners and sole traders are legally inseparable from the business, a limited company is itself a separate 'person' in law. It has its own liabilities and obligations, quite apart from those of its owners, directors and employees.

The private limited company is the form most often used. If you wish to sell shares on the stock market and have a share capital of £50,000 you can become a public limited company (plc), but few starters do.

The company itself is responsible for its debts, not the owners or directors, the shareholders' responsibility being limited to the paid-up share capital. Since most small companies are authorized to issue £100 of shares, yet issue only two or three shares of £1 each, their paid-up capital is limited to that £2 or £3. Because of this, institutions lending to limited companies almost always insist on a charge on the company's assets, which are usually worth a lot more than £3 (meaning they can send in the bailiffs if need be) and guarantees from substantial people, usually the owner-directors.

Shareholders own the company but need not be involved in running it. Directors are appointed by shareholders and are responsible to the owners and the law for the way the company is run. They can also be employees of the firm and/or shareholders.

Although this situation has the potential for all kinds of arrangements between people, almost always the small limited company's shareholders are its directors, owning just one or two shares each. Once the company expands and needs extra capital, it might attract an investor.

If, for example, the investor requires a one-third share of the firm, more shares will be issued within the authorized limit of £100 to make that possible. The existing directors could issue to themselves a further two shares each, bringing the total between them to six, then issue another three shares to the investor. Nine shares would then have been issued, giving each of the three one-third of the issued shares and hence one-third of the company.

Under this arrangement the directors could issue the shares to themselves at face value, £1 each, while selling the investor's portion at the value of the investment made. More often, the firm will have made money that has been allocated to the directors as income, which they have not withdrawn but have left in the firm, appearing on the balance sheet as 'directors' loans'. Those loans will be converted into shareholdings, their shares being sold to them at a more realistic price than £1.

Although that is the situation in principle, in real life an investor would want more than three shares, so as to give flexibility if he or she wanted to sell on part of his or her holding to someone else. Owning three shares, the investor could sell only one-third, two-thirds or all of his or her holding; whereas, owning 300, the investor could sell much more finely tuned proportions. For that to be possible, the authorized capital would have to be increased and the other shareholders' holdings increased accordingly, but while the number of shares held by each shareholder would change from the simpler model, the proportion held by each of them would still be one-third. Each would still own one-third of the firm.

If the firm should go broke, the directors have no personal responsibility unless they have been negligent or are guilty of the offence of wrongful trading. The liquidator takes over, collecting the firm's debts and selling its assets. First to be paid are the government (wouldn't you know it), next employees, after them the secured creditors and finally the unsecured creditors, usually other businesses who have sold to the firm on credit. If anything is left it is split between shareholders, but usually there is nothing.

There is no obligation to record the existence of the business if you are a partner or sole trader, but a limited company must be registered at Companies House. A solicitor, chartered accountant or company formation agent will set one up from scratch for you, but a popular option is to buy a firm that has already been set up and is ready to trade. This costs up to £300 or so.

The accounts of limited companies must be audited professionally once they reach a certain size or under particular conditions. For most small firms auditing is not required. The main exceptions are once turnover reaches £5.6 million or assets £2.8 million, or if the firm is regulated by the Financial Services Authority (FSA).

The accounts, in the form of a balance sheet and other documents, must be filed at Companies House by a certain deadline, with a fee (£30 at the time of writing), and also be sent to members (that is, shareholders).

Naming the firm

Choosing a name for the business

The choice of business name is a marketing decision, but there are legal ramifications. Ideally, a business name is expressive, attractive, memorable and has a leading initial near the start of the alphabet so that it appears high in listings. As with all marketing activity, look carefully at the name from the point of view of your customer. Ask other people for their opinion.

The rules governing the names that limited companies may use are operated by Companies House. Generally, they exclude names that:

- are criminal;
- are offensive;
- are already registered;
- suggest government approval;
- are misleading.

There is more to it, all explained on **www.companieshouse.gov.uk**, the Companies House website. Anyone, limited company, sole trader or partnership, may use a trading name other than his or her own. If someone does so, his or her true name and address must be disclosed on all business documents for suppliers, employees and customers. In addition, a notice must be displayed 'prominently' in parts of business premises accessed by customers. The notice must take a specific form, as shown in Figure 16.1.

Finally, this information must be disclosed in writing immediately it is requested by anyone with whom anything is discussed or done in the course of business. It is important to comply or you could commit a criminal offence and moreover might not be able to make your contracts stick.

There are rules about what qualifies as someone's own name. Take someone whose given name is John Smith:

- John Smith;
- J Smith;
- Mr J Smith.

FIGURE 16.1 Notice to be displayed by businesses using a trading name

```
PARTICULARS OF OWNERSHIP OF
(insert trading name)
AS REQUIRED SECTION 29
OF THE COMPANIES ACT 1981

FULL NAMES OF PROPRIETORS:
(insert names)


ADDRESSES WITHIN GREAT BRITAIN AT WHICH DOCUMENTS
CAN BE SERVED ON THE BUSINESS:

(insert addresses)
```

John goes into partnership with his mother, Jane. Their 'own names' are:

- J & J Smith;
- Jane and John Smith;
- John and Jane Smith;
- Smiths.

Mother pulls out and John forms a partnership with Tom Brown. Their own names are:

- T Brown and J Smith (and vice versa);
- Thomas Brown and John Smith (and vice versa);
- Messrs J Smith and T Brown (and vice versa).

In due course Jane Smith buys a limited company off the shelf, called Tetrablank Ltd. She trades in that name, the company's own name.

In all of the above examples, using any of these 'own names' means there is no separate business name to disclose. However, any of these individuals or combinations of people might sense that marketing reasons dictate the use of a name that says what they do, rather than who they are.

They might choose a name like John Smith Engineering Supplies or Victorian Woodworkers. None of those names is the name of a person or company involved. They may use the names, but only if they disclose the ownership, as described earlier. In everyday dealings they will describe themselves as 'T Brown and J Smith trading as John Smith Engineering Supplies' or 'Tetrablank Ltd trading as Victorian Woodworkers'. 'Trading as' is often abbreviated to 't/a'.

In those last examples the letterhead would feature the trading name prominently across the top. The declaration of ownership will be in small, but clearly legible, print along the bottom, along with the other details such as VAT registration, registered office address for a limited company and so on.

Conclusions

- Choice of business name is primarily a marketing decision.
- Variations from the company's or individual's name may have implications for disclosure.
- The choice of entity is important as it has wide implications, personally, legally and for taxation.
- Banks have heard of limited liability and do not allow borrowers to shelter under it; all other creditors are affected, though.

17
Criminal and civil law as they affect business

In this chapter

LEARNING OUTCOMES

By the end of this chapter you should be able to:

- understand the two codes of English law: civil and criminal;
- know how civil and criminal law affect businesses;
- explain the place in law of tort, a civil wrong;
- understand its extensive implications for business.

(Employment law is covered in Chapter 23.)

Civil law and criminal law: two separate codes

Civil law

The two systems of law, civil and criminal, have grown from completely different roots. Civil law came about from old statutes, often laws made by the Saxon kings before the Normans took over in 1066, which have been interpreted – and therefore changed and developed – in innumerable decisions by judges down the ages. The result was a generally agreed set of rules for the way people should behave, backed up by sanctions for those who did not.

The system stemmed from an aggrieved person taking his or her complaint to the local lord and asking him to order the alleged transgressor to make good his or her loss. If my fences were so poor that my pigs got into your field and ruined your crops, natural justice demands that I make good in some way. After all, that might mean your family could not eat or that you lost a lot of income, so it really mattered. The lord did not want a couple of his subjects conducting a blood feud so he would try to sort matters out and impose his authority on the situation. At the trial we might both bring along witnesses who would back up our different stories. The lord would decide if the testimony of my wife was more reliable than that of a passing priest you had brought along. He would hear your arguments and mine, challenge us and our witnesses and ask questions to clarify. Once he was satisfied that he had the facts he would issue a judgement, either making an order against me or telling you to stop wasting his time. Whatever the outcome, it was no longer a matter between the two of us but the word of the lord, something to be respected and feared: only a brave person would go against it, for example by exacting his or her own form of revenge.

In a civil case today the principles have not changed much. The state has no involvement, other than providing the framework within which cases can be fought, by substituting learned judges for the variable performance of local lords, premises and higher levels of appeal courts should they be needed. The police and the Crown Prosecution Service (CPS) stay away: the battle is between two or more parties and their lawyers. There is no requirement to hire a lawyer but as the entire system depends on the adversarial approach, which demands knowledge of many fine points of law, most litigants and defendants do.

An award by the judge in a civil case still results in one party compensating the other. As anyone who watches too much television knows, the test placed before the jury in a criminal case is that the accused should be guilty 'beyond reasonable doubt'. In civil cases the burden of proof is the less demanding 'balance of probabilities'.

Many a hollow victory has been won in the civil courts, where plaintiffs have won their case and been awarded damages: when the lawyer's bill came in the celebrations stopped abruptly. Some people have used the civil courts to prove a moral point, perhaps asking for damages of one penny, as the main issue was that they wanted the court's endorsement of their belief that they were in the right.

Criminal law

Criminal law is completely different. It arises from laws passed in Parliament and not yet abolished. The sanctions are fines, imprisonment or community service (no longer hanging, for any offence, even for arson in Her Majesty's Dockyards which was kept on until the 1970s). Criminal law is enforced by the police and the CPS, as well as many other public servants, including HM Coastguard, Trading Standards officers and others.

There are two golden rules: for a civil case, keep the action short and settle well before it comes to court. For the criminal law, stay on the right side of it.

The civil law affects business owners mainly through two of its many branches: contract law and tort.

Tort

Tort in English law

Tort is defined as a civil wrong. The word is, appropriately, modern French for 'wrong' and came into English law via the Norman Conquest.

A range of civil wrongs has grown up over the centuries as the civil law has developed and extended. The civil wrongs are as follows, with a brief thumbnail sketch of the implications for businesses:

- Nuisance: causing or allowing smells, noise, obstruction etc, all torts that any business is capable of generating through accident or carelessness.

- Defamation: damaging reputations, which is easily done by an entrepreneur in a moment of enthusiasm while selling against a competitor.

- Conversion: selling stolen goods, even if acquired innocently, which anyone, whether or not in business, is open to committing.

- Trespass: entering property uninvited, which is possible to do when visiting a sales prospect and could be done by another on your property. The plaintiff has no rights to recompense unless they can prove damage (walkers' organizations recommend straying ramblers offer 50p to enraged farmers as damages, thus neutralizing any court claim for damages).

- Passing off: pretending that goods came from someone other than their true source, which is not easy for the honest person to do.

- False imprisonment: unreasonably detaining someone. Again this is not easy to do unintentionally, though possible as a result of a locked door slamming shut in the wind.

- Negligence: generally, this is carelessness or recklessness in the way one conducts oneself or one's business.

Of that list, negligence is the tort most likely to be committed by businesses. Having a loose stair carpet at your office is careless. To ignore a warning about it is reckless. If someone then trips, falls and suffers injury, they may sue you for negligence.

In practice the matter is likely to be handled entirely by the insurance company, who would take on responsibility for defending the court case and paying out any damages awarded. However, if the policyholder is found by the court to have acted negligently, it is possible that the insurer will be able to deny responsibility, for some insurance policies require the insured not to act negligently. Anyone to whom that happened would be in for a shock, as they might be liable not only for the damages, but also the insurance company's and the plaintiff's legal costs. As mentioned previously, these sums may be far greater than any damages award.

As if that is not enough, whether or not the firm is found to have acted negligently (in civil law), in an example like this the criminal law may be invoked by the Health and Safety Executive (HSE), which might decide to prosecute you under the legislation under which it acts. Since that legislation is part of the criminal law, there might be a fine or even a prison sentence as well.

Quite apart from events at the firm's premises, the main source of negligence claims is alleged dangerous or damaging effects of products or services sold. The only answer is rigorous attention to design and specification, with an emphasis on quality in production, installation and servicing. In many ways this risk accounts for the many pages of paperwork pointing out the blindingly obvious, often blamed solely on a culture that places health and safety above everything, yet also due to insurance companies' requirement to demonstrate that every possible avenue for dangerous misuse has been closed off.

Conclusions

- The two codes of English law, civil and criminal, are quite separate.
- Civil law is exercised by individuals (including companies) against each other.
- Criminal law is enforced by the state via the police and CPS.
- There is a variety of torts which a business can fall foul of.
- The tort of which business most needs to be aware is negligence, though the others should not be ignored.

18
The law of contract

In this chapter

LEARNING OUTCOMES

By the end of this chapter you should be able to:

- understand what a contract comprises;
- avoid contractual trouble;
- know that the forming of contracts is a serious matter that can be done unwittingly;
- agree that the contract to sell should be part of the usual communication with the customer, written by the seller but checked by a solicitor;
- explain the distinctions between conditions, warranties, guarantees and exemptions as they affect selling and buying;
- recognize the implications of product liability;
- distinguish between copyright, registered designs, trademarks and patents;
- decide when it is worth going to law.

Contract law is part of the civil code, meaning that the police are not interested in normal commercial matters, such as whether or not your bills get paid. The civil law of contract is extensive. Knowing some aspects of it helps the small business to form contracts that are valid and to recognize infringements of its rights.

In law, a contract is formed when three conditions are present:

- offer: an offer to buy, which may be subject to conditions;
- acceptance: an acceptance of the offer;
- consideration: some sort of exchange, in business usually money.

Thus if I offer to wash your car (the offer) for £1 (consideration) and you accept (acceptance), we have a contract. I must do the work and you must pay me. But where is the work to be done? Who supplies the water and equipment? When must it be completed? To what standards of cleanliness – do I have to leather-off as well as washing and rinsing? When will you pay me? How can I prove that you agreed £1, not 50p?

Those questions illustrate why, in business, only fools fail to confirm their more important contracts in writing. Except for land sales in England, Wales and Northern Ireland, an oral agreement is still a contract – but, unless there are reliable witnesses, it is difficult to prove its exact nature unless it is written down and accepted by both parties. This is, of course, where the lawyers come in.

If I offered to wash your car in return for a bag of plums from your tree, or in return for you to babysit my children, and the offer was accepted, it would still be a contract. If I said I would do it for nothing, no contract would exist as the third condition, 'consideration', would be absent.

When forming contracts, perhaps surprisingly one is not advised to employ a lawyer to look over every simple agreement that an entrepreneur might make. A dash of informed common sense can go a long way. In general, the best guide is to:

- Tell the truth.
- Keep your promises.
- Know your obligations and keep to them.
- Know and respect your customer's rights.
- Never promise what you cannot or may not be able to deliver.
- Always express clearly any doubts or uncertainties.
- Be able to prove what you say is true.
- Behave fairly and reasonably.
- Make conditions clear.
- Read and understand before signing.
- Keep dated written records.
- Confirm your understanding of any agreement in writing.
- Make proper use of professional and official advice.

When buying from a larger firm there is a risk that the entrepreneur will be up against all the small print that an established business can deploy, most of it printed in light grey five-point type on thin white paper that shows through the black print on the other side. In such cases reading the small print can be difficult as well as depressing but, sometimes, it is the only way to understand what one is committing to. Be sure to check carefully that your understanding of the offer is the same as the seller's and, if it's a valuable purchase, get a written statement of exactly what the proposal is. Check it carefully for any shades of meaning that may not immediately be clear.

That said, most disputes, especially with big suppliers, do not arise from deliberate misbehaviour but much more often by accident or some simple misunderstanding. The obvious answer is to cut down the area open to misinterpretation and thus reduce the risk of dispute.

The firm's contracts

The matter of contracts needs to be looked at from two opposite ends: contracts to buy and contracts to sell. Where the firm is selling it has obligations and expectations and its customer has the same; where the firm is buying, the situation is no different. However, in most commercial transactions there is a great deal of difference between the situation of each party to the contract, buyer and seller.

Contracts to buy

Pop into the newsagent's, put a coin on the counter and say '*Sun*, please'; when the newsagent hands it over the contract to purchase is complete. Leaving aside your taste in newspapers, as you collect your change you can reflect that most contracts to purchase are formed just as unthinkingly as the one you have just concluded.

When buying for business a more rigorous approach is strongly recommended. Examination of the signature box on an order form will disclose that a signature means you accept the terms and conditions of sale, which no member of staff is authorized to vary. As mentioned above, these terms may be on the back of the form, in a tiny typesize, in a tasteful shade of light grey. Few people except their creator have ever read them. Yet the point of them is to absolve the seller of responsibility for pretty well anything.

In 1977 the Unfair Contract Terms Act came into law to limit the exclusions allowed. Specifically, excluding liability for death was disallowed. Excluding liability for losses due to negligence, or for poor-quality and defective goods, is permissible only if reasonable.

'Reasonable' is a wonderful word that crops up all over the place in law. The courts usually judge it on:

- what information was available to each side before the deal;
- whether it was a standard-form purchase or the deal was negotiated;
- whether the purchaser had the power to get better terms.

Essential checks to perform are that the written contract gives accurate:

- prices;
- quantities;
- delivery dates;
- payment terms.

During the negotiation phase the buyer may be able to improve the position by asking for:

- unfavourable terms to be deleted from the standard conditions;
- deletion of the seller's protection from the consequences of negligence or the supply of defective equipment;
- better terms than are on offer as standard, such as free training or after-sales support.

Do not just ask but treat it like a sales task. You have to show why the offending condition is wrong for you and for your relationship with the seller.

Contracts for the few major purchases are likely to be gone over carefully because everyone can see that the costs of getting something wrong are high. It is in the more minor activities, the business equivalent of popping into the newsagent's, where most of the risks lie. See the example in the box below.

CASE STUDY Purchasing case study

You need 200 3-foot lengths of timber. The product is sold in 2-metre lengths.

You allow for 5 per cent wastage and calculate that you will still get two 3-footers out of a length, so you order 100 of the 2-metre lengths.

When the load arrives a lot of the lengths are under 2 metres, too short once your wastage is taken into account.

You phone to complain and the supplier tells you there is a condition on the back of the order you signed, which also appears in the back of the company's brochure, to say it can vary length by up to 10 per cent. That 10 per cent plus your 5 per cent makes the offending pieces under-length.

You conclude there is nothing to be done. You deliver late and too few to your customer and have the substandard lengths cluttering your store for the foreseeable future.

You resolve to specify more carefully next time.

When any purchases arrive, check to see if there is any sign of damage and do not be afraid not to accept them. For example, if a carton is broken and there might have been theft, either refuse the delivery or sign for it with the words 'damaged and unexamined' next to your signature.

Always open up packaging and examine deliveries in detail on the day of arrival. There will be rules in the small print about how soon after delivery complaints will be entertained – usually a matter of hours or days – and the seller will retain paperwork only in line with that timetable. If there is a complaint, make it immediately and always confirm in writing the same day, keeping a copy.

Contracts to sell

Here the tables are turned; you are now the one seeking maximum advantage, or at least not to be disadvantaged. While terms and conditions (T&Cs) of sale are necessary legally, they can also serve a marketing function by communicating your reasonable expectations and requirements of your customer. That means writing in clear language and legible type in a way that a human being with normal eyesight can decipher.

If the presentation of terms and conditions is seen not just as defensive, but as a marketing issue, it follows that firms should not reproduce what the solicitor recommends, but should construct their own. In that way customers will be addressed in a way that is consistent with the rest of their dealings. Only once they have been written should T&Cs be handed over to the solicitor to ensure legal effectiveness.

Trying to foresee the matters that T&Cs should cover can be a daunting prospect. Consequently, a prototype is offered of a set of terms and conditions of sale (see Appendix 2). Its purpose is to provide a draft that any entrepreneur can customize to personal circumstances. Hack it about freely: that is what it is for. But do get your solicitor to check the result.

One final thought: people of a light-hearted disposition could unintentionally form a contract to sell as a result of joking. They didn't mean it but the other person did. If that were to happen in front of a witness a lot of avoidable trouble could be caused. Much though it goes against human nature, jokes should not be part of the relationship with customers or enquirers.

Other legal matters

In addition to the matters so far discussed, the law affects business in a number of other ways.

Conditions, warranties, guarantees and exemptions

Any contract, whether for buying or selling, incorporates conditions and warranties. **Conditions** are really important matters, the breach of which entitles the other party to its money back plus damages. There are also **implied conditions** which need not be spelled out but are automatically present in all contracts:

- The seller has the right to sell – eg the goods are not stolen or on HP (that is, owned by the hiring company).
- Goods comply with the description – eg if reconditioned, they are not sold as new.
- A sample corresponds with the bulk: the example you have been shown is truly representative.
- The goods are of suitable quality and fit for use.

The final item needs expansion. 'Suitable' quality is that which is 'fit' for the use to which the customer can be expected to put the purchase. Exceptions are allowed, where the seller points out a fault or the buyer gives the article the sort of inspection that might reasonably be expected to reveal the fault.

Warranties are less important, entitling the injured party to damages only. They include many of the topics covered in the draft terms and conditions in the appendix referred to above.

Guarantees may be given with items bought in as components. That may be helpful, but does not deflect liability for the finished article that the component is built into.

The customer's redress is to the person who supplied the goods, so you have to put things right at your expense and then chase your supplier for satisfaction. Where guarantees are issued, the issuer must make it clear that they do not affect customers' statutory rights. Whatever the written guarantee may say, in law there is no time limit to the customer's rights, only what is 'reasonable' in the circumstances.

Exemptions can be criminal offences, where the trade or public are deprived of their legal rights – hence the disappearance from the shops of signs such as 'No refunds on sale goods'. The law is more relaxed about hired goods and sales to business customers, where there may be 'reasonable' exclusion clauses. If it affects you, take legal advice for it is a complex field.

Product liability

Until recently the UK did not have the level of product liability that exists in the United States, but we are moving rapidly in that direction. A supplier's responsibilities are to:

- Warn about potential risks – 'This product may contain nuts'.
- Inform consumers about risks and precautions – 'Once cooked, it will be hot: handle with care'.
- Monitor products' safety by recording and investigating complaints.
- Test products – even where an issue is obvious to any adult, do carry out and record the results of tests. Act if a problem is found – and it is wise to keep a record.
- Don't sell something you know, or ought to know, is unsafe.
- Notify the authorities of unsafe products.

There are obviously special risks in certain categories: food and drink, toys, medicines, and mechanical or electrical items come to mind. Specific regulations apply to many such categories: the Trading Standards website gives information on **www.trading-standards.gov.uk**. In general, Trading Standards officers, based at county, unitary and city councils, are willing to give advice on how to avoid breaking the law in this and other ways, including the labelling of packaging.

At the back of all this is the threat that the authorities may take enforcement action if you do not comply, resulting in fines or imprisonment, and that injured parties – not just direct customers – could sue. Once again, insurance cover is advised.

Copyright, registered designs, trademarks and patents

Under these headings the law gives varying degrees of protection to intellectual property (IP).

Copyright gives the weakest protection. It gives automatic protection to anything original on paper – text, music, names, drawings, etc. Copyists need not change much to claim that theirs is also an original work. To make potential copyists aware that you know your rights, insert a ©, your name and the date at the start. If it could be important later to prove the date, send a copy to yourself through the post, conspicuously sealed; check that the postmark is legible and keep it safely.

Copyright in artistic products lasts for the life of the author plus 50 years. There are moves to change this, prompting Sir Cliff Richard to voice fears of his impending impoverishment. For industrial designs protection is for 15 years from the time the product goes on sale.

A **trademark** can be registered at the government's Intellectual Property Office (**www.ipo.gov.uk**) and you can search its database to ensure that yours really is novel. Trademark agents will do this for you if you prefer. In case your first preference has been taken, think up a stock of five or six names you would be happy to use as a trademark and work through until you find a vacant one.

Registering your own trademark gives unequivocal protection to you as its owner, or it should. Unfortunately, it is not foolproof as there is no requirement for a mark to be registered, so you could unwittingly use one not registered, but in widespread use for decades and therefore entitled to protection.

Registered designs give better protection than copyright. For both trademarks and registered designs the services of an agent are necessary. Protection is for 15 years from registration, provided it is renewed every five years. The cost of this will be £500 to £3,000.

Patents give the highest level of protection. When applying it is vital to be able to declare that you have never 'disclosed' the item, that is, told anyone about it except for a patent professional. A full patent gives 20 years' protection from the date of filing the first application.

An agent will probably advise an initial application, cheaper and simpler than a full application, to establish your place at the head of any queue and give you a year in which to test the market, study feasibility, work out manufacturing methods or even find a buyer and decide whether or not to proceed. You will need a patent agent and deep pockets, as the cost of an initial application could be £2,000 and a full application £20,000 to £30,000 over three or four years.

As with any other protection scheme, the real test comes when you have to repel a copyist. Patent lawyers are even more expensive than their 'common or garden' counterparts, so it is wise to ensure that you have legal expenses insurance that covers the cost of defence in all the markets in which you are likely to operate.

Going to law

There is a temptation to replace the whole of this section with a quotation from Ambrose Bierce's incomparably funny *The Devil's Dictionary*: 'Lawsuit: A machine which you go into as a pig and come out of as a sausage.' Not much more need be said.

As Bierce implies, going to law is best avoided. If it cannot be avoided, keep your involvement short. In most cases small businesses have more to lose by loss of management time and concentration than by settling the case quickly. As a famous judge, commenting on the cost of lawsuits, once remarked: 'The law is open to anyone, just like the Ritz Hotel.'

There is one exception, where you are owed £5,000 or less. The case will go to the County Court, but you may elect to have it dealt with by the Small Claims Procedure. This is a simple arbitration procedure designed for straightforward cases, conducted in private by the arbitrator with just yourself, the defendant and any witness or representative that may be needed. The procedure was designed to encourage DIY lawsuits, so you may not need a representative unless the case is at all complex. If you win, you will get back the court fees plus your costs in addition to any award. If you lose, you forfeit the fees and meet the other side's costs. A phone call to the local County Court will produce the forms.

The cost of solicitors deters people from using them, but there are occasions when they can actually save money by getting quickly to the nub of an issue. The worst way to use them is to try DIY, get into a tangle and then ask them to sort things out.

Contingency fees are a mixed blessing. This is the arrangement where a solicitor takes on a case, not for a fee but for a share of the award. It does ensure that poor people have access to the law, but no lawyer takes on a contingency fee case unless they are sure of victory. So the plaintiff could have won, paid a fee after the award and been better off. Fees might even have been awarded against the defendant.

If entanglement with the law is inevitable, ask around for a solicitor with a reputation for success in the kind of case concerned. Pay whatever is necessary, giving clear instructions that you want the action concluded quickly and cheaply.

The risk of an adverse result is small, but if it happens to you the cost will be high. You may wish to consider legal expenses cover as part of the firm's insurance. It will not pay awards or fines, but it does meet the legal costs which, as previously discussed, can be crippling.

Conclusions

- Contracts exist only when offer, acceptance and consideration are present.
- Most potential trouble can be avoided by the use of informed common sense.
- Contracts are complex but the vast majority of problems can be covered by some simple precautions.
- T&Cs can become part of the firm's marketing communications, showing it to be open and above board in its dealings, while still conferring proper protection.
- Selling and buying must take into account the implications of conditions, warranties, guarantees and exemptions.
- The implications of product liability should be considered.
- Copyright, registered designs, trademarks and patents give different levels of protection at different levels of cost.
- Going to law should be avoided where possible: the costs of avoidance are often lower than those of compliance.

PART 6:
Premises, operations, records and taxation

19
Premises – options and implications

In this chapter

LEARNING OUTCOMES

By the end of this chapter you should be able to:

- understand the implications of working from home;
- find premises;
- deal with commercial leases;
- understand planning consent and its implications;
- make a successful planning application;
- appeal against refusal;
- understand Uniform Business Rates (UBR);
- understand water charges and sewerage charges.

Premises

The need for premises

All firms need premises, even if it is a spare bedroom to house the PC or a garage in which to hang the ladders, yet the use of residential premises for business contravenes a number of regulations. Fortunately, most authorities can be counted on to turn a blind eye, exercising the legal maxim *de minimis non curat lex* (the law does not concern itself with trifles). That is not to say that there are no risks, merely that the prudent operator takes trouble never to attract attention. Clearly, the approaches that incur least cost and the lowest levels of commitment will appeal while the firm is finding its feet.

Working from home

Many firms start this way and some never leave. The potential problems are obvious and, when they arise, stem from a lack of consideration for others. Few people, especially neighbours of the new activity, would like their residential area turned into a minor industrial estate, so the main issues are:

- the amount of noise, smells and other nuisance generated;
- the number and type of visitors;
- the visible evidence of business activity;
- quantity and type of traffic created.

If there should be complaints they will end up with the local authority's planning department. Their ultimate sanction is a letter inviting the alleged offender to cease operations or apply for planning consent (which will almost certainly be withheld). Failure to comply will lead to court action and hefty fines. Consequently, this is a risk not to be taken lightly.

However carefully a firm may operate, however considerate it is towards its neighbours, there is always the possibility that someone in the vicinity is jealous, or feels that rules ought to be enforced, or for some other reason decides to stir up trouble. Knowing one's neighbours is recommended, so that they are less inclined to complain in the first place, but if they feel your conduct is intolerable they will speak directly to you, not the council.

In addition, the family may have views about losing a bedroom, garage or study. The house may be subject to covenants that prohibit business activity, but it is difficult for even neighbours to have them enforced. (Covenants are in the deeds for the property and typically forbid the keeping of livestock and the operation of a business; if I had ambitions to operate an alehouse from home they would be dashed by a specific covenant that applies to the premises.)

On the other hand, many small firms operate from home in complete harmony with neighbours, sometimes so unobtrusively that people do not realize what is going on. Therein lies the answer: the operation needs to be so low key as to be virtually invisible and inaudible, creating no nuisance and run with total consideration for the interests of neighbours. Even if some curmudgeon should report such a business to the planning authority, the supposed offender can retaliate by applying for an 'authorized use certificate', confirming that the planning category has not changed.

Although there are undoubtedly a few pettifogging officials with nothing better to do than deal with *de minimis* matters, the vast majority of those home-based firms that are closed down by the authorities deserve all they get. Work in progress parked on the verge, old engines in the front garden, the smell of paint and the noise of hammering: nobody should have to live next to it. Contrast that behaviour with my neighbour's. Everyone knows he runs his business from the garage, and those of us who are customers have been inside it. Occasionally, a big lorry delivers materials, but it presents no problems. His customers are fewer than a dozen a week and all arrive by car, a level of activity exceeded by private individuals with a busy social life. It is difficult to imagine why anyone should complain. He is also the most sociable man whom nobody would wish to offend.

Working from home does present a temptation that should be resisted, to do costings that assume accommodation is free. Better to cost in what commercial premises would cost so that when expansion or some other force pushes you out into the market prices do not suddenly jump. Other people manage to pay proper rent, so why not at least pretend to your customers that you do?

Insurance is a big issue. Running your business may automatically void your domestic cover, so disclose your plans to your insurers and get things straight. It will cost more, but still be far cheaper than having a major claim refused.

If you have a mortgage, the lender has a right to know your plans. This ought to be no more than a formality.

If your property is rented, the landlord needs to know your plans so as to notify his or her insurers. You may be asked to pay any extra insurance premium.

Government policy

The following is taken from a government website:

You do not necessarily need planning permission to work from home. The key test is whether the overall character of the dwelling will change as a result of the business.

If the answer to any of the following questions is 'yes', then permission will probably be needed:

Will your home no longer be used mainly as a private residence?

Will your business result in a marked rise in traffic or people calling?

Will your business involve any activities unusual in a residential area?

Will your business disturb your neighbours at unreasonable hours or create other forms of nuisance such as noise or smells?

Whatever business you carry out from your home, whether it involves using part of it as a bed-sit or for 'bed and breakfast' accommodation, using a room as your personal office, providing a childminding service, for hairdressing, dressmaking or music teaching, or using buildings in the garden for repairing cars or storing goods connected with a business – the key test is: is it still mainly a home or has it become business premises?

If you are in doubt you may apply to your council for a Certificate of Lawful Use for the proposed activity, to confirm it is not a change of use and still the lawful use.

(www.planningportal.gov.uk/permission/commonprojects/workingfromhome)

Finding premises

The anti-business attitudes of the public sector in the 1960s and 1970s have taken a long time to change. They did much damage in limiting the amount of accommodation provided for small firms. Only in the first decade of the 21st century did a reasonably free market in small business premises begin to emerge.

The premises now being provided are a far cry from the retired chicken sheds in which earlier generations of entrepreneurs began work – miserable places with the huge benefit that they cost almost nothing. Newer premises are built to modern standards of heating, insulation and finish, take modern health and safety and environmental requirements into account and, consequently, are not cheap.

In country areas there may be the chance to rent a disused building from a farmer or landowner. The system requires you to get planning consent and to convert the building to modern standards. Many new firms overlook this point, running in the way their forebears did, on the lowest overheads possible and with no security of tenure. This may not matter unless you need to borrow: lenders want to know if you have the right to operate from your premises at least until their loan is paid off.

If you should go along the conversion route, allow for the costly extras of mains water, drains, lavatories, electricity, gas if available, security, disability access vehicle parking spaces and turning areas, plus possibly acceleration or deceleration lanes into the entrance, depending on the character of the road outside. There may also be charges from the water company for periodically pumping out a sewage tank. The authorities will insist that everything is done to the highest standards. Once in the official system there are no short cuts.

Commercial leases

No lease should ever be signed without professional advice. Some negotiation may be required before a lease is in a condition that you are prepared to sign. Especially if premises are in short supply, a landlord may try to swing all kinds of liabilities on the unsuspecting potential tenant. The tenant, in turn, will want to reject them, but that is only possible if he or she has actually read the draft lease, worked out what it means and discussed it with a solicitor wise in the ways of landlords.

In addition to the rent, further costs are usually incurred:

- landlord's legal fees;
- your legal fees;
- landlord's buildings insurance premium;
- repairs during your tenancy;
- redecoration periodically and at the end of the lease;
- your surveyor's fees.

In the case of a brand-new building, a full professional survey is unlikely to be necessary. However, tenants should always protect themselves by examining the building closely, inside and out, and photographing and making notes on anything they think looks odd or ill-finished. In a conversion or in the case of an older building it is wise to have a professional check and report on the state of the fabric, as well as to record the condition before the start of the tenancy. Otherwise you could be required at the end of the lease to make good all sorts of dilapidations that took place before your time. For the same reason, take large numbers of photographs with the date recorded on them. A chartered surveyor will produce a schedule of condition for the landlord to agree to.

The lease may be FRI (full repairing and insuring). This means that you have to insure and maintain the building to the standard in which you found it.

The planning system

Planning permission

Using any land for industrial or commercial purposes requires planning consent. Former occupants may have got away with not applying, but you may not be so lucky. When renting or buying formally, this is unlikely to be an issue, but the informal market is different.

If you can trace back continuous usage to 1964, you may apply to the planning authority for a Lawful Development Certificate, a document that says, in effect, that you have consent to continue something that has gone on for so long that it is part of the scenery. The only problem with this is that it will tie you down very tightly to specific activities, constraining your flexibility in the future. Even so, local authorities do make mistakes. One property developer bought a site reserved for 'engineering', by which the authorities had visualized small workshops, but he successfully argued that civil engineering was part of what his firm did so he could operate his building business from the site.

If you want to move from the existing planning consent, the government-imposed fee will be at least several hundred pounds, with no guarantee of success. There is a fee calculator at **www.planningportal.gov.uk**. If the planning officer seems helpful you might feel confident enough to do it yourself, but otherwise a planning specialist (architect, town planner, surveyor or solicitor) may be needed.

Six to eight weeks after the application, the decision will arrive, under one of four headings:

- full planning consent, giving the right for anyone to put the land to the permitted use in perpetuity;
- temporary planning consent, allowing anyone the right to perform the specified activities for the period stated, usually from one to five years;
- personal planning consent, permitting only the applicant to use the premises as specified;
- refusal.

If the site is sensitive or the activity potentially contentious, a combination of temporary and personal consent may be given. Application can be made to renew temporary consent.

Temporary consent is better than refusal, but may constrain the enthusiasm of lenders, who want to know you can earn so as to pay them back. It may also constrain your enthusiasm to renovate a building that you might occupy for only a brief period of time.

It is unwise to rely on a wink and a nod from a planning officer, still less from a councillor. In this field, believe nothing until it is officially confirmed in writing.

Any consent may have conditions attached. These may range from the innocuous, such as not storing in the open air or working after 7.00 pm, but others might be obstructive. If the latter, talk to the planning officer and explain the difficulty; he or she might be able to have the condition varied, or you could appeal to the Secretary of State.

Applying for planning permission

The formal system requires you to complete and submit forms, plans and a fee. Then the planning committee hears the case and decides and the decision comes in writing several weeks after the application.

All that needs to be done, but long beforehand you begin the campaign. Planning officers (the full-time officials) and councillors (the part-time elected representatives) are busy people and capable of getting the wrong end of your stick. You need to influence them favourably.

To see why, start with the arrival of your forms at the local authority office. They are checked for accuracy and copies go to water, gas, electricity and highways authorities for comment, as well as to the parish council. Immediate neighbours are notified. Thus many people get to hear of your plans and have the opportunity to protest before the committee hears your case.

Most resistance is usually based on ignorance, misunderstanding of the true nature of your plans and consequent hostility. If that is all the committee hears, it would be natural for it to incline towards refusal. To redress the balance, you should adopt a particular course of action.

Contact the planning officer and invite him or her to the site. Explain your plans and answer questions. Describe your activities and show how yours will be a small-scale business. With any luck, the result will be that official working for you rather than against you.

Next, contact the parish or town council. Follow the same process as you did with the planning officer. Invite the borough councillor for the area and the councillor who sits on the planning committee for that area too. Call personally on any neighbour likely to be affected and explain yourself. Remember how important to all these constituencies the prospect of local jobs is, especially jobs for young people.

Then you are ready to fill in the forms. Immediately afterwards get every business organization you can think of to write to the council in support of your application. Now you can sit back and let matters take their course.

You may attend the planning committee meeting but usually are not allowed to speak. Nonetheless, it is worth telling the chair that you are present should he or she feel the need to call on you for clarification of any point. You will hear the decision that evening and will get it in writing (probably with a number of conditions attached that were not discussed) a few days later.

Appealing against a planning refusal

Despite all the preparation advocated here, some planning applications do fail. In that case the right to appeal exists, above the heads of the local authority to an inspector appointed by the government.

An appeal may be launched against any of the types of decisions discussed here. There are two approaches: the written appeal and the public hearing. For most purposes the written appeal is strongly preferable, being quicker and cheaper. The appeal must be made within six months or special permission must be given for delay.

Complete the appeal forms and return them. The council gets copies of what you write and responds in turn, a copy of which comes to you. An inspector from the Planning Inspectorate visits the site by appointment and may ask questions. You may not question him or her but may only answer questions. Within six months you will get the decision, which is usually a common-sense one.

To appeal, it is important to have advice from a planning specialist. Ask about his or her record of success on appeals and get quotes for the work.

Rates, and water and sewerage charges

Uniform business rates (UBR)

UBR are charged on business premises by local authorities and water suppliers in a way similar to the imposts on houses. The difference is that, whereas councils set their own levels of council tax, UBR are set centrally by the government. UBR are not cheap and, compared to the council tax charged on domestic premises, are poor value as councils are forbidden to collect waste from many business premises unless they charge extra.

To give an example from one small town in the south Midlands: a 30-year old 134 square metre (1,440 square foot) workshop to let by the local authority for £7,500 a year has a rateable value of £7,900, with rates payable (the important figure) of £3,420. Thus UBR are adding about half to the cost of rent. And that does not include water and sewerage rates, of which more later.

UBR are calculated by applying the standard multiplier (SM) to the rateable value. In this case, the SM is 43.3p, as it is across the whole of England outside London, so the sum is: £0.433 × £7,900 = £3,420 payable.

Here the situation gets complicated. While the calculation above is accurate, there is a slightly lower rate for small businesses and a temporary reduction or even exemption in certain circumstances. The situation is too complex to explain here in full, but the Business Link website's section on business property deals with it in detail: **www.businesslink.gov.uk/bdotg/action/layer?r.s=tl&topicId=1086951342**.

No appeal is possible against one of the components of the calculation of UBR payable, the SM, but the Rating Assessment (£7,900 in the example) is open to challenge. However, it is not to be appealed against lightly, as appeals can result in the opposite of what is desired, a rise in the Assessment. As with rent, it may be best to accept the inevitable, recognize that competitors struggle under the same yoke and get on with doing things better than them.

Water charges

Business premises with water meters are charged for their consumption just as domestic premises are: a standing charge plus a cost for the quantity measured. In cases where no meter is fitted the supplier may simply assess a charge (temptingly open to challenge) or apply a number of pence to the premises' Rating Assessment (its rateable value). Businesses run from home are not charged separately for water: they simply pay the domestic charge in the normal way.

The water companies give advice on their websites on reducing water consumption and hence the size of metered bills. A business customer may select a water company to buy from; details are given on the Ofwat website (**www.ofwat.gov.uk**). Savings may be available by choosing various kinds of tariffs.

Sewerage charges

Charges for discharging water into the sewage system are usually levied by reference to the quantity of water coming into the premises, plus a standing charge. In Scotland, users may choose their sewerage company as well as their water supplier.

Conclusions

- Working from home is desirable for its low costs but needs careful evaluation and management. The chief risk is of effective complaints by neighbours to the local authority. Banks may be reluctant to lend in view of this risk.

- The supply of premises varies in different areas, but there is little low-cost accommodation available in the formal system. Entering the informal system may cut costs but banks are reluctant to finance businesses with no certainty of tenure.

- Commercial leases are often highly negotiable and must be taken on only with professional supervision. Property matters are too complex for the layperson to manage unaided.

- The planning system is best complied with, especially if the firm has plans to grow. It can be difficult to get advice from local authority officials but the effort can be made. Commercial property agents understand local policies and politics.

- Making a planning application involves much form filling and expense. To ensure that it succeeds first time the firm should lobby decision makers.

- Appealing against refusal is usually done cheaply by written appeal but may be done more expensively by public hearing.

- UBR can be a high cost and this is easily overlooked in the rush to find premises.

- Water and sewerage charges, while usually not so high as UBR, also need clarifying before taking on premises.

20
Planning, control and purchasing

In this chapter

LEARNING OUTCOMES

By the end of this chapter you should be able to:

- plan operations;
- monitor performance against your plan;
- understand the need for proper control;
- exercise control;
- avoid the risks inherent in purchasing;
- undertake purchasing in a planned way.

Planning of operations

Operational planning

'Operations' is the catch-all term for all the day-to-day things done to make the business operate. The management of operations therefore has two aspects: dealing with the complexity created by a teeming number of small things that are often interdependent; and developing a strategic vision of how it is all to be handled.

The human brain is good at seeing an overall strategic picture; it is also good at working out the many tiny details that have to be in place for the overall vision to work. What it is not good at is doing both at the same time. Consequently, it is easy to start off with the grand vision, consider some troublesome detail that threatens to obstruct progress and be so caught up that one remains at the level of detail for the rest of the day, never getting round to resolving the matter that was started.

Nonetheless, it is important for a grand overview to be established. This overview will include what premises will be needed, what equipment, which people; how orders will be obtained, processed and fulfilled; how records will be kept, what reports the records' data will generate, how often and for whom; what systems will be in place to keep the whole thing under control... and so on.

Once the overall vision is in place, systems need to be set up to deal with the detail. The aims here are: to standardize everything as much as possible; and to minimize the number of individual decisions to be made.

The latter is usually accomplished by creating routines, with rules and conventions for how things are done. Thus perhaps 95 per cent runs like clockwork, with only 5 per cent of exceptions popping up for special treatment, a much lighter load on people than if everything was dealt with as if unique.

The areas covered include for every firm:

- sales;
- purchasing;
- order processing;
- customer records;
- production;
- delivery;
- invoicing;
- payments in and out;
- stock control;
- payroll;
- staff records;
- financial records and reporting.

In particular firms there will be additional areas specific to the industry or activity.

At the strategic level a decision needs to be made about the place of technology. Our ability to automate activity accelerates all the time, so the temptation to put in every bit of technology to do things cheaper is rising. But be warned. As Simon Caulkin, Management Editor, reported in an article published in *The Observer* on 18 February 2007: 'Dell made the classic nerd's mistake of underestimating the human factor – the first and last link in the supply chain – and trying to fill it with IT. As most companies do, it put computers in charge of the thing humans do best and vice versa, thus making everyone unhappy.'

The argument is not that IT has no place, just that it is unsuitable for the 'soft' areas where human interaction is needed. As Caulkin argues, these are the areas that interact directly with customers, both when selling and when delivering to them. Two more groups should be added to that item: dealings with suppliers and with staff, both areas in which the 'soft' skills of dealing with human beings are to the fore – or ought to be.

Planning before action

Planning the operations of the business is vital, yet some people resist it. Reasons to resist it include an emotional resistance to paperwork, a conviction that plans always go wrong and a preference for doing something practical instead. None of these justifies neglect of one of the owner's key responsibilities.

Some arguments for planning appear in the bullet list below. If you are not yet convinced, please consider them very carefully. If you remain unconvinced, talk these points over with an adviser to get a different view.

If you share this book's view, you will plan for each of the areas in the bullet list. If your operation is to be small, easily handled by a few hours' work a week by yourself and a part-time clerk, you do not have big volumes to consider. However, if you could find yourself handling a lot of activity, you will need to plan staff numbers.

- Making mistakes on paper is cheaper than making them in your business activities.

- When starting up you know least. Without knowledge, you need to think and imagine.

- Plans are always wrong, but preparing them makes you see important linkages.

- Even the simplest business is more complicated than it looks. No business can be planned and controlled in your head.

- After running for a time you put the plan right and set out on the new course. This teaches you why it was wrong.

- Without the plan you would not have learned.

- If you don't have a plan, you don't know where you are going. If you don't know where you are going, any road will do. Some roads go to strange places.

- Thinking first means you make or save more money.

For each area of activity in your business, create a spreadsheet table that allows you to insert the time the activity takes, multiply it by the number of those activities in a day, then multiply them by 350 days to arrive at annual volumes. Once you know the volumes, you can divide by the output of each member of staff, allowing for each full-time member of staff 220 days at five productive hours a day. The figure of 220 may seem pessimistic, but it allows for holidays and sickness. The calculation is, for the UK:

365 days – 104 days at weekends – 8 Bank Holidays – 20 days' holiday
= 233 days available, less (say) 13 sick = 220 productive days.

From the resulting plan will come the requirement for office space, workshop space, equipment, furniture, parking spaces, restroom space and so on, for that particular activity. Repeat the exercise for each element of operations to arrive at the overall total.

Once the plan has been developed (and perhaps tested by running it past a business adviser) it can be put into action. As with all other plans, the story does not stop there. The plan is wrong – all plans are – so it is important to monitor progress against it in order to learn, and hence to improve the plan for the future.

Control of operations

Control

So far we have dealt largely with looking ahead – making plans and forecasts – and to some extent the matter of putting them into operation. However, that is only part of the picture. All the plans in the world have no meaning unless outcomes are compared with them, otherwise they are no more than wishful thinking.

Thus at some point the entrepreneur wants to know if outcomes vary from the prediction and, if so, to what extent. Keeping on top of developments by the intelligent comparison of outcomes with plans is the essence of control.

There are six components to the process of control:

- planning, expressed numerically (eg production quantities, cash-flow forecast, staff's productive hours, P&L budget, etc);
- activity, carrying out the plan;
- measurement of activity;
- comparison of measurements with the plan;
- evaluation of any differences, whether they are trivial or important;
- decision, possibly to revise the plan.

Once that cycle is complete, the entire process begins again: control never stops. To control business operations it must be known what ought to be happening (from the budget and other plans); and what has actually happened (from the management information system: the MIS). To be of any use, the information needs to be timely and sufficiently accurate for its purpose. This can sometimes mean a trade-off. If you had to wait for months to know last week's sales figure, the information would be useless by the time it reached you. If you could have it at 4.00 pm on Friday, but to only 60 per cent accuracy, it would be equally useless.

Accuracy is desirable, but takes time. Speed is desirable, but can compromise accuracy. For each operational area the following need to be thought out:

- what management information is needed frequently;
- how often it is needed;
- when it is needed;
- an acceptable level of accuracy.

It is difficult to generalize about what levels of accuracy might be acceptable, but for most purposes something in the range of 90–95 per cent would provide the basis for decisions. It is known probably not to be accurate but it is 'good enough'. The concept of 'good enough' is not a recipe for sloppiness but a recognition of the need in the practical world for the trade-off between speed and accuracy mentioned above.

The firm's MIS has been referred to. This grand-sounding term can cover many degrees of sophistication, from the four-drawer accounting system (see below) to an integrated PC-based package.

The four-drawer accounting system requires a desk with two drawers on either side. Invoices payable go into the top left-hand drawer and as they are paid they move down to the drawer below. Copies of invoices receivable – the bills the firm has sent out – go into the top right-hand drawer and when payment comes in they migrate to the drawer below. At any one time the firm can see who is owed what and when it is due, and who owes what. The need to pay a creditor can be balanced by chasing debtors owing the same amount. This system is not advocated, but it is used by many small, stable firms.

As a general principle, information needs to be presented in a form that easily allows comparison with budget. The quality of presentation of information will almost certainly vary in different areas of the operation. Accounts are likely to be computerized and so should provide management with comparisons of performance against budget immediately and accurately (assuming everything that ought to have been keyed in has been). On the other hand, raw materials stock records may be kept on paper and staff might be lax in recording what they withdraw, so that a physical count is needed to see if the firm is about to grind to a halt for lack of supplies. The armed forces say nothing moves without a piece of paper, a maxim that can be carried too far, but it does make sure that not many things get lost or forgotten.

Controls should start from the smallest unit and work outwards. In production, for example, the key document is the job card. It could look like Table 20.1.

The job card travels with the job through the production process. Thus, at any time, anyone can check on where every single job is in relation to plan, who did what to it and whether there is catching up to do. It should be kept in a clear envelope and attached firmly to a relevant part of the work.

Its usefulness is governed by the extent to which people complete it, so management eyes need to watch for that. Staff will be encouraged to do the paperwork when they see that their productive time is being calculated from the totals shown on the cards. Incomplete records mean they seem to be slacking. The remedy is in their hands.

When the week starts, summing up the cards will show what output is needed during the week, enabling detailed planning, moving staff around, asking for overtime or shifting some work into the following week, and so on. At the end of the week, each job card is reviewed to see where the delays were and to consider action.

These checks will lead to thinking about:

● extent of forward commitments and what should be done;
● spare capacities;

TABLE 20.1   Job card

JOB CARD	Ref no:	Description:	Order no:
Customer:	Customer ref:	Plans:	Order date:
Special instructions:	Special components:	Packing:	Delivery:
PRODUCTION RECORD	Dept:	Dept:	Dept:
	Operation:	Operation:	Operation:
	Operative:	Operative:	Operative:
COMPLETION	Start:	Start:	Start:
Target	Finish:	Finish:	Finish:
Actual	Time elapsed:	Time elapsed:	Time elapsed:
NOTE: THE JOB CARD STAYS WITH JOB!			Dispatch date:

- scheduling of the next work to come along;
- holiday schedules;
- maintenance timetables;
- whether budgeted capacity is excessive or inadequate;
- scrap and rework rates;
- stock levels.

By this simple means you are on top of the production activity. If the same sort of discipline is applied to each of the other areas, control of the operation will be as complete as it needs to be. It will never be 100 per cent, but it will be enough to reduce surprises to a manageable minimum at the same time as leaving management free for other work.

In the planning of capacity it is important to look at people as well as machines. People need:

- training;
- supervision;
- the right materials, tools and equipment, in the right place and in working order;
- safety equipment and an understanding of its use and importance;
- understanding of their work and how it fits into the whole;
- good working relationships;
- rest and refreshment;
- secure storage for belongings;
- understanding of the rules, why they exist and the penalties for infraction;
- a sense that their contribution is recognized and valued;
- decent treatment.

The real expert on a job is someone who has been doing it for a time. Learn from your staff: go round and speak to each of them twice a day, inviting comments on problems and how things could be done better.

Staff who have some discretion over how they spend their time can choose to chase the wrong target. Meet each of them for five minutes at Friday lunchtime. They should bring a list that shows:

- things they plan to work on during the following week;
- where they are now;
- where they plan to be in a week's time.

You can ask how they plan to tackle the things they list, using the opportunity for mentoring and guidance. If the list seems unambitious you can suggest additions, or if it is too full, counsel a reduction. Above all, you can guide their sense of priorities.

The meeting is repeated every Friday, with a review of how things went against the plan as well as a projection for the coming week. You gain impressions of staff's effectiveness and they get advice they need. If they can see that this matters and that you take it seriously, you are in control at a cost of no more than 15 minutes a week for each key employee.

As signalled in the discussion of charge-out rates, it is unrealistic to expect employees to work productively for every minute of the day. You will impress on them the expectation that they will, exhorting their supervisors to make sure it happens, but in your planning you assume output for 70 per cent of the time you pay for. If you are lax it could fall lower, even disastrously so, but strong management should find 70 per cent a good guide for planning purposes.

Time you have paid for can evaporate easily, especially from:

- a slow start to the working day, chatting with colleagues instead of starting work;
- poor punctuality, arriving late and getting ready to leave early;
- tea and meal breaks extending in length;
- time spent gossiping after a business matter has been discussed;
- smoking, popping out for 10 minutes every hour;
- putting business PCs, copiers and phones to personal use;
- poor planning, requiring trips out to collect supplies.

Control of these matters can bring useful rewards. Equally, laxity will be punished. If these matters slip the workforce might have to increase by 10 or 20 per cent – which is no mean addition to the pay bill.

Purchasing

Purchasing: essential but troublesome

Purchasing for a business is a serious matter. It affects the equipment with which the firm operates and the environment it operates in; the materials it incorporates in its finished product or service; and therefore influences the way it is seen by staff and customers.

The problems of purchasing are not new: the Romans had the term '*caveat emptor*', meaning 'let the buyer beware'. In other words, purchasing is a risky business, and the ultimate responsibility lies with the buyer to make sure that the purchase is what is really needed and is of suitable quality.

Purchasing can teach a lot about selling, especially how not to do it. In addition to this free training it also shows just how many people make it their business to call on a firm in the course of a day, apparently believing that buying from them will lead it to a bright new future.

All uninvited visitors want attention for as long as it takes to get an order. You will be unable to spare that amount of time and so must decide on a policy. Do you see everyone, but briefly, or see nobody? Or a select few? In which case, what governs the selection? The right stance will depend on factors particular to your situation, but it is a decision that must be taken. Remember that an oral order is still a contract. One golden rule is never to give anyone an order to make them go away. There is a simpler and cheaper alternative of just asking them to leave as you have work to do.

Specification of purchases

Buying on impulse is as bad an idea in business as it is in private life. From time to time opportunities may arise that had not been foreseen, but in general most purchases can be considered in advance so as to minimize the scope for error. That involves a disciplined process of deciding what you want, resulting in the drawing up of a specification.

There are of course two approaches to buying. One is thinking about what you want, defining it and searching for it. The other is looking to see what is available and buying the most attractive proposition.

Each has its place in different contexts, but for serious investments that need to work hard the former approach makes sense. It does not preclude taking a look at what is on the market first, to see what it is realistic to include in the specification, but the general principle of undertaking thought before action has to be right. In some cases preparedness to compromise on certain details can yield great savings, since a standard product usually costs much less than something made to special order.

For planned purchases the decision as to which supplier to choose falls automatically out of the process of specifying needs. Whoever comes closest to matching those needs gets the order.

Contractual and administrative implications

When buying, make sure that potential suppliers know about any special requirements. For example, if you have an order for a job requiring delivery of materials from the supplier no later than the 23rd of the month, tell them. Make a note on the order form or include in your e-mail or letter of confirmation a sentence to that effect. Not only does that emphasize the urgency, but if suppliers deliver late and the whole transaction goes wrong and ends up in court, it may enable you to get judgment against them for the damages awarded against you.

When a sales representative completes an order form and asks you to sign, the first thing to do always is to check what has been written. Ask for a copy before anything else can be written on it. Few salespeople are dishonest, but it is prudent to protect yourself. Keep that copy and check it against the delivery note and invoice.

Also, ask if the price shown on the order reflects the total cost. Usually there is VAT to add, but sometimes a hefty delivery charge or some other fee can dilute a saving you thought you were making. Ask for delivery dates, even approximate, to be written on the order, to commit suppliers more to keep to the salesperson's promises.

When buying through the internet there is an opportunity to print a hard copy of the checkout screen. Do it and file as before. Telephone orders should be confirmed in writing either by the seller or to the seller by you.

All this may sound bureaucratic, and it is. But the advice is there for a reason: laxity in such matters causes many firms to lose money, sometimes in quite large quantities.

Vigilance is needed when the delivery and invoice come. It is wise to check immediately that what has arrived is what you ordered and that the price is correct, and to take up discrepancies straight away. Again, confirm in writing.

Conclusions

- As with all complex areas, plans for production should be formed and tested before implementation.
- The plan is a learning tool, but can be so only if performance against it is monitored and conclusions drawn about variances.
- In the absence of control planning is meaningless. Anything could happen yet people would be unaware of perhaps calamitous events.
- The exercise of control can be done by straightforward means matched to the complexity of the firm's operations.
- Control is not just about numbers but includes the activity of people.
- The risks attached to wrong purchasing decisions are so great as to justify forward planning.
- Where possible and realistic, specifications should be produced for proposed purchases.
- Events in the process of purchasing need to be recorded at every stage.

21
Safety and quality

In this chapter

LEARNING OUTCOMES

By the end of this chapter you should be able to:

- recognize a safety culture's contribution to employee motivation;
- take practical safety measures;
- understand the requirements of legislation;
- know that non-compliance can be costly;
- understand the meaning of 'quality';
- set up systems for managing quality.

Safety at work

Working safely makes a great deal of sense. Creating a culture of safe working not only avoids the pitfalls we shall come to shortly but also gives staff important messages about how their employer views them. People who believe they are as disposable as a soiled tissue will not commit to the firm and its mission; instead they will:

- put in only the minimum effort they can get away with;
- slack at every possible opportunity;
- steal;
- sabotage;
- concentrate effort on avoiding being caught out;
- lower the morale of others.

Not all staff will start their employment with such attitudes and behaviours, but if they are treated badly for long enough their approach will deteriorate.

Morale and motivation can therefore be helped by a sound safety culture. 'Sound' does not mean obsessive – one young manager was taken aback by staff with a smattering of knowledge of safety issues. The staff were expected to stand on chairs to place a banner on top of a lightweight display screen, and demanded the safety equipment required under regulations governing working at height – the equipment specified for steeplejacks and scaffolders.

If those are not reasons enough for creating a safety culture, there are hard financial arguments as well. Accidents cause a loss of productive time: the person affected may have to visit hospital, perhaps accompanied by a colleague; he or she may be away from work for a period of time, disrupting schedules; paperwork will have to be completed for insurance purposes and perhaps for the official authorities. In addition, insurance premiums may rise.

The practicalities

In the UK the Health and Safety at Work Act (HASAWA) requires employers to provide safe conditions and for everyone, staff and management, to work safely. The penalties for infractions can be onerous: fines of up to £20,000 and/or two years in prison, plus a criminal record.

HASAWA demands that employers ensure the health, safety and welfare at work of all employees, as far as that is practicable. This covers:

- safety of the workplace and any equipment;
- safety in the way work is done;
- providing necessary information, training and supervision;
- a safe and healthy environment;
- facilities and arrangements for staff welfare.

Staff are not the only people affected. The employer is also responsible for the health and safety of visitors to the premises on legitimate business.

Employees, too, have responsibilities. They must:

- take reasonable care for the health and safety of themselves and others;
- cooperate with their employer on safety issues;
- neither misuse nor damage safety equipment.

While you will be duly careful for staff and visitors, it is vital to be even more careful for yourself, since if you were unable to work for a month or more, or lost some key faculty such as your sight, the firm would probably fold. Even if your injury were less onerous, life could be miserable. Ask anyone with a bad back.

If you employ people, even if only occasionally or part time, you need to give them an initial safety briefing and further briefings as new hazards arise, for example when new equipment comes in. Record the briefing's contents, get the employee to initial it and file the record. Be especially sure to require the accident book to be completed for anyone hurt, however trivial the incident, and make sure staff know where the first-aid box is and how to use the contents. There are companies who will visit periodically to check that your first-aid box has the contents required by regulation and top up any shortages, at a cost.

Spring cleaning ought not to be an annual event. Clean and tidy workplaces tend to be safer, and are certainly more efficient. Make cleaning a task done at the end of each day, with everything put away and cleaned down. Neglect it for a week and you, and visitors, will know the difference. Keep on top of it and mess never becomes a problem.

Before starting up, contact the Health and Safety Executive and check everything you are required to do (**www.hse.gov.uk**).

Quality

'Quality' is a term surrounded by much misunderstanding. People talk of 'quality' clothes, meaning well cut and made with skill from good materials, or a 'quality' car, that is, one designed and built to high standards. Neither sense has a place in the business use of the word.

Quality is defined differently by many thinkers, but they have in common more than they differ. The consensus has gathered around the idea of quality as meeting customers' needs, while complying with any relevant regulations.

There is a school of thought that holds it to be better not simply to meet customers' needs but to exceed them. If that is done to the product itself it can be wasteful: there is little point in making a woman's fashion shoe that will last for a decade when it will be discarded after only a couple of years. It is usually less wasteful to concentrate the under-promise and over-delivery outside the product or service itself, applying it instead to the ancillary parts of the offer – delivery or spares back-up, for instance. As so often, what is best depends on the business you are in.

Managing quality

The management of quality is another matter besides. There is even a set of British (and international) Standards to cover it. Managing quality, brutally paraphrased, is a matter of specifying the requirement, eliminating error and recording actions so that the process of production can be traced back if need be. And very useful it can be, too. If a turbine blade fails in an Argentinian airliner, all the engines of that kind worldwide can be traced immediately and those with blades from the same batch isolated for checks.

In some industries it is expected that suppliers will be BS EN ISO 9001 registered (details from **www.bsi-global.com**), but for most it is an option. The decision to choose registration should be made only after careful consideration, for qualifying for and maintaining registration does involve a great deal of work and the creation of new working systems and recording methods.

When a delivery is late it is tempting to skip the final check and get the delivery onto a vehicle. Consider the implications: which will be remembered and punished more in the circumstance in question: a few hours' lateness or a faulty installation?

The answer will vary with circumstances but it is important to know in advance what it is, so that the decision to send or withhold can be immediate.

Conclusions

- A culture of safe working encourages motivation as it contributes to a sense of employees being valued.
- Unsafe working can incur considerable costs and penalties.
- Staff and employer share responsibility for safety.
- Quality, in business, means meeting customer specifications and complying with regulations.
- Quality does not mean over-specifying.
- The management of quality is an important task for managers.

22
Financial records and taxation

In this chapter

LEARNING OUTCOMES

By the end of this chapter you should be able to:

- understand the need to manage finances;
- decide on whether or not to use PC-based accounting and record-keeping;
- deal with the business taxation system;
- address National Insurance (NI), pensions, income tax and corporation tax;
- deal with the principles of VAT;
- understand VAT as it relates to the customer;
- handle a VAT return.

Financial management

Record keeping

Managing finance is of crucial importance, and is conducted with figures that result from aggregation of many detailed records. Therefore it is vital that those records are set up properly and maintained frequently.

The hierarchy of record keeping runs like this:

- no records kept, but all paperwork given to an accountant at the end of the year to sort out income tax, etc;
- simple DIY records, on paper or PC, enabling day-to-day management of finance;

- a bought-in paper system such as Safeguard or Kalamazoo;
- conventional double-entry books;
- a computerized accounting and financial information system.

The first on the list is far more expensive than a record system need be, but it can work for the simplest businesses dealing entirely in cash. Very few businesses are like that.

At least the second approach is needed if the facts of the firm cannot all be carried in the owner's head. It is often coupled with the 'four-drawer' system met previously or the 'two-shoebox' system, its even simpler cousin, where invoices payable are kept in a shoebox on the left of the desk and those receivable in another shoebox on the right. In the case of cash shortage, a handful of debtor invoices are pulled out and phone calls or visits made.

The advantage of these systems is that no invoice ever gets lost and that understanding the cash situation is simple; you know what is due to come in and go out by totalling the drawers or boxes. Combining this with records of orders placed (which will have to be paid for), the bank statement (saying where you started from), credit-card slips (bills not yet settled) and chequebook (showing what has been paid but not yet gone through the bank) reveals the current and immediate future cash situation.

The bought-in systems, third on the list, can handle more sophisticated operations. Double-entry books used to serve mighty commercial empires until the advent of mechanical, and, later, electronic systems. However, instead of employing one of these you should consider jumping straight to the final stage, given that:

- You will almost certainly have a PC in the firm anyway.
- The convenience will probably outweigh the cost (Amazon and others discount the list prices).
- Once the chore of inputting invoices is complete, all recording and analysis is instantaneous and accurate.

To take a look at the kind of thing on offer, try: **http://shop.sage.co.uk/software-landing.aspx** and click on 'software and services'. Sage offers a number of bundles including an 'instant business package' at the time of writing costing £310 including VAT, covering accounts, payroll, customer management and advice on managing staff and health and safety. This is not a recommendation, simply a mention of a user-friendly site listing small-business software. When shopping, ensure that the software conforms to the requirements of HM Revenue & Customs (HMRC; **www.hmrc.gov.uk**), or your accounts could be refused for tax-calculation purposes.

A firm unsure if it will expand rapidly could look at one of the integrated small-business packages. They not only do the accounts but also maintain records of customers and suppliers.

Whichever route you choose, discuss it with your accountant before acting, and build into your timetable a specific time daily or weekly when you do the accounts.

Bank accounts

Many sole traders operate only a single bank account. Presumably it suits them, but there are dangers in confusing the state of business and personal finances. If the account runs down, how do they know if it is because they are spending too much as a private individual or earning too little as a business?

Starting from the view that the owner ought to know what the position of the business is at any time, there is only one conclusion: that there need to be separate personal and business accounts. Each account can have its own chequebook and credit card. Some banks offer charge cards for issue to employees for a limited range of purchases for work, such as fuel for a company vehicle. Every week or month there can be either a standing order for the business account to pay over the owner's drawings to the personal account, or if cash-flow is unpredictable a transfer can be made when suitable.

Although internet-only banking is cheap, it is unwise to use it as the sole way of paying bills and receiving money. A PC crash could easily freeze the whole firm. However, some banks offer internet access to conventional accounts, which is a great convenience.

NI, pensions, income and corporation taxes

Taxation of businesses

As this is so complex a field that is, moreover, constantly changing, only a broad outline can be given here. Where figures are quoted they may have changed since publication, so the current situation should be checked before any action is taken. Fortunately, HMRC has gone to great pains to be clear and comprehensive in the information it provides, including through an admirable website **www.hmrc.gov.uk.** It even runs a series of free workshops to train the newly self-employed in record keeping and taxation.

The principal taxes on income which a SME needs to recognize are:

- National Insurance (NI);
- income tax;
- (if a limited company) corporation tax.

Since this can be a confusing area for people, HMRC runs a helpline for the newly self-employed on 0845 915 4515.

Though it is not strictly a tax, employers are forced by law to contribute to employees' pensions, so pensions are dealt with here, too.

In essence, as soon as someone becomes self-employed he or she should notify the income tax authorities. From then on, the person will be required to complete an annual tax return. Tax liability will be assessed under Schedule D, which confers the ability to offset certain business expenses against income before tax is calculated.

NI

This tax on employees and employers began life as a government insurance scheme, covering people for unemployment benefits. It is now just another payroll tax under which both employer and employee pay at pre-determined rates into the central taxation fund.

In addition to income tax, a self-employed individual is required to pay NI contributions in Class 2, a fixed weekly amount, and Class 4, a proportion of income. For the year 2012–13, Class 2 was announced in 2012 as £2.65 a week and Class 4 is 9 per cent of profits between £7,605 and £42,475. Above £42,475 2 per cent is charged. These rates and boundaries change frequently.

Pensions

In 2012 pension reforms are expected to come into force. Under the Pensions Act 2008, all employers will have to provide a qualifying workplace pension arrangement to all eligible staff, and make employer's contributions to it. All eligible staff must be automatically enrolled; the scheme can be any that the employer chooses subject to certain criteria. Schemes are likely to be offered by the private sector, and the government has introduced the National Employment Savings Trust (NEST).

Employers must contribute at least 3 per cent of staff's pay, based on a band of earnings, to top-up staff members' own contributions. In addition, tax relief equivalent to about 1 per cent will apply. Employers *must* enrol staff automatically, unless anyone wishes to opt out. There are penalties for offering incentives to opt out. Business Link's website gives more details of this complex matter at: **www.businesslink.gov.uk/bdotg/action/layer?r.l1=1073858787&r.l2=1084822773&r.s=tl&topicId=1074452901**

Income tax

No tax is paid on the 'personal allowance', which varies with circumstances. Until 5 April 2013, that is set for a single person under 65 at £8,105. After that and any other tax reliefs, tax is charged as follows:

- up to £34,370, 20 per cent;
- £34,371 to £150,000, 40 per cent;
- over £150,000, 50 per cent.

Note that these are the rates applying to earned income. Different rates can apply to interest and dividends (such as those paid to you as a shareholder if you run a limited company).

Since Class 4 contributions and income tax are billed after the event, unless your personal cash flow is excellent something should be put by weekly. After the first year the authorities will, to some extent, save you the trouble. Under the self-assessment scheme for income tax they will estimate your income in the next year to be the same and bill you in advance for half of the tax due. This, again, needs to be saved up for.

Corporation tax

Corporation tax is quite separate. It is like an income tax, except that it is paid by limited companies on their profits, not by individuals. For the year ended 6 April 2012, the rate for small companies (up to £300,000 profit) was 20 per cent. After that it climbs until it is at 24 per cent on profits of £1.5 million. It will reduce to 23 per cent in 2013 and 22 per cent in 2014.

The government has announced new plans for a shake-up of tax arrangements in the poorer parts of England, aimed at stimulating enterprise. At the time of writing no details are available, but if you plan to locate outside London, the east and the south-east, it would be wise to search the Business Link, BIS, Treasury and HMRC websites before committing yourself. If their proposals prove to be especially generous, relocation may be on the cards – especially if you are close to the boundary anyway.

Tax relief

Tax relief is worth a brief mention. Before starting the business, check with your accountant how you should set things up to minimize the tax bill. Especially check if you plan to work from home, claiming a share of domestic expenses against tax. When you come to sell the house you will not want a bill for capital gains tax on the increase in the house's value which the accountant could have ensured that you avoided.

Individuals and companies alike are allowed to calculate their profits for tax purposes after taking account of legitimate business expenses. The websites **hmrc.gov.uk** and **businesslink.gov.uk** give further details on a complex topic.

TABLE 22.1

Net profit before tax	£5,000
Tax allowance (eg from buying equipment)	£15,000 –
Tax loss	£10,000

You have not lost money; you made £5,000, but offsetting the £15,000 tax allowance has meant that for tax purposes you can legitimately claim a loss. You do not have to pay tax on the £5,000 profit as it has been wiped out by the 'loss'. Moreover, if you have paid tax in previous years you can claim back tax relief on the £10,000 against it. Alternatively, the £10,000 can be carried forward to relieve your tax liability in the future. There is a limit on the proportion of income that can be claimed for relief from personal income tax: either £50,000 or 25 per cent of income, whichever is higher.

This arrangement is subject to conditions. If you might want to use the facility, careful timing of your start date is advisable, as is the advice of your accountant. Tax losses may seem far-fetched but, given the generous allowances for any investment made in the first year, many new firms can make them.

VAT

VAT in outline

In the EU, VAT is charged every time most goods are sold commercially. There are exceptions, including sales by very small firms and sales of certain 'exempt' products.

In the UK there are three rates of VAT at the time of writing:

- zero rate, in effect 0 per cent, on some food, books, newspapers and certain other items;
- 5 per cent, on fuel and power, children's car seats, static caravans and some construction supplies;
- 20 per cent on everything else.

The zero rate exists so that, should the government decide, VAT can be imposed easily. There are also some goods that are exempt from VAT or entirely outside its scope.

Registration can be compulsory or voluntary. A business must register for VAT if any of the following apply:

- Its VAT-able sales in the previous 12 months exceeded £77,000.
- It takes over a VAT-registered business.
- Its taxable supplies, acquisitions or distance sales will exceed £77,000 in the next 30 days.

(These numbers applied early in 2012 and are often changed in the Budget.)

An unregistered firm, or one selling exempt or zero-rated goods, will be paying VAT on its purchases but may not charge VAT on sales. This is fine if you sell to the public or other unregistered firms. On the other hand, your prices to business-to-business (B2B) customers will be a bit higher, or your profits on those sales lower, since you will have to pay out VAT on what you buy but cannot recover it on what you sell. To such firms voluntary registration may be attractive.

Voluntary registration can be useful to the small firm in either or both of two circumstances: it buys in a lot of equipment on which it pays VAT, in which case it can claim the VAT back; it sells mainly B2B, so that the cost to the customer is ex-VAT. However, you do have to have proper VAT accounting and to keep the system going. There are provisions for de-registration, which can be found on the VAT website, **www.hmrc.gov.uk**.

It is extremely unwise to try to cheat the VAT system. The penalties include seizure of business assets, effectively closing the firm.

As well as sanctions and punishments for misbehaviour, HMRC has a range of schemes for smaller business aimed at simplifying VAT accounting and smoothing-out payments. The website has details.

Practical workings

The way VAT works for a VAT-registered firm running the standard system is this:

> **Buying**
>
> Your supplier invoices you for the cost, plus VAT, say £100 + £20 = £120.
>
> You record the invoice in your system as £100 of purchases and £20 of 'input' VAT.
>
> **Selling**
>
> You invoice your customer for the cost, plus VAT, say £300 + £60 = £360.
>
> You record the invoice in your system as £300 of sales and £60 of 'output' VAT.

The VAT return

At the end of the accounting period (which can vary, depending on the scheme you are on, but in the standard scheme is three months) you total all inputs and outputs and enter them on the return. Subtract one from the other and send a cheque for the difference to HMRC or, if the figure is negative, request a refund.

In the example above, if the firm were registered and those were the only transactions in the period, the VAT return would show:

Outputs	£60
Inputs	£20
VAT payable (£60 – £20 =)	£40

That makes VAT look simple, which it is in principle, but the actual operation and detailed rules represent complexity raised to the level of high art.

Conclusions

- Keeping accurate and timely accounts helps maintain control.
- PC software is available to handle most record-keeping functions.
- Control is helped by separate bank and credit-card accounts for business and personal use.
- All taxation is complex and the detail is easily misunderstood by the layperson. The entrepreneur cannot avoid the need for some understanding of the field.
- Professional advice is vital.
- The tax implications of a limited company are different from those of an individual.
- The VAT position of firms is subject to complex rules.
- VAT is, in principle, nonetheless simple: it is a sales tax.

PART 7:
Employing staff

23
Why employ, planning to employ and employment law

In this chapter

LEARNING OUTCOMES

By the end of this chapter you should be able to:

- make the economic case for employing staff;
- understand the principles of staff management and performance;
- describe approaches to staff management;
- see how the legal framework affects plans;
- define a job;
- specify a person;
- explain the main principles of employment law, dismissals and unfair dismissal.

Why employ staff?

The benefits of staff

When discussing costing we noted that there are two major benefits from employing people: a reduction in the cost of a product and the ability to turn out more. Thus a firm that takes on staff can afford to reduce prices or promote more heavily, thus raising demand, and satisfy that demand through the higher output that the work-force can produce. In turn, if the transformation is managed effectively, it raises its profits.

To take advantage of this effect the owner must recognize some key facts:

- People need special treatment.
- There are many similarities between individuals, and many differences.
- Managing people is different from other managerial tasks.

Managing staff

Anyone who has prior experience of working with people will recognize those truths (or clichés), but many entrepreneurs stumble towards them only through bitter experience. Some take on staff but manage them poorly, then blame the staff for doing badly; the usual response of such managers is to turn the screw even tighter which does not correct the situation but tends to worsen it. There is a moral point here: employers have the right to expect a good day's work, loyalty and commitment, but they have no right to make people miserable. Yet misery is the state of too many people working in business today.

Thus, before staff are taken on, as a potential employer you should undertake some self-examination. Ask yourself:

- Am I a loner who gets on better when solitary?
- Am I gregarious or insecure and do I want staff largely for my own psychological reasons?
- Do I think the only way to exploit the opportunities available is to employ people, and recognize I may have to change to make it work?

The only 'yes' you should score is, of course, to the third question. For many business owners, evolving from entrepreneur to effective manager of people can mean quite big changes of attitude and behaviour.

Most entrepreneurs are driven people, always pressing for higher performance and better results. That is what entrepreneurs do, and it is right that they should. Too often their flaw is to assume that other people:

- are as driven as they are themselves;
- will respond favourably to pressure;
- are fundamentally lazy and need constantly to be pushed.

In some cases that will be true, at least in part, but in the majority of instances it is not only false, but behaving as if it were true demotivates people and makes them resentful. A resentful employee still gets paid, but, instead of directing energy towards the job, thinks of getting back at you. This is clearly not what you want.

Getting results from people

The US writer Douglas McGregor delineated his theory X and theory Y over 40 years ago: the theory X manager is cynical about people, believing they must be driven and threatened if they are to perform: in his or her world, people's feelings and beliefs come nowhere; much of such a manager's behaviour is that of the bully. The theory Y manager, on the other hand, believes and acts as if staff want to work well and effectively and respond better to encouragement than to the threat of punishment. (McGregor, 1960). A combination of factors is clearly present when people work well, and is absent when they do not.

For some reason, in general, the British are not good at getting the best performance out of their people. A large car-assembly plant run by UK management had severe quality problems and was crippled by strikes and poor productivity. That plant was taken over by a Japanese firm and in a very short time was performing excellently. Astonishingly, the workforce remained the same: only the plant's management changed.

The new managers took a very different view from the typical 'top-down' style of management. They saw their shop-floor staff as partners in the enterprise of making good cars. They asked for, and listened to, ideas for doing things better, many of which were implemented. Instead of isolating themselves in remote, wood-panelled offices far from the shop floor, they visited the production area several times a day to see how things were going and took an interest. They wore the same overalls issued to production workers and ate in the same canteen.

The difference in attitude? In a few words, respect in place of contempt, springing from convictions that:

- People want to do their work well.
- The people closest to the problem are those best placed to solve it.
- The management team's motivational job is to set the course, communicate it, provide the necessary equipment and stand back, allowing people to get on with working effectively.
- The management team also has a responsibility to monitor and correct the course, intervening to clear obstructions so that work continues unhindered.

That is an approach that worked in a particular setting but it also contains the seeds of universal truth. Every business owner needs to think through his or her philosophy of management to suit the task, the context and the people. Once you have decided exactly how you and your firm relate to the staff, you are ready to move towards taking some on.

Another social scientist who studied the reasons for variable performance at work was Frederick Herzberg. His 'hygiene factor' theory established that there are positive motivators, like encouragement and appreciation, and 'hygiene factors', things that do not motivate positively but can demotivate if absent, such as decent office furniture. (Herzberg, Bloch and Mausner, 1993). From Herzberg we see that certain aspects of the work environment are taken as read and only noticed if they are not there or are inadequate. It may seem obvious, but many firms ignore the point.

Planning to employ people

Looking for good staff

The military believes that there are no bad soldiers, only bad officers. Some might feel this takes too rosy a view of the perfectability of human beings, but it does serve the useful purpose of focusing attention on the role of the manager in getting results from people.

Taken to extremes, it would mean anyone could be recruited and turned into effective staff, irrespective of his or her past record, present ability or future aims. To dismiss that belief, as most people would, is to accept the need for discrimination. So how can we discriminate?

'Discrimination' is a word that has acquired undesirable overtones. Choosing or refusing people on grounds of gender, colour, nationality or race, religion or philosophical belief, marital status, sexual orientation, disability, pregnancy and (under certain conditions) age is illegal in the UK. The burden of proof falls on the aggrieved applicant, but quite apart from matters of principle, the time and trouble absorbed by even an unsuccessful claim make it unwise to place the firm at risk. The way to avoid the risk is to be clearly fair in all aspects of the recruitment process, and to be in a position to prove you were fair. This implies written policies and records and means that everyone is put through the same hoops to test their suitability. While this introduces an undesirable degree of mechanization into the organic activity of meeting and assessing a person, the risks of a simple, informal approach are too great to run.

Put out of your mind any idea that it is your firm and you can please yourself whom you employ. To all intents and purposes, you may not. But the lawmakers allow you still to be, to some extent, the boss.

You may discriminate legally on grounds of most of the things that really matter in staff:

- education;
- experience;
- qualifications;
- ability;
- personality;
- skills;
- articulacy and literacy;
- numeracy;
- motivation;
- intelligence;
- likelihood of fitting in with the team.

Be aware that some of these items could be interpreted as surrogates for impermissible discrimination. For example, 'not likely to fit in with the team' is risky, where the team is all black and the applicant white. Or vice versa. Or all of one gender. People might question your true motives.

The traditional method of discriminating is the interview, but research shows that it is a most unreliable predictor of performance in the job. Many experienced interviewers say they make their mind up in the first few seconds, one even stating that he chooses people on the way they walk across the room to greet him. Some rely on references, but not all applicants have them, some positive ones are written in the hope that they will help a nuisance to move on and some negative ones are revenge on a good person from an unworthy employer.

There is hope, in the form of the assessment centre, which attempts to mimic some of the situations the successful applicant will be faced with, observes performance and draws conclusions.

These matters will be explored shortly, but there is one more area to deal with under this heading: the process of finding good people. It falls into a logical sequence:

- Define the job in writing.
- Define in writing the characteristics of a person who could do the job well.
- Create advertising copy, choose the right media and advertise (or go to a recruitment agency).
- Receive and shortlist applications against the criteria in the first two items above.
- Interview candidates and send to an assessment centre.
- Select the recruit, check references, offer the job and receive acceptance.
- Decline unsuccessful candidates.
- Induct.

The following sections address these issues one by one. Nowadays it is prudent to make sure that a paper trail exists to show that things have been done 'fairly', so while some of what follows may seem excessive, it is merely a part of wise management.

Defining the job

There is more to this than simply writing 'SQL programmer', 'driver' or 'clerk'. The job specification should include the following headings:

- job title;
- purpose of the job;
- post to which the postholder reports;
- posts that report to the postholder;
- location;
- duties and responsibilities;
- hours of work;
- special conditions, if any.

Job title is self-explanatory. Purpose of the job briefly summarizes what the job is for.

When specifying reporting relationships a family-tree type of organization chart can be used to express more complex relationships and responsibilities. Location should include any mobility required, such as weekly visits to other sites, work on customers' premises, etc. Duties and responsibilities are itemized and numbered, starting with the most important or most time-consuming and always finishing with the item: 'Any other duties that may be required from time to time.' Hours of work includes any requirement for overtime, shifts, etc. Special conditions could include any other important aspects, such as the need to provide a serviceable vehicle, foreign travel, changes of schedule at short notice, etc. Some firms include pay on job descriptions, but usually that is more conveniently and flexibly dealt with by other means.

Writing a portfolio of job descriptions covering all posts has a useful purpose in exposing any clashes of duties between different jobs.

Specify the person

The person specification lists the qualifications, skills, abilities and experience of the person able to do the job to an acceptable level of performance. Take these steps to create one:

- Take the job description and cluster together any sets of duties that require similar characteristics in the postholder.
- Identify and list the work and life skills needed to carry out each cluster of duties.
- Consider and record the educational or skills qualifications needed.
- Consider and record the previous experience needed.

You have now completed the planning phase and are now ready to move on to execution of the plan. But first, some aspects of the law should be considered.

Legal aspects of employment

Employment law

The law on employment can occasionally be, as on other matters, an ass. It represents a move by the state into the civil law of employment, which has raised a few eyebrows. Fortunately for most employers it never presents a problem provided they:

- behave well;
- communicate clearly and thoroughly;
- know the rules;
- create and observe appropriate procedures;
- keep records;
- do not act in haste.

FIGURE 23.1   Employed or self-employed?

EMPLOYED OR SELF-EMPLOYED?
GOVERNMENT GUIDANCE

As a general guide as to whether a worker is an employee or self-employed, if the answer is 'Yes' to all of the following questions, then the worker is probably an employee:

- Do they have to do the work themselves?
- Can someone tell them at any time what to do, where to carry out the work or when and how to do it?
- Can they work a set amount of hours?
- Can someone move them from task to task?
- Are they paid by the hour, week, or month?
- Can they get overtime pay or bonus payments?

If the answer is 'Yes' to all of the following questions, it will usually mean that the worker is self-employed:

- Can they hire someone to do the work or engage helpers at their own expense?
- Do they risk their own money?
- Do they provide the main items of equipment they need to do their job, not just the small tools that many employees provide for themselves?
- Do they agree to do a job for a fixed price regardless of how long the job may take?
- Can they decide what work to do, how and when to do the work and where to provide the services?
- Do they regularly work for a number of different people?
- Do they have to correct unsatisfactory work in their own time and at their own expense?

SOURCE: www.hmrc.gov.uk

So far it has been assumed that the staff are conventional employees on the firm's payroll. However, hybrid arrangements exist and you need to be sure of the status of your staff for a wide variety of reasons. An excerpt from the HMRC website appears in Figure 23.1 to help you decide.

Employment rights are many, though most are common sense and well known. The website **www.thepersonneldept.co.uk** is worth reading to get a picture of all the areas you need to be aware of.

One important right is that to a written statement of the contract of employment. It must be provided within two months of the start of employment. Business Link's website offers a downloadable blank PDF of a written statement at: **http://online. businesslink.gov.uk/bdotg/action/stmtEmpLanding?r.l1=1073858787&r. l2=1084822756&r.s=tl&topicId=1075225309**. The rest of its content on employment matters is worth reading, too.

If employees believe they have been unfairly dismissed they can lodge a case with an Employment Tribunal (Industrial Tribunal in Northern Ireland) within three months. The period can be extended under certain conditions. To exercise that right they have to have been employed for two years – though there are some offences for which entitlement begins at the time employment starts (dismissal on racial or gender grounds, for example).

If an award is granted it may comprise two components. One is a basic award, the other a compensatory award, gauged by the tribunal's view of past and likely future loss of earnings, pension rights, etc. Compensation can be unlimited – yes, unlimited: just think what that could mean – on certain grounds involving health and safety and some forms of discrimination.

Before the matter comes to the Tribunal, the Advisory and Conciliation Service (ACAS) will offer to mediate via their Arbitration Scheme (LRA Arbitration Scheme in Northern Ireland). For the straightforward cases it is preferable, on both sides, to a full tribunal hearing.

Entire books have been written about employment law, so here we do no more than summarize some of the key issues. It is an area that business owners need at least to be aware of, and preferably to have some familiarity with.

Disciplinary and grievance procedures

Written disciplinary and grievance procedures are required by law for every employer. Each is the mirror-image of the other; discipline is when an employer is dissatisfied with an employee's conduct or performance; grievance is when the employee objects to actions by the employer.

The procedures must have three features as a legal minimum:

- The written statement: a statement of the alleged misconduct.
- The meeting: a meeting to try to resolve matters. The employee has a right to be accompanied by a 'friend' (in unionized organizations, probably a union official).
- The appeal meeting: following written notice that the decision is thought unfair.

If you wish only to warn an employee, the disciplinary procedure is not invoked, nor is it for suspension on full pay. If you want to punish by deduction from wages, demotion, dismissal or in other ways, the procedures apply. These procedures must be notified to the employee in writing within two months of the start of the employment. Conversely, the employee has the right to invoke the grievance procedure about any suspension or warning.

If an employee is guilty of gross misconduct it may be unwise to dismiss instantly. Instead, suspend on full pay and write later to notify your intention to dismiss and the reasons why. Offer the employee the chance to appeal. Use the time to collect evidence, information and witness statements to inform your case. Sometimes employers find that the employee was, after all, in the right, in spite of apparent misbehaviour.

Fair dismissal

Despite all of this, there are grounds for fair dismissal. You may dismiss employees for these reasons:

- They cannot do the job.
- Their conduct is unacceptable.

- Redundancy.
- The law forbids the job to continue.
- Some other substantial reason justifies it.

Nonetheless, it is vital to follow the procedures.

Redundancy is when a job ceases to exist: the job is redundant, not the person. The Business Link website lists 37 ways in which selection for redundancy can be unfair, thus laying the employer open to action for unfair dismissal. Most usefully, it also gives guidance on the safe process to follow.

For further reference the Citizens' Advice Bureau website, **www.adviceguide.org.uk**, explains situations of employment difficulty from the point of view of the employee. The websites for the DBIS and Business Link, **www.bis.gov.uk** and **www.businesslink. gov.uk**, address business concerns and responsibilities.

Conclusions

- Employment law is a minefield but informed common sense, fairness and sound record keeping confer a great deal of protection.
- Any potential employer should prepare carefully before taking on staff.
- The considerable financial and time investment in staff will be repaid only if staff are managed effectively.
- Studies show that best results come from management teams who trust staff to want to work well, provide the resources necessary and offer encouragement and appreciation.
- Employers do not have a free hand to employ whom they like but must conform to ideas of fairness as embodied in anti-discrimination legislation.
- Defining the job and the person suitable to fill it are useful disciplinary exercises as well as helping to ward off potential threats of legal action.

24
Executing the recruitment plan

In this chapter

LEARNING OUTCOMES

By the end of this chapter you should be able to:

- put a recruitment plan into practice;
- advertise for staff;
- plan and conduct interviews and activity centres;
- undertake induction.

Moving on from the plan

The plans for staff recruitment in place, the firm now moves on to actual recruitment activity. The first consideration is attracting the right applicants.

Advertising

Advertising costs money, but not getting the right applicant could cost more. It is important to:

- produce an attractive advert;
- place it in the right media;
- have staff time, stationery and procedures in place to deal with an influx of enquiries and applications bigger than you expect, so as to look professional.

You may be tempted to cut corners with the sort of advert suitable for the local paper; remember it will be seen by not only potential employees but also customers and competitors. At a minimal cost your designer should be able to create an appearance for the advert that stands comparison with adverts from major organizations. You want the best staff, so it might pay to look like the best employer.

If writing copy is not your strength, do your best but then get an adviser to review your advert and comment. It is important that the first attempt comes from you, rather than handing the task over entirely to someone else, so that you establish in your own mind what the advert is trying to say and can therefore consider critically what the adviser says.

The media to choose are dictated by the nature of the post. For a civil engineer you would advertise more widely than in the local press, possibly finding you had to go no further than the Institution of Civil Engineers (which, like many professional institutions, advertises jobs on its website). On the other hand, advertising nationally for a receptionist would be wasteful.

Advertising on the web is uncertain but as most job applicants beyond the purely local expect to apply online it is important. Since individual adverts, like yours, will be swamped by the sheer volume of recruitment adverts, it may be worth placing the advert with one of the recruitment agencies. Equally, if your agreement with the agency will allow it, advertising on your own website and more generally on the web will do no harm.

The closing date for applications will need to be specified and, outside special times like the summer holiday period and Christmas, ought to be about a fortnight ahead. You will be asked about the date of interviews, so fix that too.

Responding to the effects of the advert can be difficult to plan for, which may be an advantage of dealing through an agency. However, agency staff are not all thoughtful and professional, especially when there are more applicants than jobs, so good candidates' applications might not get through.

You may get no applicants or you may be flooded. Know what you will do in the latter case, especially if it would tie up all the phone lines for a day or two. Nonetheless, response ought to be same-day, first-class post (or e-mail), with an application form and the job description, and any further information you want applicants to have about the firm. Insist on written applications so that, should there be any later dispute, you have clear, written evidence of the applicant's claims.

Examples of application forms can be found by Googling 'job application form'. These should give you ideas for constructing your own.

Shortlisting of applicants

Here applications are compared with the person specification. Those that do not show evidence of meeting major requirements are immediately discarded. The remainder are ranked in order of desirability against the criteria in the person specification.

Decide how many applicants you want to interview and allow between 20 and 40 minutes per interview, depending on the nature of the post. A further five minutes each will be needed to write up your notes while the memory is still fresh. Thus in a day of interviews from 8.00 am, with the last one starting at 6.00 pm, with 30 minutes for lunch, you can comfortably plan for between 10 and 20 interviews. Or you may wish to spread it over two half-days instead.

Once the desired number has been selected the candidates are immediately invited for interview with a letter or e-mail. Include a map, an offer of reasonable travel expenses and – if by post – a tear-off confirmation slip with stamped addressed envelope.

Interviewing

Before the interview you need to prepare six items:

- accommodation and a timetable for the interviewing day;
- a standard set of questions to be put to each candidate;
- an interview record and evaluation sheet for each candidate;
- an assessment centre;
- a record and evaluation sheet for each candidate's performance at the assessment centre;
- a grid on which to plot the results from interviews and assessment centres.

Preparing the timetable helps to highlight and address any scheduling difficulties in a complicated exercise.

The standard questions form the core of the interview for every candidate. They relate directly to the person specification and the responses are noted on the interview record.

The records are needed both to aid a final selection decision and to create a defensive record in case of challenge. The form used for the interview record might look like Table 24.1. You will need a similar record for the assessment centre.

The assessment centre itself represents an attempt to reproduce the jobs that the successful candidate will be expected to do and observes how well candidates tackle them. All the requirements relate back to the job description.

Using the example of a sales executive, the requirements might include composing a well-presented sales letter, making a sales presentation to a small group of people and dealing with a complaint. There would also be other demands, but examples are given for these.

The presentation should relate to a standard brief that you send each candidate with the invitation to interview. The brief should obviously require a task that is not too far in nature from the kind of thing the successful candidate will be called on to do. To show the sort of thing you can do, a (completely imaginary) example relating to recruiting a sales executive for a specialist industrial adhesives firm is shown in Figure 24.1.

TABLE 24.1 Interview record

The Supremacy Company INTERVIEW RECORD			
Candidate	**Post**	**Date**	**Interviewer**
J Smith	Sales Exec	3.6.11	Jenny Bird
*Criteria	**Score** 1–5 (1 LOW)	**Evidence**	**Comments**
1 Social manner			
2 Persuasive-ness			
3 etc			
4 etc			
5 etc			
6 etc			
Overall suitability			
Decision			
Action			

* Taken from person specification

FIGURE 24.1   Presentation task briefing

The Supremacy Company

PRESENTATION TASK BRIEFING

As part of the recruitment process for the post of Sales Executive, we ask each candidate to prepare a sales presentation of **no more than five minutes'** duration.

Each candidate will deliver their presentation to a small audience of Supremacy Company staff and associates on the day of the interview.

The aim is for us to be able to assess each candidate's ability to construct and deliver a sales presentation to a small group.

We ask you **not** to use PowerPoint if you wish to use visual aids; a flip chart on an easel and an overhead projector will be in place on the day. If you wish to use them, you will have to create your flip charts or OHP slides in advance.

The brief to which candidates are required to work is as follows. Please do **not** introduce further product or market information.

* * * * *

You are about to call on GalactiCo plc, a large manufacturer of domestic appliances. Their response to the threat from the Far East has been to automate production fully, almost eliminating human beings from the production process. This is a preliminary meeting, following an invitation you had from one of their engineers at a trade fair. You expect there to be present representatives from their design engineers, production engineers, management accountants and buyers, and the chair to be a senior figure from R&D.

The engineer you met, Jim McLean, will be present. You have five minutes in which to persuade them that your company should be involved in a new development involving the use of revolutionary new adhesives in place of the mechanical fixings (nuts, bolts, etc) to hold their products together. The cost of metallic products, especially stainless ones incorporating nickel, has rocketed over the past few years, whereas chemicals have not. The environmental impact of a switch might be equivocal, there would be global savings in energy use, but an increase in emission of VOCs (volatile organic compounds). Use of adhesives would simplify end-of-life recycling. The supply of chemicals is less politically vulnerable than that of metals.

You think your case has significant strengths and weaknesses.

STRENGTHS
Energetic company
Good technical expertise in adhesives applications to hostile environments including heat and wet
Used to problem-solving on joint ventures
Joint MD is technical leader in the field, having part-time chair in materials science at a major university

WEAKNESSES
Low output but could gear up
Narrow field of specialism
Neither MD is a good salesman
Up against major international firms
Firm only four years old

In judging performance against this particular brief, you might look out for:

- a straightforward sales story – there are no whizz-bang items in the brief;
- ability to address sensibly a knowledgeable audience, for example they already know that volatile organic compounds (VOCs) are nasty;
- playing to strengths, such as the joint MD's expertise, while acknowledging weaknesses with a positive spin;
- social points, such as knowing to pronounce McLean as 'Mc-Lane';
- a standard structure of 'tell them what you're going to tell them; tell them; tell them what you've told them'.

A superior performer would recognize subtly the improbability of getting the contract and GalactiCo's probable motive of seeking a tripartite arrangement between themselves, the company and one of the international giants.

There is no obvious use for visual aids, but marks should be awarded for any instinctive attempt to use them. It is a good characteristic in a salesperson.

If this seems like a lot of extra trouble, consider that in no other way would you have a clue about how any interviewee is likely to do the job – until you have taken the person on. It is a little late then to start learning about his or her shortcomings.

To buttress the presentation, our sales executive should also conduct an 'in-tray' exercise, taking various simulated documents and recording on them the implications seen, priority to be given and the action he or she would take. In practice you would load the in-tray with many examples; in Figure 24.2 we show just a sales letter and a complaint. Note that today's date is 3 September.

FIGURE 24.2   Sample element of assessment centre (1)

From: MD	To: Sales Exec	Date: 25 August

I shall next be in on 2nd September for a couple of days. Could you draw up a letter from yourself to Janet Jones at GalactiCo, telling her of the new superpolymer and how preliminary tests show it meets their heat resistance standards? You and I need to meet them to talk it through.
Thanks, MD. (Note to candidate: please draft this letter and hand in.)

Assessors will be able to tell if the draft letter meets the needs of the moment. It must be done as soon as possible, given the fact that the MD is away after tomorrow and has already allowed a week for it.

Figure 24.3 records an issue that is both urgent and important. Three lorry-loads represents a large and expensive shipment. It is probably out of doors and at risk of being damaged by passing diggers, etc. Candidates should stress the need for immediate action, starting with some internal fact finding: was the correct stock sent? Was it at the end of its shelf-life? Then over to the customer to establish the facts of the problem, probably involving a site visit at 8.00 am, and alerting a technician that he or she might be called to drop everything and rush over. All of these points should be noted by the candidate on the document (continuing overleaf if necessary).

FIGURE 24.3 Sample element of assessment centre (2)

From: Switchboard	To: Sales Exec	Date: 29 Aug

Sorry I forgot to tell you I had a call from Mr Durrant of Sierra Construction a few days ago. He was not happy with the latest stock we delivered and wants to send it back. He shouted a bit. He says there are three lorry loads of it blocking the site and said something rude about not paying for it.

That's all I can remember. Sorry, I've been off sick and only just remembered.

An assessment centre needs to be planned for and staffed. One person or group can witness and evaluate it for one candidate while another is being interviewed: candidates then change places.

Although the illustrations are of paper-based activities, other skills can also be tested in this practical way. If you wish to do this, insurances should be checked to ensure that cover extends to non-employees operating equipment.

Deciding

Interviews and assessment centre activities complete, you can now pull together all the results on to a single sheet. An example that follows on from the previous illustrations appears in Table 24.2.

By following this template a firm would not have proof against mischievous claims or those driven by grudges. However, it would have a strong paper trail of having behaved properly and defensibly. Should a challenge occur, a strong defence can be mounted as the recruitment was undertaken in a way that:

- relates to laid-down criteria based on legal ways of discriminating between candidates;
- is recorded;
- will appear 'fair' if challenged.

Keep the records for two years, just in case. Then destroy them in confidential waste.

After the interview

You telephone the successful candidate that evening to make the job offer, subject to satisfactory references. You write to confirm, sending two copies, one for the candidate to retain, the other for signature and return.

Take up references immediately. At least one referee should be a current or recent employer. This person should confirm the post and its responsibilities, dates of employment, precisely, and at least not indicate that they are pleased to see the back of your candidate. Expect some guardedness, for conscientious people are careful how they speak of others to people they have never met. On this matter, when asked for a reference be careful not to over-praise any employees. If they are poor performers,

TABLE 24.2 Assessment summary

ASSESSMENT SUMMARY	CANDIDATES						
	Browning	Tennyson	Eliot	Hopkins	Gray	Milton	Thomas
Interview **Score 1–5 (1 low)**							
Criterion 1							
2							
3							
4							
5							
6							
Assessment centre **Score 1–5 (1 low)**							
Criterion 1							
2							
3							
4							
5							
6							
OVERALL							
DECISION							

and someone employs them on the strength of your reference and they then fail, you could be sued. Best to confine yourself to dates and have a policy of making no further comment. Many companies do that.

Once satisfactory references are in, write to unsuccessful candidates thanking them for their interest and regretting that they have not been successful. Don't overlook this step and be sure to be courteous; if your first choice candidate pulls out you may have to go back to unsuccessful candidates 'cap in hand'.

Induction

Work out a programme for the new member's first days in the new job. Hand responsibility over immediately the person arrives, but shadow and mentor until he or she is able to handle it with justified confidence. Expect there to be a heavy load of questions and supervision, but be patient; every bit of help you give enables the new person to grow. One day he or she will be able to operate independently, but it will not be in the first week. Without gushing, make a point of recognizing achievements.

Before any new members of staff join, send matter to enable them to read themselves into the job and the company. If there are important meetings, consider inviting them as an observer. New members of staff are 'family' now, and need to feel like it. Remember that they will be anxious about their degree of ignorance and be keen to perform, which may drive them to do silly things to impress you. Tell them, in advance, that you are looking for good, solid performance in the medium to long term, not flashiness now. Bear in mind, too, that they may have come from a firm with a very different culture from yours and that it will take time to adjust. If these matters are ignored, a new recruit – who may have had more than one offer – might decide that another employer offers a more congenial home.

Conclusions

- The disciplined plan should be executed in an equally disciplined way.
- Advertising may best be done via an agency, especially if the natural recruitment medium is the internet. If the catchment area for staff is purely local, local media and staff agencies may be the most cost-effective.
- Results from interviews and assessment centres need careful recording.
- Induction is a critical phase, during which a candidate could easily decide to take an alternative offer, throwing plans into turmoil.

PART 8:
Managing risk, developing the firm

25
Risk management and insurance

LEARNING OUTCOMES

By the end of this chapter you should be able to:

- create risk-management strategies;
- understand the place of insurance;
- specify the required insurance cover;
- understand the sources of insurance.

Strategies for risk management

To be alive is to be exposed to risk. The problem lies in knowing which risks are worth planning for and how to deal with them. As a human, one accepts the occasional cut finger as the price of a little gardening or woodworking; there is also the chance that some more serious event will make one unable to repay the house mortgage. In that context it is easy to see which eventuality needs careful management and one acts accordingly via insurance. In business, especially to the new entrepreneur, the issues are not so clear-cut.

The business owner approaches risk systematically by:

- identifying those risks that could present problems;
- assessing them for importance, from qualitative and quantitative viewpoints;
- selecting and concentrating on the ones that would seriously damage costs or ability to operate;

- ·reducing the chance that the risks will materialize;
- reducing the impact, should the risks materialize;
- having contingency plans for recovery.

Such assessments can only be individual to each firm, but all will include the issues of what happens if the following occurs:

- A key customer or supplier drops out.
- Key staff (owner included) fall sick, leave or die.
- The firm ceases to function through an IT failure, fire, flood, etc.
- Vital equipment fails or is stolen.
- Key staff lose their driving licences.
- A major customer fails to pay.
- The authorities close your premises or the access to them.
- There is a regional or national emergency.

Many firms will find their list encouragingly short, but that should not be used as a reason for not spending some time thinking about the matter. Moreover, risk should be reviewed from time to time as the firm evolves, forms new relationships and, perhaps, grows.

As with coronary patients, so with small firms: the first hour after the event is the most important. As part of contingency planning, make sure that staff programme into their phones the numbers for:

- insurers;
- the local council;
- key customers;
- key suppliers;
- your security alarm company;
- utilities;
- the landlord;
- the neighbours, domestic as well as business;
- plumbers, locksmiths, glaziers, IT specialists, carpenters and electricians.

In addition:

- Keep an emergencies file at home, including building plans of the business premises that can be given to emergency services.
- Involve staff in assessing what to do under various conditions and train them to react appropriately.
- Prepare to deal with interest from the media.

Business Link, on **www.businesslink.gov.uk**, has an advisory thread that follows the process of planning for risk. It includes a case history that should convince even the most sceptical that this issue matters.

Insurance strategies

One tool for reducing the impact of disaster is insurance. People often regard insurance as a necessary evil, buying the least necessary at lowest cost. That is not always the wisest approach.

The new firm *needs* only a single category of insurance: that which the law requires and is therefore compulsory. It is strongly *advisable* to add insurance against catastrophe, as part of the risk-management strategy. These insurances are discretionary.

Statutory insurances for business include insurance for employer's liability, motor vehicles, lifting tackle and pressure vessels. In addition, some professional organizations require members to take out professional liability policies as a condition of practising. Some industries, for example travel, require bonding to protect clients' money.

Some say that catastrophe is not worth insuring for, as it is unlikely to happen. If so, insurance would be cheap. Since a catastrophe would, by definition, threaten the firm's existence, the small premium must be worth paying.

Insurances

Insurance for the smaller business

Many insurers offer bundled packages of policies for small firms, which can offer good value. They vary in cover and cost, as well as in the way they treat claimants, so shopping around is advised.

All tangible property should be covered for full replacement cost (not current market value) and the sums insured should be kept up to date. Otherwise there is a chance that the insurer will pay out only a proportion of a claim. Make a mental note always to tell the insurers of a change of circumstances, even at the level of having unexpectedly to use the family car to take samples to a customer. Without cover for commercial travelling, you would be driving uninsured.

The infallible guide to which discretionary cover to buy, and which to avoid, is the analysis undertaken to arrive at the risk-management strategy. Its quality will be greatly improved if you involve a commercial insurance broker in the process.

Needless to say, insurance cover documents should be read with great care to ensure that you have the cover you expect. It is a tedious business, but very important.

Insurance suppliers

The real test of an insurance supplier is not how cheap it is but how it behaves when a customer has a claim. No insurance firm pays out claims joyfully with a generous heart, but there are some that are less obstructive than others. It pays to shop around, not just for price, important though that is, but for the claims-handling reputation.

The best advice of all for the small business is not to buy direct from the insurer. Instead, buy from a registered broker.

A registered broker is quite different from an agent, consultant or other class of seller. Everyone else is out for themselves, or works for the insurer, but a registered broker is responsible to the client. In other words, such a firm has to put your interests first, in every way.

Not all brokers are the same; you need one who specializes in business insurance. Talk to a few, brief them on your plans and assess the responses. Ask to be put in touch with small clients who have recently settled claims as a way of taking up references.

Conclusions

- Even though a risk is remote, if its implications could be grave it should be covered for.
- Major risks should be covered by insurances.
- Bundled insurance policies covering the firm's operations may offer the best price, but value should be checked by reference to the insurance strategy.
- Registered insurance brokers with commercial experience are the best source of cover for small businesses.

26
Expansion and culture

In this chapter

LEARNING OUTCOMES

By the end of this chapter you should be able to:

- understand the basis for and timing of expansion;
- explain entrepreneurial aims;
- recognize and describe the three stages of growth;
- devise an expansion strategy;
- describe and design an organizational culture.

Expansion

The time to expand

There never is a one-size-fits-all answer to the question of when it is right to expand. Some firms, usually through planning but sometimes by accident, take off like skyrockets from the word go. Others plod on quite satisfactorily for years, only ever employing the founder.

In an ideal world in which everything would run with the logic and exactitude of a Swiss watch, a certain pattern would be followed. The first stage of getting the firm established is quite demanding enough without imposing on it the demands of expansion. That phase safely passed and people and systems bedded down, the anxiety and hard work of foundation and launch is behind the entrepreneur. Now it is possible to look beyond the day to day, out towards the wider world and other possibilities.

While life may rarely be like that, it is sometimes, and that is the pattern to be explored here. If practical experience and the excitement of specific opportunities carry events along faster, it may be hard to resist. Still, the knowledge that there is a template for bringing growth about in an orderly way may help to impose some pattern on the rush of events and help dangers to be foreseen.

The founder's experience

Once the firm is established, maybe after its first couple of years, thoughts will inevitably turn towards the future. You will have been on a roller-coaster experience of learning. New opportunities present themselves constantly, many disguised as difficulties; the real problem may be choosing which opportunity to take. Although everyone's experience is different, there are common threads, which will be explored here.

Equally, if the situation is less romantic, comprising little more than a desperate, hourly fight to stay afloat, expansion may offer a route into waters that, if not exactly calmer, do not threaten existence every minute. That may occur by moving into new fields, possibly ones associated with the existing sphere of operation, by expanding the scale of operation so as to become more the predator than the prey or – rarely – shifting to a completely new field entirely.

Key issues

If you grow the firm it will create hassle and involve further risk. Are you really ready for them? It is just as respectable to employ yourself alone as it is to be the next Sir Richard Branson. This entire exercise, after all, is meant to be for you rather than for the spectators.

This is the time to decide what the firm is really for. At one extreme, it is there to give you little more than a job with perhaps a dash of independence; at the other, to make you very rich. Will it make you rich by founding a family dynasty, or by being built up to sell to a known buyer in maybe 10 or 15 years' time? Whatever you want, decide on it and go for it.

Being inundated with work does not mean you must expand production. You could subcontract the extra to someone else. Or put up prices to choke off excess demand, making very big profits as a result, but possibly inviting in new competition.

Doing the latter might change you into a specialist, high-quality, high-price niche operator, which might impose new demands on all aspects of the firm. It might also make you moderately rich for relatively little extra effort.

If you go for growth, recognize the key truth that **growing a firm is a different job from founding one**. At a strategic level you need to consider:

- Your expansion strategy – how you will actually go about it.

- Developing yourself as a manager – acquiring the new skills needed to operate differently.

- Consultants and how to use them – good ones can have wonderful effects.

- Your mission statement – you need one, and it mustn't be waffle.

Expansion strategy

If you do all the extra work in-house you may have to:

- take on staff;
- expand premises;
- increase equipment;
- fund capital and revenue aspects of the expansion.

If you subcontract you must:

- manage the subcontractor(s);
- ensure quality and timeliness;
- ensure confidentiality (if relevant);
- fund extra demands on cash flow.

Perhaps you do not have to choose. You might be able to begin with subcontracting sales or production, thus freeing your attention for whichever aspect of the expansion exposes you to greatest risk. The 80/20 rule might help. However, it might ease your cash flow (at the expense of your supplier's).

It is a decision that will be improved by applying expert involvement. Call in a consultant.

Funding your growth

Many growing firms find that expansion plans are thwarted by exhausting their capacity to raise more loan capital. This need not be the bank acting difficult; for perfectly proper reasons, it is wrong to get the balance between loan and equity (the owners' fixed capital) too far out of kilter. Conventional wisdom says a pound of loan should be matched by a pound of equity.

Most small firms are financed by arrangements to put that formula in the shade. That is usually because there is hidden equity, in the form of a bank lien on the owner's house, behind the loans.

When the day comes that more funding is required than can be supported, assuming that the owners have no personal source of funds they want to invest, the firm will need to become a limited company and sell shares.

The high street banks do not buy shares in small firms. That is done by private individuals or investment banks. Most investment banks are not interested in investing the odd million or two, but there are specialist firms who are keen to consider such opportunities. Their motives are simple and clear. They want to be able to sell their shares within only a few years for a greatly inflated price.

An investment bank will press you hard for performance. It does not mind who it sells to as long as that person's or firm's money is good. You, on the other hand, might mind a great deal.

The three stages of growth

As organizations grow, they pass through discernible stages, with the result that the firm at the end of the process does not much resemble itself at the outset. Each stage has its own particular characteristics.

Stage 1: Foundation (you have come from here, but remind yourself of what it is like)

- Staff or contractors: are there few or none?
- Other people's tasks are minimal and menial tasks, entirely under your direction.
- Your tasks comprise everything that involves importance and responsibility.
- Your knowledge of other people's tasks is total.
- Your focus will be getting the work in, getting the jobs out, collecting payment.
- The reporting structure is wheel-shaped, with you as the hub and everyone else looking to you.

During this first stage you are working extremely hard with little support, turning a hand to everything that needs to be done. Consequently, the structure is simple and the task in hand completely clear, even though complex and calling on a wide range of skills and abilities.

Stage 2: Development (where you may be, or may be headed, at present)

- Staff or contractors: 5 to 50 (approximately).
- Other people's tasks are specialized but still under your direction, either directly or via a supervisor.
- Your tasks: you are still carrying overall responsibility and requiring others to do things your way.
- Your knowledge of other people's tasks is variable – limited in some cases to a general view, total in others.
- Your focus is getting the work in, getting the jobs out, getting payment and managing staff.
- The structure may possibly be a pyramid, with you firmly at the top, or possibly something less geometrical but moving in that direction.

Still working very hard, you are no longer on top of every aspect of operations as too much is going on, and this may worry you. You are developing ways of coping by beginning to manage the people who have taken over aspects of your former duties. Things generally run well, but too often something falls through a gap in the organization when everyone assumes that some task is someone else's job.

Stage 3: Delegation (where you want to be)

- Staff or contractors: 50 (approximately) upwards to thousands.
- Other people's tasks are specialized, delivering their small part of the big jigsaw.
- Your tasks: you are still carrying overall responsibility but unable to exercise direct leadership of the workforce. Now you are operating entirely through intermediary managers or supervisors.
- Your knowledge of other people's tasks is highly variable and constantly falling as far as the mundane is concerned, growing in the case of the challenges facing your subordinate managers.
- Your focus is the business environment, key customer and supplier relationships, company culture, managing and developing your managers.
- The structure fits the traditional organization chart or, in some cases, a soft systems diagram (there's no space here to go into what that is, but if you know the jargon you'll recognize it; if you don't, it's not important).

At last things seem to be in some sort of order. Not that mistakes never happen, but mostly they don't, and when they do the managers below you usually sort them out. You are still worried about your lack of control over the day-to-day issues and often have to force yourself not to jump in and do managers' jobs for them. Instead, you use what you see as material for your mentoring of them, encouraging them to learn from those experiences. Letting go of much of the detail has given you a sense of isolation from the real world, but the time it has liberated enables you to play externally on a much wider field, looking at opportunities that in stages 1 and 2 you did not even dream of.

Needless to say, if the firm is to grow effectively you must complete the journey to stage 3. Some firms grow but get stuck in or between stages 1 and 2, never fulfilling their potential, usually with three consequences:

- Good staff don't stay.
- The staff who stay become demoralized.
- The owner overworks and becomes ill.

In many cases, these firms would have been better off if they had stayed at stage 1.

Culture

Organizational culture

The 'culture' of an organization is extremely important to its success but hard to define. Nevertheless, it is easy to spot when you see it. It is 'the way we do things round here', a set of assumptions about the world and our response to it that the group takes for granted. It shows in the atmosphere of the place. It shows in the way people deal with each other. It shows in attitudes to customers and suppliers. A good culture is probably the main factor in retaining and developing good people – which, along with customers and cash flow, will become your main preoccupation.

One respected academic believes that creating and maintaining the organization's culture is the only really important thing a leader does (Schein, 1990). That may apply once the organization has grown to considerable size, but within the scope of this book it makes too many assumptions about the competence and effectiveness of subordinate managers.

However that may be, the fact remains that if the leader does not define and maintain the culture, constantly reinforcing it by example and reflecting it in his or her own behaviour, it will drift and dissipate. People will set up their own private groups, or will act as freelances, doing things *their* way rather than *your* way.

You set the most important example in the firm. You show the standard of behaviour, the level of integrity, the way of addressing people that becomes the norm. Staff will watch and copy you, so if you want them to be the sort of people your customers, suppliers and colleagues would be happy to deal with, be that sort of person yourself. Here is no room for double standards, no place for 'do as I say, not as I do'.

Culture springs from the values held by the leader. They lead to certain types of behaviours and influence the way people think, deciding what is 'the way we do things around here'. In a well-run firm that does not take place in isolation, but within the framework of structures – formal and informal – that have come into being, the formal ones via rational processes and the informal as a function of the interactions of individuals.

The formation of culture, and development of leadership style, are endlessly fascinating and highly complex matters that repay further reading and thought. There is not space here to develop them further.

Outcomes of undesirable cultures

The reasons to develop a culture of constructive, generous and helpful attitudes towards people may not be evident to all. Thus thought should be given to what can happen if the culture goes wrong.

In a discouraging culture people first become defensive, less interested in furthering the firm's aims than in defending their own position. They see others as a threat, rather than as helpful colleagues and work to undermine them on the principle allegedly espoused by the great Welsh rugby coach, Carwyn James, who is said to have instructed his team: 'Get your retaliation in first'.

The next stage in the decline is that politicking takes over as the main focus of effort. Information may be withheld or false information provided, in order to ensure that a supposed rival fails. There is a clamour to spend time with the powerful, especially you, in the hope of reinforcing a position and spreading poison about others. Some people whom you thought you could trust may even seek to misinform and mislead you.

Ask yourself: is this really what I pay people for? If it is not, take action before it all goes wrong and set up a benign culture within which people can flourish.

Conclusions

- Expansion can be for offensive as well as defensive reasons.
- The personal aims of the individual entrepreneur are key to the shape and destination of the expansion.
- Movement from one stage of growth to the next needs to be recognized and the nature of the firm to change accordingly.
- The penalties for growing but not evolving the organization can be dire.
- Expansion calls on different skills and abilities from founding a business.
- Selling shares can have uncomfortable implications for independence and control.
- The organization's structure must be properly designed and operated.
- Setting and maintaining the organization's culture is one of the leader's principal jobs.
- If culture goes wrong, the firm goes wrong.

27
Leadership and management

In this chapter

LEARNING OUTCOMES

By the end of this chapter you should be able to:

- understand expansion's personal challenge to the entrepreneur;
- see means of meeting the challenge;
- see the need for management skills;
- understand how to acquire management skills.

Leadership

The new job

Before embarking on expansion the entrepreneur will have become used to being the one person who is on top of everything important in the firm. If the business is to expand successfully the source of some of that authority will have to be relinquished.

You may have got used to being the sole decision maker on everything. You may also have done a number of manual tasks yourself. That must all change. Your job in a bigger firm is to manage processes, oversee performance and encourage people. Other people – not you – do the 'work'.

Most entrepreneurs find this transition hard to make. Some even force their firms into failure by not even trying to make it. How does that come about? How does an energetic, intelligent person who has successfully launched a new business fail to discern that the needs of an established and growing firm are radically different from those of the same firm's launch phase?

It probably starts from having one's nose too close to the job in hand, constantly applying the formula that created the success without ever looking up to see if what one is doing is still relevant. Such an approach can be like treating a teenager in the way you treated the same person when they were a newborn baby. In other words, it is potentially disastrous.

What is leadership?

The word 'leadership' is often misunderstood in business. It can be taken to mean noisy, brash, abrasive, know-all behaviour, a very wrong reading of the term. So-called 'high-profile leaders' may impress a gullible journalist, but their firms often suffer as a result of their crude and ill-judged self-indulgence. True leadership is very different. Some of the best business leaders keep well away from the media, knowing that they represent a force that may massage the ego one minute, but be looking to tear it down the next. They, rightly, concentrate their energies on the business.

What does a good leader actually do? It depends on the context – and as that is constantly shifting, the leader is alert at all times to what is going on, both internally and externally. Another thing that the leader does is to deal with crises, deciding on how they are to be handled, then providing a vision for staff of a better future and spelling out the path that will get them all there.

'Vision' also comes in when a crisis is absent. The alternatives exist of either everyone wandering off in the direction that suits them best, or pulling together in the same direction – in the latter case it is the leader's vision that acts as the glue to bind them. Everyone who has worked in organizations has seen departments that exhibit both of those sets of characteristics.

In addition to having vision, the leader works in a way that may be almost imperceptible to many yet can still be firmly present. In this further role – perhaps the one that occupies most time for most of the time – the leader is helping staff to achieve their potential. He or she recognizes that all individuals bring to their work a unique bundle of strengths and weaknesses, as well as their own personal portfolio of characteristics.

The leader identifies each individual's triad of strengths, weaknesses and characteristics and works with each of them differently in order to get results. The people who are bright but self-doubting will receive reassurance and encouragement, being encouraged to 'have a go' and make mistakes from which they both can learn. Their more brash and unthinking neighbours will be reined-in and caused to look ahead at the consequences of proposed actions before plunging in.

So the leader provides a vision that drives the organization forward, takes the lead in a crisis and senses changes within and outside the firm to which it will have to respond; but above all, works with and through other people to achieve results. Thus the entrepreneur's job now is not to achieve directly, but to achieve through other people.

This is not a novel thought. In the fifth or sixth centuries BCE, the Chinese philosopher Lao-Tzu wrote:

"To lead people, walk beside them ...
As for the best leaders, the people do not notice their existence.
The next best, the people honour and praise.

The next, the people fear; and the next, the people hate...
When the best leader's work is done the people say,
'We did it ourselves!' "

(www.goodreads.com/author/quotes/2622245.Lao_Tzu)

Structure

Part of the proper management of people is to provide a formal reporting structure that fits the task to be carried out. When, in the 1920s and 30s, Alfred Sloan was amalgamating many smaller companies into General Motors – at one time, the biggest company the world had ever seen – he had no templates to go by as that sort of thing had never been done before. So he looked at examples from outside. The armed forces he copied for the clarity of their chain of command and the Catholic church for the flatness of its organization (from Pope to parish priest in five levels).

The twin principles of clarity of the chain of command, and with it clear understanding of what each post is responsible for, and flatness of the organization are worth bearing in mind whatever the scale of operations, be it global or local, large or small.

Having established the structure, you delegate responsibilities to it and in due course it reports back on progress. You hardly lift a finger, except to inspire, monitor and mentor. In a perfect world it would run itself. Set it up as close to that model of perfection as you can. You will still have plenty to do keeping an eye on the machine you have created, but with time to do the things that only the head of the organization can do.

Management

Management skills

If leadership is about deciding on the destination and which road to take towards it, management is about ensuring that you get there, and as efficiently as possible. As the firm grows, the entrepreneur's job changes and new skills and abilities are called for. To a great extent the intelligent entrepreneur will work out how to rise to these new challenges, but trial and error unfortunately involves error, something to avoid if at all possible. Put simply, too much is at stake – the staff's feelings, the firm's position and your reputation – to risk a self-development experiment, especially when alternatives exist.

A further argument is that, although your firm is unique, the path you are treading has been beaten flat by the feet of those who have passed this way before. Other people have learned the lessons and many have distilled those lessons into written accounts. Yet others have studied what earlier entrepreneurs have done and drawn many useful conclusions about good and bad practice, as well as developing useful models and templates.

When so much has been done already, it seems unnecessarily perverse and egotistical to insist on reinventing the wheel.

Some people who start businesses do so from a background of deep managerial experience and training. This chapter is not addressed to them, as they will already be tucked up with some interesting and useful reading that might extend their skills, applying the models offered to see if they yield insights into the world in which they operate. It is instead for those who have never read serious management writing or experienced the sort of education that a business school offers and, as practical people who have already proved their worth, are at least sceptical about what a bunch of scholars and thinkers can do for them. Try them. They will surprise you.

You might have the skills already to work well at stage 3; your skills might evolve through experience or you might want to take training. There is an enormous variety of training available. Time is precious; so there is no reason to buy any that is not exactly what you want.

Developing as a manager

For most people running businesses, especially during the early stages, there are not enough hours in the day. Consequently, it is understandable if they can scoff at the idea of taking time to:

- join groups of businesspeople, such as the Chamber of Commerce;
- attend meetings;
- contribute to workshops;
- meet academics;
- read books and articles (Dewey classification 658 in the public library);
- go on courses.

Yet all of these will give benefits, perhaps in a different form for different firms, so it is not possible to say which is 'best'. However, the one guaranteed to get you thinking about your firm, how it operates and its future, is the last. The temptation may be to go to a seminar on some topic of current interest: while that is important in keeping one up to date, that is not the kind of course meant.

The MBA (Master of Business Administration) is the business manager's equivalent of professional training in his or her chosen field. It aims to provide the tools to understand the firm and its environment and to see the complex interactions between its internal components and how they, in turn, interact with the outside world.

A number of organizations offer MBAs by part-time study and by distance learning. The best offer the chance to meet and work with other students and with tutors, as well as insisting that few essays and assignments are based purely on theory but on the way their employer works in practice. That last point gives a great advantage to the owner-manager in two ways. First, unlike colleagues who work for large organizations, he or she does not have to do research to find out how aspects of the business work – every activity is within his or her daily experience and, second, the academic assignments actually *require* the person to apply the theoretical tools to his or her own organization. To have your analyses of your own firm subjected to the criticism of an expert tutor is the equivalent of getting a management consultant free of charge.

Not that MBA courses are cheap, but then few worthwhile things are. Is the course value for money? It depends on the quality of the institution and the effort the student puts in, but it can have remarkable effects: 'The MBA is life changing as it enlightens you to take a holistic view of both professional and personal events. I was amazed how I am now able to see all types of situations with a fresh point of view' (Joe Synnott MBA, quoted on the Open University website, **www.open.ac.uk**).

Anyone still sceptical should remember the words of a former dean of Harvard Business School: 'If you think education's expensive, wait until you try ignorance.' Leaving aside the in-built assumption that Harvard's MBA dispels ignorance (a belief not universally shared) there may be wisdom in it.

Conclusions

- Once people are employed, the entrepreneur must assume the responsibilities of a leader. There is no alternative.

- Leadership is a specialized art that repays study. Because it is largely intuitive, its impulse comes from within and the nostrums of others may be of little use.

- Management is a complementary but different art, mainly scientific, that also repays study. Adopting techniques from other people can be richly rewarding.

PART 9:
A systematic approach to growth

28
The PLG© Programme

The PLG Programme: Prepare, Launch, Grow©

The PLG Programme leads you step by step through the process of:

- preparation – for setting up your business on firm foundations;
- launch – of the firm on the right lines;
- growth – to fulfil your potential.

More than half of new firms fail in their first few years. More fail when they try to grow. Usually it is because of poor planning, which can be avoided, especially if the PLG© Programme is followed.

Start your new business here...

FIGURE 28.1

What it's for

The overall aim is to end up with a complete business plan for your new firm. Preparing a business plan helps you by making your mistakes the cheap way – on paper. It helps banks to see what you want to borrow and why. It gives you a standard against which to measure progress.

You will need access to:

- a PC with internet connection;
- a phone;
- either a PC with spreadsheet and word processor, or a calculator, plenty of paper and pens.

It might look daunting at first, but just do one thing after another and you will get to the end.

How it works

The instructions are divided into the three PLG sections, reflecting the stages of your business: prepare, launch, grow.

Within each section are subheadings that tell you what you have to write for that part of your business plan. After a time you will find you are making real progress towards the goal and, eventually, you will end up with a complete business plan. That plan is mainly for you, to make sure you have thought about tying all the components of your firm together, but it will also be ready for the bank or investors, to support your case for borrowing.

Next...

Business plan: introduction

Executive summary

This is where you summarize the plan briefly. The idea is to give readers a picture of the complete proposal before they launch into the detail. As it is a summary of the plan, you have to write the plan first!

Once the plan is finished, return here and write the executive summary. It should be no longer than three paragraphs and should give just the main features of the business. It should be sober and sensible, not shouting or screaming with enthusiasm. The people who will read it have seen business plans come and go. They will not be impressed with shouting and screaming.

Now that we have started to think about writing, consider what style is best. Here are my suggestions:

- Use a direct, clear type of English (which I am aiming for here).
- Use short words and simple language.
- Keep sentences short, one thought per sentence.
- Keep paragraphs short, one argument per paragraph.
- Use bullet lists when appropriate.
- Make the main points well, but don't try to answer every potential question.
- Number the pages.
- Put any large mass of detail into an appendix, at the end.

Where people might want to refer in discussion to specific points, it helps if you number the relevant paragraphs or items in lists.

When you have finished the plan, get someone who does not know the industry to read it, to see if it makes sense to them. Most official readers will not understand the industry either.

Next...

Business plan Part 1: Overview

Business overview

Here you describe what the business as a whole is to do, your vision for it. It should take a paragraph, maybe three to five sentences.

If it's not clear what is needed, imagine bumping into a friend in the street. Both of you are in a hurry but want to be polite. They say: 'This business of yours. What's the idea behind it? Where does it fit in?'

You might answer: 'It's the only Polish restaurant for 30 miles; the cooks and staff will all be Polish and we'll offer families an affordable home-cooking alternative to the usual curry or chow mein. When the first one's got going I'll open another in the next town, and so on. Polish ex-pats will love it and the Brits will too.'

In three sentences the vision for the business is described. Word it a bit more formally, and it is suitable for the bank, or anyone. The bank would put your friend's questions more bluntly: 'What makes you think this idea will work?' So answer them. You already have, almost.

Expect to come back here to make changes as the plan evolves. In the sections below the headings of the plan itself follow in **bold** type with notes about what you should include.

Business background

Summarize only, giving notes on the main points. Bullet points are fine.

Principals

Who you are – qualifications, background, experience.

Start date

When you plan to start.

Present position

How far you have got.

Business identity

Legal constitution, business name, trading name.

Market background

How big the market is, how it has changed recently and how it is likely to change in the future, with reasons.

The industry

The industry at present – structure, customers, suppliers, distribution system.

Unique proposition

Why customers will want to come to you – the benefits you offer.

Market information

How big the market is, how it has changed recently and how it is likely to change in the future, with reasons. Any other important issues.

Present suppliers

How customer needs are met at present, who competitors are, their methods and the share each holds (these can be estimated, in which case say so).

Market developments

What you expect to happen and how suppliers and competitors are likely to respond.

Business plan Part 2: Operating plans

Marketing plans

Here you describe things in more detail. A balance needs to be struck between keeping it brief yet giving enough information. If tempted to write too much, remember you usually have a chance to answer questions face to face.

Positioning
How your service or product will be positioned against competition.

Sales proposition
Why the customer should buy from you rather than the competition.

Target customers
Analyse the market, specify the group you will aim at, say how many of them there are and where.

Pricing
Define your approach to pricing and relate it to your sales proposition.

Sales operations
How you will contact and sell to customers, who will do it, how many orders a week this should produce and their value.

Promotion
How you will support the sales effort and attract enquiries.

Distribution
By which channel(s) the product will reach the customer.

After-sales
Any special follow-up or opportunities to sell maintenance, etc.

Operating plans

Production
How what you sell is to be produced, maximum output capacity and how it compares with sales forecasts, longer-term plans.

Premises
Plans for accommodation, how satisfactory it is, tenure, longer-term plans.

Administration
How you will handle the administration of enquiries, orders, sales, invoices, accounts, stock, personnel.

Information systems
How stock will be controlled, how accounting information for management will be produced and when, how the systems will cope with growth.

IT
What IT you plan to acquire, how, why, who will operate it, maintenance and support.

Sales forecast
Monthly for the first two years, annually for the next three.

Financial plans

This is part commentary, part tables. Your accountant should check your work before anyone outside the firm sees it.

Capital requirements

The money needed to get the business going on a sound financial basis, divided into fixed capital (for long-term purchases) and working capital (to cover day-to-day fluctuations in cash flow).

Financing strategy

Where the money will come from, security offered, repayment period. If a limited company, how much in shares and how much on loan.

Cash-flow projection

Monthly, covering the first two years.

P&L projection

Annually, covering the first five years.

Business plan Part 3: Appendices

An appendix is where you put the indigestible lumps of information that have to be present, but are too detailed or fussy for the main document. It is up to you to judge what to include or exclude here. The main document may refer to the appendix where necessary.

A curriculum vitae (CV) for each of the principals in the firm is essential, and is best placed as an appendix. Detailed product costings might appear here, too. Each appendix should be numbered.

That's it! You have now completed your business plan... except for one small point. You need to go back and write the executive summary at the beginning.

Business plan: Presentation

To make the best impression:

- Use an inkjet or laser printer and white paper, selecting a font size of 12 pt (certainly no less than 10 pt) for the main text.
- Don't use colour or fancy effects: they do not impress and can delay or obstruct download if you send it as an e-mail attachment.
- Start with a title page, giving names, contact numbers and e-mail addresses.
- Next, have a contents page.
- Check carefully for spelling and grammar; be sure that the different pieces are consistent with each other; have others read the plan to make sure it is quite clear.
- Put it in a cover that can easily be removed by the recipient for copying.

Once you are ready, you can move to section 2 of the Programme, the launch phase of your business...

FIGURE 28.2

Business plan: Implementation

In section 2 of the Programme you put your plans into practice. Draw up a pro-gramme for implementing your plans, based on the written business plan you completed earlier, in section one of the PLG Programme.

Start on whatever will take longest to complete. Since everybody's programmes vary, there is no general pattern to offer you. You will need to put the items in your business plan into the order that makes most sense in your unique situation.

Operate your programme, keeping a strict eye on everything. Remember that, even though you put a lot into it, your business plan is only a plan. It is guaranteed to be wrong. So look out for deviations and correct them as soon as they happen. That way you should stay on course. If your plan is badly out, tell anyone who needs to know and rewrite it.

Once the firm is up and running, keep on top of things by watching the measures you have put in place. Report regularly how things are going to those who need to know.

Involve advisers and listen to their views. If they give you bad news, that is what you most need to hear.

Once the company is running well, you may want to plan for further growth. That is addressed in the final part of the PLG Programme...

FIGURE 28.3

Business plan: Growth

You have decided to grow, or at least to plan for growth and see what the implica-tions are.

If it sounds strange to do all that work, and then decide not to grow, remember that it is perfectly possible to find that growth at this moment will mean, for example, taking on unacceptably large loans, or require skills that your staff do not have. Only planning will reveal those facts.

The method followed is to repeat the business plan headings used earlier for the new firm, but with changes to reflect the fact that you now have a history. For that reason some of what follows may seem familiar.

The growth plan starts here...

Growth plan: introduction

Executive summary

This is where you summarize the plan briefly. The idea is to give the reader a picture of the complete proposal before they launch into the detail. As before, you have to write the plan first.

Once the plan is finished, return here and write the executive summary. It should be no longer than three paragraphs and should give just the main features of the business. It should be sober and sensible, not shouting or screaming with enthusiasm. The people who will read it have seen business plans come and go. They will not be impressed with shouting and screaming.

Now that we have started to think about writing, consider what style is best. Here are my suggestions:

- Use a direct, clear type of language.
- Use short words.
- Keep sentences short, one thought per sentence.
- Keep paragraphs short, one argument per paragraph.
- Use bullet lists when appropriate.
- Make the main points well, but don't try to answer every potential question.
- Number the pages.
- Put any large mass of detail into an appendix, at the end.

Where people might want to refer in discussion to specific points, it helps if you number the relevant paragraphs or items in lists.

When you have finished the plan, get someone who does not know the industry to read it, to see if it makes sense to them. Most official readers will not understand the industry either.

Growth plan Part 1: Overview

Business overview

Here you describe what the business as a whole does and your vision for it. Imagine you are answering a bank manager who has asked: 'What is so special about this firm and what makes you think this idea will work?'

Your first bit of writing will say how it looks to you now, but as the plan evolves you will come here and change it. Again, the headings of the plan appear below in **bold** type with notes beneath about what you should include.

Business background
Summarize only, giving notes on the main points. Bullet points are fine.

Principals
Who you are – qualifications, background, experience.

Business history
How long you have been in business, financial and other performance in that time.

Present position, future prospects
What is holding you back, how you want to develop.

Business identity
Legal constitution, business name, trading name.

Market background
How big the market is, how it has changed recently and how it is likely to change in the future, with reasons.

The industry
The industry at present – structure, customers, suppliers, distribution system.

Unique proposition
Why customers come to you – the benefits you offer.

Market information
Market size, history and important issues.

Present suppliers
How customer needs are met by you and competitors, competitors and their methods and the share each holds (these can be estimated, in which case say so).

Market developments
What you expect to happen in future and how suppliers are likely to respond to your planned initiative.

Growth plan Part 2: Operating plans

Marketing plans

Here you describe things in more detail. A balance needs to be struck between keeping it brief yet giving enough information. If tempted to write too much, remember you usually have a chance to answer questions face to face. In most cases you are asked to describe the current situation.

Positioning
How your service or product is positioned against competition.

Sales proposition
Why the customer buys from you and not a competitor.

Target customers
Analyse the market, specify the group you aim at, say how many of them there are and where.

Pricing
Define your approach to pricing and relate it to your sales proposition.

Sales operations
How you contact and sell to customers, who does it, how many orders a week this produces and their value.

Promotion
How you support the sales effort and attract enquiries.

Distribution
By which channel(s) the product reaches the customer.

After-sales
Follow-up or opportunities to sell maintenance, etc.

Operating plans

Production
How what you plan to sell is to be produced, maximum output capacity and how it compares with sales forecasts, longer-term plans.

Premises
Plans for accommodation, how satisfactory it is, tenure, longer-term plans.

Administration
How you handle the administration of enquiries, orders, sales, invoices, accounts, stock, personnel.

Information systems
How stock is controlled, how accounting information for management is produced and when, how the systems will cope with growth.

IT
IT equipment and arrangements, who operates it, maintenance and support.

Sales forecast
Monthly for the first two years, annually for the next three.

Financial plans

This is part commentary, part tables. Tables for cash-flow forecasts, P&L forecasts and product costings are best set up on spreadsheets. That enables you to make the inevitable changes with the minimum of extra work. Your accountant should check your work first.

Capital requirements
The money needed to expand the business on a sound financial basis, divided into fixed capital (for long-term purchases) and working capital (to cover day-to-day fluctuations in cash flow).

Financing strategy
Where the money will come from, security offered, repayment period. If a limited company, how much in shares and how much on loan.

Cash-flow projection
Monthly, covering the first two years.

P&L projection
Annually, covering the first five years.

Growth plan Part 3: Appendices

An appendix is where you put the indigestible lumps of information that have to be present, but are too detailed or fussy for the main document, such as quotes for equipment. It is up to you to judge what to include or exclude here. The main document may refer to the appendix where necessary.

A CV for each of the principals in the firm is essential, and is best placed as an appendix. Detailed costings, historical accounts, copies of brochures and quotations for proposed purchases would all fit here too. Each appendix should be numbered.

Past accounts for the firm should also appear as appendices.

Growth plan: Presentation

To make the best impression:

- Use an inkjet or laser printer and white paper, selecting a font size of 12 pt (certainly no less than 10 pt) for the main text.
- Don't use colour or fancy effects: they do not impress and they can delay or obstruct download if you send it as an e-mail attachment.
- Start with a title page, giving names, contact numbers and e-mail addresses.
- Next, have a contents page.
- Check carefully for spelling and grammar; be sure that the different pieces are consistent with each other; have others read the plan to make sure it is quite clear.
- Put it in a cover that can easily be removed by the recipient for copying.

You have now completed your business plan, your plan for growth and the PLG Programme.

Congratulations, and best wishes for the future.

Learning resources

In this section

This section contains:

- mini case studies of entrepreneurship in action from around the globe, for use in class and group discussion;
- suggested topics for class and group discussion;
- reminders of theoretical models that may prove useful;
- sample assignment titles, with suggested approaches to answers, to help students to understand what is expected from them.

Associated resources

Further materials specific to this book can be found on the Kogan Page website: http://www.koganpage.com/editions/a-practical-guide-to-entrepreneurship/9780749464886. There are:

- over 350 PowerPoint slides for lecturers to download, covering the entire book's contents, chapter by chapter;
- the set of 20 worldwide mini case-studies that appears below, with added discussion notes and key points for use in class discussion and group work;
- a link to Durham University's free GET (General Enterprising Tendency) test, to assess suitability for entrepreneurship;
- a link to Business Link's free library of 200+ video and learning resources for new starters;
- a link to the University of Kent's free leadership styles test;
- a link to a website where you can check the regulations that your firm will have to observe;
- creating your own, personal, start-up checklist via the Business Link website.

Copyright

While the material in this section is subject to copyright, its reproduction by photo-copier for the purposes of classroom discussion of matters raised in this book, by individuals working in bona-fide educational and training institutions, is permitted and encouraged.

Mini case studies

The mini case studies are drawn from actual business histories of 20 firms set up all around the world.

Some of the case-study firms have succeeded, so far at least; others seem to have disappeared, perhaps only temporarily. Note that, inevitably, any information on prices, products and company information quoted may have changed since the time of writing. If the founders appear to have acted contrary to received wisdom, if the description is incomplete or messy, such is real life. Clearly, in such abbreviated form only the main points can be made; the full story would take more space than can be spared or is needed, for the aim is to offer real-life stories of what real people did, in order to enable students to apply common sense and analytical and projective models to identify:

- what was done well, from which they can learn a positive lesson;
- what they think could have been improved upon, to encourage their critical faculties;
- which practices to avoid;
- how they might have done better.

It is hoped that exposure to real-life situations will give students the confidence to see that entrepreneurs are human, like them, and while entrepreneurs are to be admired they need not be worshipped. If that should cause students' confidence to grow to the point where they develop a realistic belief that they, too, could found businesses – or, conversely, conclude that business is not for them – an important further aim will have been met.

CASE STUDY 1. Californian smokers' den on wheels

Where else other than California would you find the CigaRV, a mobile cigar lounge?

In a state where smoking is equated by many with the works of the devil, its disciples, however devoted, feel hounded into – whisper it not – giving up or, at least, going underground. Paradoxically, for a state which is in so many ways an example of liberality, there is no social venue in which smoking is welcomed. Yet around one US resident in five is a smoker*, representing a market opportunity that's been spotted by the genius who recognized that it's legal to smoke in a car but not in a public building.

Despite its echoes of Prohibition, 'The Mobile Man Cave', as it's dubbed, is not some seedy dive. Kitted out like a cross between a smoker's shop and a gentlemen's club, replete with leather sofas, four flat-screen TVs showing sports from three separate satellite TV receivers, and extensive humidors, it lives in an enormous, adapted 26-foot long six-wheeler US 'recreational vehicle' ('motor home' in UK English).

It will turn up to your party, event, golf outing or sporting contest to allow your guests to select their favourite cigars and smoke them in comfort. Or if you fancy a change of scene, your guests can take to the road and puff away on the route to somewhere new.

It's ingenious, but one wonders how long it will be before either the equality movement starts to burn underwear in protest or (more likely) the entrepreneurs behind it note that in 2008 18.5 per cent of US women smoked* and set up a mobile boudoir exclusively for their use.

*U.S. National Center for Health Statistics, Health, United States, 2010.
www.census.gov/compendia/statab/2011/tables/11s0200.pdf; **www.cigarv.com**

CASE STUDY 2. Delhi fights back against personal violence

Apps for smartphones come at us in bucketloads, most of them trivial. But here is one that treats a serious problem seriously.

Delhi-based Whypoll already runs a website showing dangerous areas of the city, places where women in particular are most likely to attract unwelcome attention or worse. In addition, victims can report anonymously any attacks – anonymity being vital in a society where family honour can be stigmatized if a woman admits to being attacked – so that pressure can be put on the authorities to improve things.

Whypoll's innovation is Fight Back, a phone app that, with one press of a button, sends an emergency SMS with the exact GPS location to up to five recipients – including the police. Official statistics, almost certainly under-reporting, say that rape has multiplied more than sevenfold in Delhi since the early 1990s, so this meets a major need.

The service need not be limited to Delhi or even India, meaning that Fight Back could eventually save countless people worldwide from attack and force even the most misogynistic authorities to crack down on the evil of personal violence.

www.whypoll.org

CASE STUDY 3. Swiss cyclists recycle lorry covers

Too many cyclists have been recycled brutally by lorries, so it is a pleasure to learn of cyclists turning the tables, though rather more gently.

One day in 1993 brothers Daniel and Markus Freitag were staring out of the window, looking at the lorries roaring over the flyover when, suddenly, an idea formed. Daniel, at the time a graphic design student and Markus, a commercial display artist, needed water-repellent bags to carry their drawings on their bicycles; out there were lorries covered in acres of completely waterproof tarpaulin which must periodically need replacement.

Oddly, it was not easy to source old tarpaulins but the brothers persisted, constantly searching for a variety of designs and colours. The tarpaulins were cut up, cleaned and then sewn into bags that did exactly what the brothers – and therefore other keen cyclists – wanted. Word spread and before long they had a full-time business. Now they employ around 130 people, have nine shops of their own, 400 resellers worldwide and their online store.

Business successes like this rarely happen just through luck. A look at the website shows a huge range of products, all unique, far beyond the original messenger bag (which is still going), in a wide range of styles and colours. Yet all this has been done from what is one of the highest-cost countries in the world. Two factors challenge any company manufacturing in Switzerland: in the long term, the high pay and overheads that are general in the Swiss economy and, more recently, the Swiss franc's role as a safe haven for jittery investors worldwide. The latter must be a great problem for all Swiss exporters since in 2011 no less an authority than the Swiss National Bank said that the high value of the franc was a threat to the country's economy. Central bankers rarely speak so candidly.

How have the Freitags managed it? By an unremitting concentration on new ideas coupled with emphasis of their green credentials and an attractive laid-back style that projects this highly serious business as fun to deal with.

To take just one example of their creativity: they worked together with Pelé Sports to make footballs from tarpaulin, a material the resistance of which makes it ideal for play on the dusty and abrasive pitches of the townships. Following on from the popularity of football in South Africa after it hosted the World Cup, they gave away 200 Pelé balls to children in needy areas. How many other bag makers have sprinkled their product with that sort of fairy dust?

www.freitag.ch

CASE STUDY   4. Brazilian bakers seek subscriptions

Near glamorous Rio de Janeiro lies the town of Praça da Bandeira, which hosts an amazingly creative bakery.

Los Paderos, famed for its artisan breads, offers a monthly subscription of 70 Brazilian Real (about £25) for three packs of breads from its large range of completely natural speciality breads, delivered to your home. There's plenty of choice, for the packs come as 30, 70 or 80 gram samples, made up from two, three or six breads from 160 grams to 210 grams. That's probably different in itself, but there's more.

The loaves are not fully baked. Instead they come partly baked for fridge storage (they keep for up to two weeks), so that you can finish them off in your own oven to enjoy piping hot, fresh bread whenever you want.

It's an idea that could help to extend the geographical area covered by an individual bakery and thus bring in profits, while guaranteeing its customers fresh bread all the time. Demand forecasting becomes more predictable and payments go direct to the bank, reducing the headaches associated with handling cash.

www.lospaderos.com.br/pagina/?CodSecao=16

CASE STUDY   5. If the cap fits...

London-based Lucky Seven specialize in a single product, though with a wide range of variations: US-style caps in either army or mesh shapes. What makes them special is that the decorative logos are for organizations that don't exist, offering customers the chance not to advertise what are already global brands while still having 'the look'.

The source of inspiration for Jay Jay Burridge, the artist behind the company, was the many fictional organizations portrayed in books and films and on TV. The octopus logo worn by the baddies in the James Bond film *Moonraker* is one; logos from *Alien*, *Bladerunner* and *2001: A Space Odyssey* also feature, along with many others.

Variety doesn't stop there, for no fewer than 15 colours are on offer, from a shocking pink through military drab to darkest black. Sold at £30 only from the company's website, every cap is delivered in a special Lucky Seven hat box. Postage is a further £5 on a single cap but free for two or more.

Since its foundation in 2004 Lucky Seven's growth has been boosted by the likes of Jamie Oliver, Madonna and Robbie Williams, all of whom have been seen wearing the company's caps. Further growth is expected from the children's range ('from toddlers to teenagers'), Little Lucky Seven, launched in 2011.

To keep the brand fresh, the company took part in the Movember promotion, where men grew moustaches for charity, by donating £10 for every special-edition Rufus Hound cap bought in November 2011.

www.luckyseven.tv; **www.littleluckyseven.com**

CASE STUDY 6. New Zealander comic heroes explain sickness to children

Medikidz comics explain medical conditions to children in a way they can understand. The idea arose from the frustration of two New Zealand doctors working in paediatrics at finding no educational materials suitable for their young patients.

Using the 'Medikidz' – a gang of five superheroes – they have now published 40 comic books, including *Medikidz Explain... Juvenile Arthritis, Scoliosis, Leukaemia, Brain Tumours* and *Food Allergy*.

But they don't stop at diseases and conditions. Recognizing that many medical procedures cause anxiety, Medikidz have also produced brochures such as 'Medikidz explain MRI scans' and 'Medikidz explain general anaesthetic'.

Each publication is written by doctors, peer-reviewed by world-renowned paediatric specialists and endorsed by leading patient associations and academic bodies, eg Macmillan, JDRF, the British Society of Dermatologists and the British Paediatric Respiratory Society. Also soon to be relaunched is the online 'Medipaedia' with entries about conditions, investigations and medicines with an integrated fully-moderated social network for children globally to connect around illness and disease.

Since the Medikidz launch in 2009, at which Archbishop Desmond Tutu was spokesperson, it has distributed over 1.5 million copies of its publications worldwide, into 40 countries and in 20 different languages.

UK prices are £6.99 (about US$ 11) with special offers from time to time. Distribution is via affiliates who receive 15 per cent commission.

While it took two medics to answer this great need, anyone who has ever had to deal with a young child's ignorance and fear – whether friend, sibling, child or grandchild – could have had the idea and then found medically expert partners to bring the solution into being.

www.medikidz.com.

CASE STUDY   7. Indonesians walk on yesterday's headlines

Yogyakarta-based entrepreneur Bagas Jusuf Wicaksono has developed Paperflops, beautiful-looking flip-flops made entirely of locally-sourced natural materials and old newspaper. Retailing from his website for around €30 (early buyers pay less, later buyers more) the footwear incorporates not only 1 kilogram of newspaper per pair, but also the roots of old palm trees and coconut shells. 100 per cent natural rubber is used as an adhesive and a weatherproofing sealant gives long life.

The workforce is drawn from among street children and the mentally and physically disabled who are trained in the skills needed to produce these attractive products.

In the East, flip-flops are the standard footwear for most people and many ingenious ways of recycling discarded items have emerged, most notably, perhaps, the motor-tyre based sandals worn by the Vietcong. Few, however, can have looked as attractive as Paperflops, nor have helped the underprivileged so much.

www.ulule.com/paperflops

CASE STUDY   8. Where to smoke in Croatia? Simple – ask the cigarette pack

A smoker needing a puff can become desperate, perhaps searching out the tell-tale piles of extinguished butts that show where others have gone before. Croatian bright spark Ronhill brings communications technology to their rescue.

Recognizing the problem that smokers face in a world that increasingly bans smoking, Ronhill got together with an agency to develop the first cigarette pack to tell its users about nearby places where smoking is allowed. How? Each pack of Ronhill Unlimited cigarettes is printed with a QR code that can be scanned by a smartphone; it connects to a website showing a local map that displays on the phone's screen both where the phone is at that moment and the location of nearby smoker-friendly sites.

Tobacco is one of the most mature markets in every part of the developed world. Entrants to smoking roughly balance out those exiting, and in many countries advertising and promotion are severely restricted. Thus the arena for competition is seriously limited and most of the major brands long ago resigned themselves to a lengthy battle of attrition, with no prospect in sight of any kind of breakthrough. Suddenly Ronhill pops up with technology-based added value and disrupts the market with a brilliant idea. Its advertising refers to a 'new generation'; and so it is.

Are there any other dull markets that could be similarly enlivened?

www.tdr.hr

CASE STUDY 9. Kenyan recycling cleans up for all

A high-powered bunch of highly practical US idealists are tackling one of the worst disease sources of Third-World slums – their sanitation systems or, rather, lack of them.

Three MBAs, an engineer, a designer and a lawyer from top business schools realized that it wasn't enough just to send aid to sick people. It would be good to remove the source of infection; better if the waste could be turned into something useful; best of all if local people could make a living from the process. From its roots in an MBA course project, Sanergy was born.

Taking Kenya as their launch-pad the three entrepreneurs found that 8 million people lived in slums with access to only two sanitation methods. One was a plastic bag (which may have helped the individual with a pressing need, but did nothing to solve the wider problem) and the other was an open pit, crawling with disease-carrying insects and rodents, bridged by a plank to sit on.

Sanergy builds low-cost (about £350 – under US $500) concrete lavatories which are franchised to local Nairobi entrepreneurs using finance from a local microbank; franchisees charge less than 5p per use and enhance their income via sales of additional products. The sealed, airtight containers are taken daily by handcart to a central facility which turns the product over to trucks that transport it to a central plant for processing. That produces two outputs: fertilizer for the burgeoning Kenyan flower-growing industry and gas that powers generators which feed electricity into the national grid. None of the technology is new – but the organization and structure of the solution are highly innovative, and furthermore work with the grain of the local entrepreneurial culture.

It is rare to encounter an idea in which everyone, as well as the planet, wins, but Sanergy seems to have developed one.

www.saner.gy

CASE STUDY 10. Zambikes, Acirfa and Bamboosero

In 2007 two Zambian entrepreneurs got together with a couple of US cycle-building experts to form Zambikes. They were helped by the Californian charity Acirfa, which promotes local transport solutions worldwide. The aim was to supply locally in Zambia the great need for bicycles for the transport of people and goods. In its first year's trading the company sold 300 bikes, giving the entrepreneurs the confidence to build a factory and double production the following year.

The importance of availability of suitable, affordable cycles cannot be exaggerated. When the only wheeled alternatives to walking are the ox cart or the rare and expensive motor vehicle, the bicycle opens up possibilities to individuals, professionals and businesspeople that otherwise would simply not exist. Even where someone has an ox, it is liable to sickness and death and travels at less than half the speed of a bike.

Local conditions demand of bikes simple, rugged engineering, ease of use and affordable cost. These conditions were met by Zambikes, which now offers a range of bikes that includes some that, to the Western eye, look quite conventional, plus others that have grown out of local need. There is a bike that tows a tough trailer with a payload of 250 kilograms, essential in a country where much of rural life depends on agriculture, with fertilizers and equipment to be taken from town to farm and crops to be returned to the town for sale. Needless to say, this bike has a low gear to facilitate pedalling with a load. Another trails an ambulance, again needed to take patients too ill to walk to hospital for treatment. Another has an extended rear luggage carrier that will take extra-heavy loads – three grown men and 200 kilograms payload are claimed.

Together with the Californian company Bamboosero, Zambikes makes frames for the US market from what is almost a weed: bamboo (anyone who has tried to eliminate bamboo from a garden will attest to its vigour and renewability).

www.zambikes.org

CASE STUDY 11. Hangvertiser: a German's advertising idea for India

A young German in his twenties, after travelling the globe and picking up an Australian business degree, landed in India, where he planned to make his fortune. His boutique advertising agency, founded in 2009, launched the Hangvertiser, a garment-hanger carrying advertising.

Noting that Indians are careful not to throw away things that can be useful, he realized that there was an opportunity to design a hanger on which adverts could be printed. This he did, providing a large, flat area to take print. The hangers themselves are made from recycled material, again appealing to people's growing sense that it is right not to waste.

Looking around for large users of hangers, he identified dry cleaners. They paid anything from 3 to 7 rupees per hanger (about 5p to 10p) for wire or plastic hangers and needed no persuasion to use free supplies. Thus distribution of the adverts presented no problem. Hangvertiser was also able to sell to advertisers particular geographical divisions of the cities in which it operated, thus enabling its clients to fine-tune their campaigns. This made the adverts a particularly effective tool for advertisers, especially when added to the fact that the adverts are seen every time a user puts on and hangs up a garment – cleanliness is important to the fastidious Indian middle class, so high visibility of the adverts could be expected.

www.hangvertiser.in (active in 2010 but unable to access in May 2012).

CASE STUDY   12. Exotic dining, at home in California

Many cookery books on foreign cuisine, bought in a fit of enthusiasm, lie unopened on bookshelves only to be, eventually, consigned to charity shops, still in bookshop-fresh condition. Then there are the jars of expensive spices at the backs of cupboards, missing no more than a teaspoonful but now long past their use-by date.

In 2006 these observations led to the founding of Destination Dinners in San Francisco. The founders decided that this falling-off of activity implied no loss of interest in exotic food, but reflected rather the difficulty in acquiring the right ingredients in sensible quantities, before even facing the challenge of choosing and following a recipe. The cooking, in fact, was the easiest bit, but even the few people who got that far were usually deterred from a second attempt. Their response was to launch kits that contain all the cook needs to make an authentic foreign meal at home, except for the fresh ingredients, for a group of 6 to 10 adults. Customers can choose from 12 recipe kits (containing the exact quantity of spices and other non-perishables needed, a shopping list for fresh ingredients, cooking instructions and a trivia quiz on the culture concerned), priced at $20–25 (about £14–16). Alternatively, customers are offered eight dinner party kits at $60–110 (about £45–70), containing everything in the recipe kits, plus authentic utensils and a CD of the country's music. Sales tax and delivery, via the postal system, are extra and the kits are at their best for up to 90 days. Overseas customers are supplied too, though at an extra delivery cost.

People who like the idea can sign up for 3, 6 or 12 monthly selections at $132, $246 or $468, including US delivery, plus tax. Purchasers also get a surprise cooking or serving item free. In addition, the gift market is catered for and utensils can be bought separately.

www.destinationdinners.com

CASE STUDY   13. Guatemalan map maker's novel take on city guides

One of 2009's new businesses, Guatemala-based Where To Go Maps, sees opportunities worldwide for its tourist mapping products. So what, you might think – tourist maps already cover everywhere and are usually free at hotels and information points. What's new?

Quite a lot, argues the company. For a start, the quality of design of many existing maps is highly variable, making finding your way round an unknown city or area an unpredictable business – even for people used to reading maps. The location of many must-see attractions can be hard to pinpoint, leading to confusion and frustration. (I am an experienced map user who revisited Florence recently after a gap of some years. During that time I had forgotten much of the city's layout, and I can confirm both the company's points emphatically.) Moreover, with the growth of global tourism and changes in destination preferences, many places have mapping for visitors that has not kept pace with the demands of the influx. What might have catered for a few people passing through a decade ago is of little use to those staying for a week – they want to seek out different things.

Where To Go Maps claims that in all these cases it has the answer. Its special approach springs from the professional backgrounds of the principals. Skills in architecture and urban design enable staff to understand how a visitor wishes to experience a destination. On top of that, they bring a grasp of the design of maps for different purposes. (If that does not seem important, just consider the different needs of visitors to the English Lake District: a hill walker finds a caravanner's map useless, and vice versa.)

Good design and so on is all very well, but at some point it all has to be paid for. Where To Go Maps also knows the fields of advertising and promotion, so that it can bring in partners who will both advertise on and sponsor maps, and also distribute the product to the user.

www.wheretogomaps.com

CASE STUDY 14. Soup delivered to the office in Oregon, USA

The late Andy Warhol moved soup into the realm of art by his portrayal of Campbell Soups' tins. Now SoupCycle, based in Portland, Oregon, aim to shift their compatriots' focus to what's inside the packaging and how it's delivered.

Specifying the part of its city where it operates as Souplandistan, the company delivers on different days to its subdivisions of Souptopia, Soup-Urbanites, SoupCycle Central and the People's Republic of Soup. Typically, three soups of the week appear on the website, where orders are collected by Friday night for the following week's delivery. Once the orders are in, ingredients are sourced and the cooking begins.

The product is (you've guessed) soup, with rustic bread and salad, with standard orders from two helpings up to eight – but SoupCycle offers to supply anything else. All ingredients are sourced locally then chilled, ready-to-heat deliveries are made from trailer-pulling bicycles from a range of 50 seasonal recipes, including vegetarian and vegan. For those with food allergies, SoupCycle posts the ingredients on its website. The company also caters for events and meetings.

Starting in September 2008, in its first 18 months or so SoupCycle shifted 10,000 soups, saved 3,000 car miles on deliveries and spent $33,000 (about £20,000) with local farmers. About 150 local people are regular subscribers.

www.soupcycle.com

CASE STUDY 15. British bicycle manufacturer partners Malaysian company

The famous British cycle-manufacturer, Raleigh Industries, has a long and proud record of export sales. Over 125 years ago it began to trade in what is now Malaysia, becoming so successful there that in 1966 it began local manufacture and in 1969 was listed on the local stock exchange and began supplying the demanding US market with Raleigh products. By 1980, though, government restrictions on overseas ownership brought the firm low and subsequent attempts to revive the name proved doomed.

Meanwhile, over the years cycling had increasingly become seen as a leisure and sporting activity, requiring better-quality machines than the low-cost imports that addressed only that part of the market interested in basic transport. Against this backdrop, the impending formation of ASEAN, the Asian free-trade area that resembles the European Common Market of old, made businesspeople realize that an enormous new market would open up, full of opportunities for growth, but also requiring growth for defensive reasons. The dash for growth gave impetus to local firms to seek out global brands and know-how.

Montana Cycles had been in business since 1993 and had survived the 1997 Asian financial crisis, but in 2008 dropped its entire repertoire of products in favour of the Raleigh range. This sudden change represented, in effect, a start-up operation, albeit with ready-made experience of, and many contacts in, the industry. This example is included here as the situation was not dissimilar in several ways to a start-up by an industry expert in any market.

In the short time that Raleigh and Montana have been together, both have been surprised at and pleased by the way in which each side's strengths have complemented the other's. The result in the very short term is that Montana have captured for the Raleigh brand a sizeable share of the medium-to-high end of the market, the part expected to grow fastest as ASEAN takes hold and prosperity spreads. It is also a segment with better margins than those at the low-quality, low-value end, which Montana and Raleigh are happy to leave to others.

So this is a tale of an enterprising Malaysian company taking a bold decision in giving up much of what it had worked for over 15 years in order to take advantage of an enormous new market opportunity (and avoid a major threat from new competitors) by teaming up with a firm of international renown.

www.raleigh.my

CASE STUDY   16. Finns supply new tech gadgets early

Tech-hungry consumers are often frustrated by the time that passes between the announcement of a new piece of equipment and when it is available to buy from retailers' stores. The retailers themselves would dearly like access to the people keenest to upgrade or replace their devices.

A website based in Helsinki and St Petersburg aims to meet the needs of both groups. Preorder.it takes orders from potential buyers who want to register their interest, and offers the information to merchants. Merchants can then assess demand and order accordingly, while deciding on what prices would be likely to yield the sales they desire. They then make their offers to the buyers. Since all of this takes place in advance of the release of products for sale, buyers can be sure that they will be among the first to own a hot, new device.

In every market there are early adopters, who want to be first with every novelty that comes out; equally, there are those at the other end of the distribution who will adopt it only after years or decades of managing without, or even never. In between lie the majority, more or less willing to consider new things. The advantage in waiting is that in the rush to market some aspect may not have been fully thought through, leaving early adopters with the problem of upgrading after a period of frustrating performance; new users who buy v2.0 swan straight into an upgraded version without even thinking about it. They also benefit from lower prices as supplies expand and retailers compete with one another to chase market share.

Despite that, there are those for whom last month's laptop, phone or PDA simply isn't good enough. For them, registering with Preorder.it seems the right move.

No physical address is disclosed, other than that the operation is in Helsinki, Finland, despite the web-address suffix of '.it', which usually denotes Italy.

www.preorder.it

CASE STUDY   17. Canadians cycle round the world

In 2003 Tour d'Afrique was set up in Toronto, Canada, named after what was then the firm's new cycling tour of Africa, from Cairo to Cape Town. Ever since then it has steadily added new routes, all on the same heroic scale, in Europe, Asia and South America, springing from the conviction that cross-continental travel in a group, under one's own power, liberates the individual while developing body, mind and self-knowledge.

Clearly, the six people who run the company are experienced and committed cyclists. But their ideals run wider than doing just what they love. They are keen to encourage less athletic people to undertake their tours as an exercise in self-discovery, reminiscent of those great round-the-world sailing challenges for non-sailors. They also seek to pay back something to the far-flung communities whose lands, settlements and heritage lend the tours much of their magic. To do that they have set up the Tour d'Afrique Foundation, which raises money to give cycles to health professionals in Africa, thus enabling nurses and doctors to visit outlying communities and people too ill to visit the surgery or hospital.

Their latest idea is based on the principle of customer-made products and services. This stands the entire tradition of the travel industry on its head. Instead of the travel company devising and selling the tour, the customers say what they want and are then brought together by the company.

Called DreamTours, the new initiative encourages interested cyclists worldwide to specify the tour they most want to undertake, with suggestions for stops, lengths of stages, number of companions and even photographs of destinations to whet the appetite. The individual names the tour, plots it on a map, suggests costs and posts it on the website. Other cyclists comment and add their ideas and, if enough people express commitment, the tour goes ahead. Indeed, if the tour sells out completely, the originator may be given a place free of charge, or can choose to have a discount applied to the whole group.

From its launch in 2009, DreamTours committed in 2010 to a trip from St Petersburg to Venice and for 2011 a long tour of India, starting in Agra. This is clearly an idea that can be applied elsewhere in the travel market, as well as beyond.

www.tourdafrique.com/dreamtours

CASE STUDY 18. New York City baking innovation

From that tireless factory of business innovation, New York City, comes possibly the daftest innovation ever seen – cupcakes for men.

But is it so silly, after all? Butch Bakery employs six people – jobs that are needed these days, or any days for that matter. In 2008 the founder, a high-flying Wall Street lawyer tossed aside by the economic maelstrom, had just had a new job in Dubai disappear from underneath him. Seeing a big demand for cupcakes, but revolted by the frilly 1950s version of femininity that the product traditionally exhibits, he had one of those moments when the little light-bulb in his head flicked on and he thought: why not cupcakes for men? After all, New York City, like most big cities in the United States, has its share of men firmly committed to asserting their masculinity; New Yorkers also appreciate wit and are amused by products that consciously subvert social assumptions.

Covering only the boroughs of Manhattan, Queens and Brooklyn (home to a staggering 6.4 million people), Butch Bakery delivers in boxes of 4, 6 or 12 at a price of $4 (about £2.50) per cupcake. Delivery is charged at $8 for orders under $50.

Steering clear of the clichéd 'masculine' iconography of sporting equipment, the designs feature military camouflage, tartan, houndstooth, woodgrain, chequerboard and marble designs. Beneath these original but self-effacing exteriors, the creamy filling is piled high with a choice from 12 flavours that include such (pleasant-sounding) shocks as peanut butter with banana, or Bavarian cream and crumbled bacon. There are also more predictable confections incorporating rum, beer and other alcoholic drinks.

Press coverage just before St Valentine's Day 2010 put the company into meltdown: the website crashed due to demand and the phone rang constantly. Buoyed up by this success Butch Bakery planned to begin nationwide distribution during 2010.

www.butchbakery.com (active in 2010 but in May 2012 'temporarily closed').

CASE STUDY 19. Serbian/French cooperation for specialist fashion jeans

A couple of young techie people living in France became fed up with the problems of carrying their gadgets around all day. One thing was certain – the gadgets could not go, so their clothes had to adapt. They hit on the idea of designing jeans for themselves that would carry an iPhone and an iPod in special pockets – so special that carrying-cases would be made redundant by pockets lined with an i-friendly microfibre material. In addition, there would have to be a secret memory-stick pocket so they could have all of their essentials with them, all of the time.

They mentioned the idea to friends, who liked it so much that they asked if they could have some, too. Pretty soon it was clear that they had the makings of a business and WTF Jeans was born. A skilled clothing designer came on board and a top tailor made the prototypes, with the aim that not only should the finished article be functional, it should look great too. Contacts in Serbia supplied an experienced clothing factory that was up to the serious job of making the final product.

The decision taken, WTF Jeans laid down the principle that it would make no more than 1,000 pairs of this product, which adds to its scarcity. Promotion was solely via all the social networking systems to which they belong, with videos on their blog to keep followers up to date – no PR, no adverts, no news releases – just word-of-mouth. Needless to say, the website was beautifully designed in tasteful black, white and denim blue. Not only did it look good, it set an example for simplicity and logic in use.

Some software suppliers charge less for early releases, more for 'beta' versions and the full whack for the final version. WTF Jeans' pricing ran parallel to this: the first 100 pairs sold for €59, the next 400 for €79 and the final 500 at €109, to sell out the limited edition of 1,000. A sizing chart showed equivalents in the main European markets (except for Germany) and the Levi's version. Delivery anywhere was €9 and there was a refund for unhappy customers.

There is obvious potential from a database of 1,000 well-off customers addicted to gadgets, contacts with fashion designers and a clothing factory, with lower costs than in much of Europe, that's looking for its next order.

www.wtfjeans.com (active in 2010 but in May 2012 website said: 'SOLD OUT: Join our mailing list and be the first to hear about our launch date for V2).

CASE STUDY 20. Belgian PDA app remembers clothing sizes, birthdays, anniversaries

This involves a question that every partner quickly learns to avoid answering directly.

The Belgium-based website Orgasizer is doing its bit for couples' harmony by helping to sort out one term in this complex equation, the small matter of remembering what size someone takes. It goes further, covering any gift aspect of any person, child or animal that one might want to remember. If they are successful, all those men haunting lingerie counters on Christmas Eve, embarrassedly eyeing-up female assistants in the hope of finding one who resembles their loved one, will be changed for ever. Instead, they will be at the same spot but gazing at their PDAs in the certain knowledge that the secret they crave is on the Orgasizer website. Now all they have to do is remember the password...

The system allows the user, a man in the situation described above, to enter details of his sizing and preferences. Age is also given, to avoid obvious style mismatches. He can also specify other people who are allowed to access his information. With discretion typical of the worldly francophone European, no one who has access permission knows who else has permission. Thus there is no risk of spouses enquiring about the others whose statistics and preferences are listed (sociologists will regret the fun they cannot have in comparing the numbers and genders of other contacts across different nationalities).

For those unable to concentrate on relationships sufficiently to remember key dates, they too can be entered. Wish lists are possible, to prompt loved ones to get the right thing, rather than what they thought was wanted.

There is obvious opportunity for tie-ups with retailers and manufacturers interested in the gift market, via advertising and targeted offers.

www.orgasizer.com (active in 2010 but inaccessible in May 2012).

Suggested topics for class and group discussion

Experienced educators will have their own repertoire of techniques for stimulating class interaction. What follows is not proposed as superior to them, but merely as an adjunct to be employed if it seems useful.

Timings are suggested across a range from the minimum necessary for quick students to make any sense of the question, to a maximum beyond which any group would run out of challenge.

Numbers given per group are indicative only, but it is suggested that small groups should not exceed six people each. Most activities assume a class-size of 12–20 or so.

Focus should not be on students giving right or wrong answers. The aim is to maximize interaction between students so as to deepen knowledge and understanding of issues and to enhance thinking and communications skills.

1. Marketing

1.1 (10–30 minutes)

In groups of three or four people, choose a case study from the list above. Try out the analytical tools you have learned on the course. Note down your main findings. Report back to the whole class.

1.2 (10–30 minutes)

In groups of three or four people, choose a case study from the list above. Consider the sales, communication and distribution strategies, and identify strengths, weaknesses, opportunities and threats. Note down your main findings. Report back to the whole class.

1.3 (10–40 minutes)

Form into groups of two or three people. Each group is to select four different case studies from the list above. Individually, then in groups, identify their segmentation strategies. Comment on these strategies' likely effectiveness in the longer term. Suggest any desirable changes for the longer term.

2. Financial

2.1 (20–40 minutes)

Select a case study from the list above. In pairs, then in groups of four to six, consider the impact on cash flow of the company's method of operation and its past history. Identify suitable types of finance and state what form of presentation is likely to be appropriate. Identify any conditions financiers are likely to impose. Report back to plenary for the class leader to note findings down for the whole class and draw conclusions.

2.2 (20–60 minutes)

Choose a case study from the list above featuring a company that can be expected to experience seasonal variations in demand. Individually, then in fours, consider the likely production system and the demands of customers. Construct a speculative sales forecast, using an index, eg January 100, February 80, March 90, April 120, etc. Consider these indices, then arrive at views on the working capital requirements per month from January to December, dividing the requirement into raw materials stock, finished goods stock and accounts receivable (debtors). Again, use an index. The class leader will note down conclusions from each group which will form the basis for discussion and conclusions.

2.3 (20–60 minutes)

In groups of three or four, examine three of the case studies above (each group selecting a different collection). What form(s) of finance is each likely to require? Consider and note down, in descending order of importance, the key points of presentation(s) to be made to the financier(s). Report to plenary for the class leader to note down your list. Discuss the merits of each group's views.

3. People

3.1 (40–120 minutes)

Select four case studies from the list above. The class divides into four groups and for each case it divides into groups representing owners, customers, suppliers (including financiers) and workforce. Each takes five minutes to decide its strategy. Owners present their future plans (making reasonable assumptions) to the other groups. Each of the groups reacts to the plans and, if it feels it necessary, to the other stakeholders' responses. The owners defend their position and modify it if necessary. The class leader holds the ring between them, striking out any outrageous or untenable positions. At the end of each round the roles change as a new case is introduced.

3.2 (20–40 minutes)

Each group of two to four selects a different case study from among those judged capable of great expansion. Groups consider the organizational implications of growth and draw organization charts for two and seven years from the present. Conclusions are presented to plenary and discussed.

3.3 (20–40 minutes)

Groups take the role of the owner of a small but rapidly expanding SME. If they choose, they may base it on a case study from the list above or on a small firm that they know (while avoiding slander), but that is optional. The owner is aged 31, has been in business for eight years and is about to interview two applicants for a new managerial job. One is aged 54 and has worked all her life in a major multinational, retiring early with a pension that she could live on. The other is aged 23 and is an internal applicant, but from a different department. Draw up a list of issues that need to be covered at interview to ensure that all the owner's reasonable concerns are addressed, bearing in mind that interpretations of 'fairness' require that the same matters must be covered with all candidates.

4. Strategy

4.1 (30–75 minutes)

In groups of three or four, identify two examples from the case studies above with requirements for relatively high initial investment and two needing relatively low initial investment. What are the implications for competitive entry to the market? If it were attacked, how could the niche be defended? Report to plenary for recording and discussion by the class.

4.2 (20–45 minutes)

Choose a case study from the list above. Individually, then in pairs, then in groups of up to six, consider the opportunities for expansion, domestically and internationally, and identify the threats and opportunities that apply to each. Report findings in plenary for the class leader to note down for class discussion.

4.3 (15–40 minutes)

Each group selects a case study from the list above that it thinks stands no chance of real success and produces a reasoned analysis for that conclusion. Taking the original idea, it proposes ways in which it could be better done. Reports are made to plenary for class discussion.

Theoretical models

Certain theoretical models are used widely and can be applied in so many instances that it is worth summarizing them here, even though students will almost certainly have encountered them elsewhere in their studies. When any students need to refresh an overtaxed memory, the list below may help to avoid having to switch between this book, their notes, handouts and other texts.

Ansoff matrix

This is a 2 × 2 matrix labelled on each side respectively 'markets' and 'products'. Each side is divided into 'existing' and 'new'. This yields four boxes labelled 'market penetration', 'market development', 'product development' and 'diversification'. Its use is 1) to analyse an existing situation of any firm; 2) to foresee the implications of future plans for the market position. The least risky approach is thought to be market penetration (selling known goods or services into a known market) and the most risky is thought to be diversification (selling new products into new markets, both containing significant unknowns). The risk profile of the two remaining boxes is judged by reference to where the firm's strengths lie relative to competitors – whether in product or market development (Ansoff, 1957).

Boston matrix

This matrix is of little more than passing interest to the young SME as it was designed for large, mature companies. It is a 2 × 2 matrix with dimensions labelled 'relative market growth' and 'market share'. These are further divided into 'high' and 'low'. It helps to assess the organization's portfolio of products or services in relation to their ability to generate and absorb cash. The four boxes are labelled 'star', 'cash cow', 'dog' and 'problem child' accordingly. The aim is to shift problem children towards star status, to exploit stars to become cash cows and to remove dogs from the system altogether. Its concern with cash relates it to the product life cycle (see below).

Hygiene factors

Hygiene factors are not motivators. Their absence causes upsets but their presence is assumed and accepted as the norm (Herzberg, Bloch and Mausner, 1993).

Pareto analysis

Pareto analysis is based on the 80/20 rule. This rule states that 20 per cent of inputs determine 80 per cent of outputs and, conversely, that as much as 80 per cent of inputs produce a meagre 20 per cent of outputs. Thus, if applied to a manager's time, four-fifths of results come from one-fifth of effort. It can be applied widely to any population and, while the proportions will rarely come out as exactly 80/20, it helps to focus attention on the need to distinguish the few, significant issues that are really important in any situation from the mass of relatively trivial matters.

Porter's five forces

This model assesses the fierceness of competition in any market under consideration by evaluating the barriers to entry, the threat of substitutes, the competitive rivalry and the power of buyers and sellers. The observer may come to the facile assumption that relatively less competition may be preferable, whereas there is a reason why the wasps are thickest around the jam-pot. Whilst the small business can rarely change the rules governing the degree of competition within an industry, it can at least see what entry to that industry might involve (Porter, 2008).

Product life cycle (PLC)

The proposition is that all products go through a standard pattern of launch, growth, maturity and decline. In some cases the cycle lasts for decades or even centuries, in others days, weeks or months. The conclusion of any cycle is usually disappearance, but in the case of the PLC it can be postponed indefinitely by relaunches which are ideally placed late in the maturity phase so as to revive flagging sales. The PLC is linked with the Boston matrix (see above) as the degree of success of a product linked with its cash situation – whether it generates or absorbs cash – determines where in the Boston matrix it should be placed.

STEP, PEST, STEEPLE

The acronym STEP or PEST stands for sociological, technological, economical and political, representing the four essential dimensions on which an organization's environment may be assessed. The factors of significant influence are listed under each heading. This highlights matters that the organization's strategies need to address. The later addition of 'LE' stands for legal and environmental, matters that were formerly thought to be encompassed by 'political'; it does no harm to expand the model in this way.

SWOT

This stands for strengths, weaknesses, opportunities and threats. Strengths and weaknesses are internal to the organization; opportunities and threats are external, being outside in the environment. Strengths allied to opportunities suggest the strategic way forward; weaknesses and threats highlight matters for improvement or defence.

Sample assignments and notes

Assignments

The titles below and their accompanying notes are essentially formative so that educators may wish to tailor them to meet the requirements of summative assessment models. As presented, none of them addresses a single disciplinary area, thus reflecting some of the realities of business.

Assessment guides are provided, rather than suppressed, as an insight for students into the considerations their assessors might take into account when evaluating submitted work.

1. Reflective self-assessment for entrepreneurship

Take any list of entrepreneurial characteristics that you feel rings true. Lists may be found in this book, in other books and on the internet. Divide a sheet of paper into three columns. On the first, rate yourself against each of the criteria in a way that enables comparison with other results (eg by using a scale of 1–10, with 10 being high). Next, interview someone who knows you well, preferably in a task-based context rather than purely socially. Ask them to rate you in the same way and record their answers in the second column. (Do not disclose any of your own ratings until after you have finished the interview.) Next, compare the two sets of answers and discuss them. In the final column record any change to your rating in the light of that discussion, noting reasons for any changes. Then go to **www.get2test.net** and take the General Enterprise Tendency (GET) test.

(i) Compare the results of the GET test with what you and your interviewee thought. Identify and consider similarities and differences.

(ii) Imagine that you are dealing not with yourself, but someone whom you are advising. In no more than 2,000 words, write a reasoned report to that person on his or her suitability for entrepreneurship, any ideas you may have for the sort of firm the person should start and any issues you believe he or she should address.

Assessment guide

An **excellent** answer would have entered into the spirit of the assignment, interviewing thoroughly and recording a discussion of changes of view in some detail, using the interaction and the results of the subsequent test to provide insight. The report will be written objectively, the author referring to himself or herself in the third person, and make cogent recommendations based on the evidence presented. The form will follow an adaptation of the standard report-writing model (executive summary, recommendations, background, research, discussion, conclusions).

A **good** answer would show industry in the collection and review of data. Viewpoints may not have shifted but where they have no more than an adequate discussion is offered. There may be faults in the approach of the report's presentation but its general direction will be sound.

A **poor** answer will show low commitment to the project with possibly slapdash analysis and low-level interviewing and thin discussion. The presentation of the report is likely to be poor.

2. Strategy

Identify two small firms in any business from anywhere in the world, one with a strategy you believe to be successful and the other with a strategy you believe either to be failing or risking failure. In no more than 2,000 words, analyse the reasons for their situations, using suitable theoretical tools where it is useful. (This assignment could be extended to require, in the one case, proposals to exploit the success further and, in the other, to halt and turn round the failure.)

Assessment guide

An **excellent** answer would be based on two clearly contrasting situations drawn from real life which illustrate conspicuous success and at least the probability of failure. Analysis would apply correctly SWOT, STEP/STEEPLE, Porter's five forces, PLC, Boston, Pareto and Ansoff in the search for explanations (some of these tools may be ineffective here). A persuasive and integrated explanation would follow.

A **good** answer would have less well-selected cases and/or use less than a large repertoire of analytical tools and/or apply the tools not fully adequately. Its explanation would therefore carry something less than full conviction but would be along the right lines in general.

A **poor** answer would not use contrasting cases or would analyse inadequately, either through the use of only one or two tools or by applying tools wrongly. The conclusions would be unsupported by evidence or in other ways be unconvincing.

3. Marketing

Sitting next to a man while travelling, you fall into conversation. He owns a pearl farm on the Chinese coast near Hong Kong. He tells you that he can sell all the near-globular white and pink pearls he can get, but misshapen, tiny and oddly coloured pearls are not in demand, despite being genuine, cultured pearls. He has a continuing problem disposing of large quantities: a bag of 200–300 would sell for only US $10. You see a business opportunity and exchange contact details. On returning home you identify types of jewellery to incorporate these materials, estimate finished product costs and begin to draft a business plan, starting with various analyses. State the headings of the business plan and write notes under each.

Assessment guide

An **excellent** answer would seek assurances of continuity of supply, identify export and import taxation and transport costs, allow for delays between order and delivery in its estimates of time to market and show evidence of obtaining approximate costings from the jewellery industry or some assembly activity analogue with commentary on the effects on pricing, margins and volume. Plausible strategies would be devised for production, communications and distribution. Pricing would be based on an assessment of the existing market, supported by evidence.

A **good** answer would follow much the same pattern, but have significant weaknesses in one or more areas.

A **poor** answer would show little evidence of effective application to the task, or poor judgement or unrealistic calculations. Estimates would be unsupported by credible evidence.

4. Finance and financial planning

Identify an empty shop that is to let and find the rent and other costs of taking it on. Using a product category of your choice, estimate your staff costs (not just wages). State assumptions about pricing and margins and from this calculate the sales volume and value needing to be sold to break even.

Assessment guide

An **excellent** answer would show evidence of serious research that produced factual information. The example category chosen would be plausible as would estimated staff costs, with current rates of employer's NI and pension contributions applied, volume, sales and margin assumptions. Extra marks would be available if depreciation on fittings and cash flow are discussed. An accurate break-even calculation would be shown and its realism commented on.

A **good** answer would show that adequate research had been done; estimated premises costs would be allowable if supported by credible sources. Volume would appear credible. Calculations of operating costs would be sound and the break-even calculation reasonably accurate.

A **poor** answer would evidence little research and an inadequate basis for estimations. Staff on-costs would be incomplete. Pricing, volume and margins would lack conviction and the break-even analysis would be inadequately done.

5. Ideas generation

5.1

Identify problems felt by your friends or family that really annoy them. Pick one of the problems and design a commercial solution that would solve the problem. Describe the solution, its pricing, any ancillary benefits offered, the distribution method, the communications strategy you would employ to sell it and approximate costs and gross and net profits.

Assessment guide

An **excellent** answer would produce a rich crop of problems of real everyday annoyance to consumers, select one with well-argued potential for commercial exploitation on some scale, apply suitable theoretical models (SWOT, STEP, five forces, Pareto) appropriately and imaginatively. It would analyse the product by core and ancillary aspects and propose distribution and communications strategies that appear relevant and cost-effective. Costs and selling prices will necessarily be speculative but should have some grounding in reality.

A **good** answer would identify plausible consumer problems, select one with a degree of apparent potential for commercial exploitation and undertake some theoretical analysis competently. Strategies, pricing and costs would appear credible.

A **poor** answer would produce a thin list of problems or select one with little commercial potential. Little or no appropriate use of theory would be evident. Strategies would be based more on wishful thinking than reality.

5.2

A cruise ship recently went aground and sank, settling in shallow water with a heavy list to port. Lives were lost for what are thought to be multiple reasons, but two factors listed in early analyses were the lack of lighting and illuminated emergency signs in corridors and the difficulty of launching lifeboats. Here is a problem that causes your inner entrepreneur to think of solutions.

Consider the problem of a ship aground with the port (left-hand) side against rocks: lifeboats cannot be launched from that side. Lifeboats on the other (starboard) side are so far out of the water and at such an angle that they cannot be swung clear. If she were a cargo ship, the crew could enter their enclosed lifeboat which sits on a slipway above the stern: all climb aboard and the lifeboat launches into the sea. But this is a passenger ship which must have far more lifeboat capacity. Also the engine room is flooded so that no electricity is available from generators, so lighting is not available at night.

(i) Invent simple systems that would, as far as possible, use existing features of the ship and examples from other forms of transport to facilitate safe escape for passengers.

(ii) Identify the stakeholders towards whom marketing effort for this device would need to be directed.

Assessment guide

An **excellent** answer would recognize the applicable management theory and create practical solutions that would introduce as little disturbance as possible to existing ship design yet, apparently, be feasible in construction, installation and operation. It might devise some system such as escape pods made from a detachable version of the existing corridors along side-decks, designed as seaworthy in their own right, which could be made waterproof by the closing of doors and released by explosive bolts with a braked descent into the sea. They would be equipped with survival stores. Escape lighting would be provided by the method used in aircraft – emergency lights set along corridors, with illuminated signs pointing towards muster stations – powered by a sealed battery system. Stakeholders would be identified by a STEP/STEEPLE analysis. Governments and international marine regulatory bodies would be the primary target. Safety is a hygiene factor and thus not saleable to shipowners nor appealing to passengers – it is assumed as a given.

A **good** answer would recognize and deploy the management theory models adequately but be less inventive.

A **poor** answer would fail to recognize or apply properly suitable managerial models and would fail to describe an apparently workable solution that would resist the forces of the sea.

APPENDIX 1
Cash-flow forecasting explained

A simple example may help to explain the principles. John runs a very straight-forward business selling apples from a market stall. On his first day in business he does the following:

- He borrows £200 from his granny, interest free on the promise of repaying her as fast as possible.
- He buys a market stall for £100 cash.
- He pays the council £10 for a day's pitch on the market square.
- He buys apples for £90 cash.
- He sells half the apples for £80, all in cash.

At the end of that Monday his P&L account looks like Table A1.1.

TABLE A1.1   John's P&L account for Monday

	£
Sales	80
Cost of goods sold	45
Value added	35
Overheads	
Rent for pitch	10
Profit	25

But where are the £45-worth of apples he still has, and the stall worth £100? And for that matter, where is the £80 we know he has in his pocket? The answer is that the P&L account records only the sales, and the expenses relating to those sales. It could not show where stock, cash or equipment is. The 'missing' items will appear on the balance sheet, an entirely separate document. The balance sheet pretends that you stop all the buying and selling for a split second and record where money is tied up at that moment. It also shows where the money in the business has come from. At the end of Monday, John's balance sheet looks like Table A1.2.

TABLE A1.2   John's balance sheet

Where the money came from	£	Where it was at that moment	£
Loan from granny	200	Fixed assets (stall)	100
Retained profits	25	Current assets	
		Stock at cost (apples)	45
		Cash (the day's takings)	80
	£225		£225

This way of showing a balance sheet is now old-fashioned, but it is easier for beginners to understand – so don't worry if balance sheets you have seen are laid out differently. They all mean the same thing.

You do not need to concern yourself further with balance sheets at this stage of your firm's development, so we'll leave them there. The point in mentioning them is so that you can see that they are basically simple documents, to illustrate the sort of information they contain and to confirm, yet again, that profit is only one of the two key matters you must deal with. Therefore, the young business needs to monitor its P&L account but need not worry about the balance sheet. Instead it pays hawk-like attention to its performance against the cash-flow forecast, which is a more flexible way of controlling and concentrating on the high-risk areas of the balance sheet.

To return to John. It is now Tuesday morning and he sets up his stall in the market again. He pays the council's superintendent another £10, and sells the rest of his apples for £80. The result of Tuesday's trading is shown in Table A1.3.

For the rest of the week John repeats the same pattern, ending up with profits of 6 × £25 = £150 by Saturday night, all in cash. Having made £150, and being a nice young chap, John thinks of paying off some of granny's loan. He knows he must keep some cash back to pay for stock on Monday, to pay the council, and to pay his £30 weekly keep. So he does a cash-flow forecast. He works out what cash he can expect to come in and when, and what he will have to pay out and when. Follow what John wrote down; even if it looks a little difficult at first it is not complicated. As usual, brackets mean a minus figure.

TABLE A1.3   John's P&L account for Tuesday

	£
Sales	80
Cost of goods sold	45
Value added	35
Overheads	
Rent of pitch	10
Profit	25

Table A1.4 shows that the result of Monday's trading is expected to be a fall of £50 in John's holding of cash, even though he will have made his usual profit. That profit, plus another £15, will be tied up in apples for sale on Tuesday. So can John pay off granny? Bearing in mind that he must start each day with enough cash for his outlays that day, he looks to see what he can pay granny and when. He will start week 2 with his £150 (the next to last figure in the Monday column) and he must finish the week with at least £130 for his outlays at the start of week 3. Try working out what he can pay, and when. The answer is in brackets below. If you found that a little challenging you will see why John did it on paper and not in his head. The calculation is not difficult – it is only simple addition and subtraction – but there are so many steps to it that you cannot do it in your head. John could easily have taken the short cut and paid out of his profits. Had he done so he would have run out of cash and out of business. As it is, he still owes granny £60 but he is still in business.

(Answer: This week, John can pay £50 straight away, £20 on Monday evening, £50 on Wednesday evening, and £20 on Friday evening. If he tries to do it faster, he runs out of cash – so he still owes granny £60 at the end of the week.)

TABLE A1.4   John's cash-flow forecast for week 2 (£)

	Mon	Tue	Wed	Thu	Fri	Sat
Cash taken in the day (a)	80	80	80	80	80	80
Cash paid out at the start of the day						
– keep	30	–	–	–	–	–
– rent	10	10	10	10	10	10
– apples	90	–	90	–	90	–
Total cash paid out in the day (b)	130	10	100	10	100	10
Net cash taken in the day (a – b)	(50)	70	(20)	70	(20)	70
Cash in hand at the start of the day	*150	100	170	150	220	200
Cash in hand at the end of the day	**100	170	150	220	200	270

* He will start the week with £150 left over from the previous week.
** The figures on this line become the 'cash in hand at the start of the day' for the following day.

APPENDIX 2
Draft terms and conditions of sale

What follows is a list of suggestions. Some may be right for your business, others wrong, and some right after rewriting. Yet others may be needed that do not appear here. Use the list to build your own conditions of sale that reflect the way you want to deal with your customers. Then, and very importantly, let your solicitor put it into proper shape.

Terms and conditions of sale

Descriptions shown in brochures, advertisements, and by way of samples are correct at the time of going to press, errors and omissions excepted. They are liable to alteration at any time without notice.

This is meant to protect you from minor complaints about changes in specification, and mistakes in price lists and catalogues. You might want to change a specification but not throw away catalogues. But it would not override the customer's right to goods that are 'fit for use'.

We may revise prices without notice. Prices will be those ruling at the date of dispatch. Any invoice query should be made in writing within 10 days of the date of the invoice. All prices exclude VAT which is due at the rate currently in force. Quotations and estimates remain current for one month.

This is some protection against cost increases that you might have to pass on. This stops you being bound by old quotations and makes it clear that VAT has to be paid – if you are registered.

All accounts are payable in full within four weeks of the invoice date.

Or state whatever your terms are – it is very important to specify them clearly.

We cannot accept liability for delay in dispatch or delivery.

It is not your fault if the delivery firm loses the parcel for a month.

Orders for goods may be cancelled only with the written agreement of one of our directors. Orders for goods made to special order cannot be cancelled.

Only a director or the owner should give this permission, not salespeople or others. Special orders are usually unsaleable to anyone else.

All orders over £100 will be delivered free within 10 miles.
Elsewhere, carriage may be charged in addition to the quoted price.
Orders for less than £100 are not normally accepted for a credit account.

Whether you charge for delivery and what you charge needs to be carefully controlled, as does the cost of administering a lot of small accounts. There is nothing special about £100; it is just an illustration.

Shortage of goods or damage must be notified by telephone within three days of delivery, and confirmed in writing within seven days of delivery, or no claim can be accepted. Delivery of obviously damaged goods should be refused. Notifications should give delivery note number, a list of quantities of the products damaged, and details of the type of damage. Damaged goods must be retained for inspection.

This should be written in the light of what your carrier's conditions say. As the carrier will destroy all papers proving delivery after a short time, it wants speedy notification of any claim. It is essential for damaged goods to be saved and eventually collected by you to stop dishonest collusion between customers and lorry drivers, and multiple claims against one damaged item.

Liability cannot be accepted for non-delivery of goods if written notification is not received within 10 days of the date of invoice.

See the comments above: tie in with the carrier's conditions.

No liability is accepted for any consequential loss or damage whatsoever, however caused.

In cases of extreme negligence by your staff or yourself this would probably not stick, but your solicitor might want to see it included.

Acceptance of the goods implies acceptance of these conditions.
These conditions may not be varied except in writing by one of our directors.

Now the customer cannot take the goods but complain about the conditions. Nor can he or she bully your salesperson into giving unlimited credit, for instance.

Under some circumstances we may cancel the contract without notice or compensation. Such circumstances would include inability to obtain materials, labour and supplies, strikes, lockouts and other forms of industrial action or dispute, fire, flood, drought, weather conditions, war (whether declared or not), acts of terrorism, civil disturbance, acts of God or any other cause beyond our control making it impossible for us to fulfil the contract.

This covers you for the times when snow blocks the roads and so on. You might even want to add the insurance policy favourites of damage by aircraft, falling trees, radioactive and biological hazards... but, there again, you might not.

Until they have been paid for we reserve our title in goods supplied.

When a customer goes into liquidation everything in his or her possession is sold to pay the creditors, even if it has not been paid for. The exceptions are items on lease or hire purchase, or that clearly belong to somebody else. You cannot normally snatch back the last delivery you sent. Clause 12 gives you protection, by saying that they remain yours until paid for. You could show the liquidator this term on the copy of the order form signed by the customer, and walk out with the goods. It will not work, however, if what you supplied has been incorporated in something else. Nor will it work if you cannot identify those items as precisely the ones on the invoice.

*Any invoice not paid in full by the due date shall attract interest payments. These will accrue from the due date at the rate of ** per cent per annum. ** The rate is calculated as eight per cent plus the 'reference rate', namely Bank of England base rate.*

Unless you have a licence to offer credit you must not charge the public an interest rate. It is suggested that you think about using a clause like this to encourage payment in line with your terms. You would probably never need to actually charge it, as the threat would be enough to make most firms pay up. Any customers who query it can be told that it does not apply to them, but only to people who break their promise to pay on time. It is your legal right to do so.

If a 'quotation' is given it is a firm price for the job but subject to these terms and conditions. An 'estimate' is our best estimate of the final cost but may be subject to fluctuation due to exigencies of the job which may be difficult or impossible to foresee.

In some businesses it is difficult to give a price for some work, as time may have to be spent to uncover the root of the problem before a proper quotation can be given. It is fair to the customer and yourself to make this clear.

APPENDIX 3
Starting a green business

Why a green business?

Successive governments, as well as the UN, have emphasized the urgent need for the human race to clean up its act. In the UK in the 19th century a reaction took place to industry pouring its waste into rivers, lakes and the air and despoiling the environment for all. During the 20th century practical action ensured that UK rivers were cleaner and that the poisonous smogs became a thing of the past. Rose-growers lament the cleaning-up of the atmosphere, as the fungal disease black spot is now rampant: formerly air-borne SO_2 killed it off, but most would agree that their distress is a price worth paying to keep forests alive.

Now the great drive is to reduce man-made atmospheric CO_2, in the belief that it is causing an unprecedented and potentially catastrophic warming of the planet. Governments are pouring in, or at least promising to pour in, vast sums of taxpayers' money to help industry to adjust, and taxing those activities seen as socially undesirable. Hand in hand with that runs an entirely reasonable pressure to reduce waste in all its forms: putting reusable materials into holes in the ground itself costs money, as well as ignoring a chance to recycle. The general public seems largely to have been convinced that something must be done and many are cheerfully paying over the odds for purchases that appear to be green.

Times of great social, scientific or economic change throw up new opportunities for entrepreneurs. The environmental revolution represents one of those times. Ten years from now the opportunities will seem obvious, for the businesses formed today will have established themselves and grown. Today they are less obvious, but the chances are there nonetheless.

The opportunity is therefore clear: a business that either helps others to reduce their carbon footprint or waste, or that can demonstrate in its own operations lower carbon use and waste than its competitors should thrive. Less idealistically, a firm that wishes to supply large companies may find itself locked out if it does not possess, or is not working towards, certification of its environmental management system.

Why not a green business?

The wrong motive is to be attracted by the subsidies on offer. Any business that depends for its existence on government handouts relies on a variable income which can be withdrawn at any time and can be a nightmare to negotiate. That does not rule out their use, but suggests that no long-term commitments should be made on the assumption of that income continuing.

The evidence on which global warming, now known as climate change, is based, is under scrutiny. If it is found wanting, much of the impetus towards greenness may evaporate. Meanwhile, and perhaps permanently, greenness can be a powerful promotional tool.

What is a green business?

The main ways of being commercially green include:

- running a conventional firm, but using fewer resources than is usual in that trade or industry;
- helping others to use fewer resources, through consultancy or ideas;
- inventing products or processes that will increase the efficiency of other businesses;
- inventing new, greener products that supersede existing products.

The spectrum covered by that list is enormous. At one end is the guest house that improves its heat insulation and sources as many of its purchases as possible locally, thus cutting down the energy required for deliveries and heating. At the other end is the engineer who develops a way to capture and store underground the carbon emissions of coal-fired power stations.

There is a further dimension: certification. If a business is to argue that its operations are green, it might decide to try to get away with no more than the fuzzy statement that they are. It might think that all it needs to do to support it is take a few token measures – a windmill on the roof, a solar panel or two dotted around and a hybrid car in the car park. In dealing with undemanding customers among the general public that may be all that is required to convince. However, some buyers are rather more hard-headed, demanding evidence of compliance with written standards. Typically they are in large-scale industry.

Examining the standards that exist means entering a world of alphabet soup: British Standard (BS) 8555 Environmental Management System, or to give it the full title, 'Guide to the phased implementation of an environmental management system including the use of environmental performance evaluation', links Environmental Management Systems (ISO 14001) and Environmental Performance Evaluation (ISO 14031). There is a special arrangement for smaller firms, called the IEMA ACORN scheme – **www.iema.net/ems/acorn_scheme** gives further details. Its workbook shows some useful case studies of how firms have dealt with the issues. Nobody should be under any illusion about the challenge of conforming to the requirements of a major certification scheme at the same time as trying to set up a business.

Where are the opportunities?

The key tool is the Pareto analysis (discussed in Chapter 5). This helps to identify where the big offenders are – those that offer the greatest chance of a big saving in waste or carbon footprint, which will also be keen to reduce it, and are therefore worth concentrating on.

For example, most people, asked who are the greatest producers of atmospheric carbon might answer 'motor vehicles' or 'aircraft'. They would completely overlook shipping, which accounts for around twice aviation's quantity. Only research and a close inspection of the figures would reveal information like that, so an investigation of the facts might lead to all kinds of new perspectives on the opportunities available. One fact that such a search might throw up is the apparent nonsense of London's new hydrogen-powered buses. The fact that their exhaust emits no carbon dioxide is admirable, but after the coachwork has been built they are taken by sea from the UK to California to have their engines fitted, then brought back to go into service. Even if it can be justified in terms of the ultimate saving, it is a PR disaster and must offer business opportunities to some UK-based firm.

Consistency – can you keep it up?

Anyone who runs a green firm needs to be a believer; anyone else would not be able to stop the mask from slipping. They need to have, and stick to, green policies on every aspect of their firm's operations; for those in a certification scheme, procedures will all be laid down. For those who are not, here's a checklist:

- premises: heating, lighting;
- travel to work: minimize the use of motor vehicles;
- staff: live locally, preferably walk or cycle to work;
- meetings: face-to-face locally, video or phone conferencing remotely, wherever possible;
- business travel: public transport wherever possible, minimizing shipping and flying;
- business accommodation when travelling: environmentally responsible hotels;
- motor vehicles: as few as possible, and the most environmentally responsible available, irrespective of comfort, etc;
- services and consumables: bought locally, from suppliers who themselves source locally;
- equipment: should have the best environmental performance;
- product or service design and delivery: maximum resource efficiency;
- waste: minimized, but where unavoidable, reuseable or recyclable.

To keep to that list you would need really to be convinced and, moreover, would need to persuade your staff to adopt a similar level of commitment. Anyone who was less than convinced would inevitably show their hand at some point and lose reputation, perhaps catastrophically.

Summary

Before following this track much thought is needed. In particular, consider:

- whether you really are green, and define the firm as green only if the answer is a resounding 'yes';
- the need for much research into what is going on, constantly looking for green opportunities;
- the fact that 'green' is much more than just a promotional sticker to add to a conventional firm; it is more a way of life that has to be lived 24/7;
- whether or not your likely customers will demand membership of a certification scheme.

USEFUL WEBSITES

Selected (free) websites useful to start-up entrepreneurs

The internet offers many sites offering advice and resources to small business and start-ups. While we cannot accept responsibility for their quality, the following offer useful information and advice, free of charge. The point of this list is not to produce a large number but to simplify the search task by confining entries to no more than a couple under each heading.

Start-up information

www.businesslink.gov.uk
www.startups.co.uk

Entrepreneurial characteristics

Dr Sally Caird, General Enterprising Tendency test: **www.get2test.net**
University of Kent Leadership Styles test: **www.kent.ac.uk/careers/sk/leadership.htm**

Finance

www.businesslink.gov.uk
www.startups.co.uk

Law

www.businesslink.gov.uk
www.startups.co.uk

Regulations

www.businesslink.gov.uk

Marketing

www.businesslink.gov.uk
www.startups.co.uk

Staff

www.businesslink.gov.uk
www.startups.co.uk

Premises

www.businesslink.gov.uk

Financial control

www.businesslink.gov.uk
www.startups.co.uk

In addition, membership bodies exist that, while they charge for membership, offer valuable services as well as representing the SME case to government and others.

Membership bodies

Federation of Small Businesses: **www.fsb.org.uk**
Forum of Private Business: **www.fpb.org**

Websites for further information on aspects of entrepreneurship

General availability of bank finance

The Department for Business, Innovation and Skills (BIS) commissioned IFF Research to conduct a survey of SMEs to investigate issues around the availability of bank finance, and also the cost and terms and conditions experienced by businesses that obtained bank finance in 2009: **www.bis.gov.uk/assets/biscore/enterprise/docs/ 10-636-2009-finance-survey-smes-results**

Ethnic minority finance

'Finance for small and medium-sized enterprises: comparisons of ethnic minority and white owned businesses', *A Report on the 2005 UK Survey of SME Finances Ethnic Minority Booster Survey* can be found at: **www.bis.gov.uk/files/file39925.pdf**

The Enterprise Europe Network helps SMEs profit from the single market, claiming €2.5 billion to boost business competitiveness and SMEs for the period 2014–2020: **http://portal.enterprise-europe-network.ec.europa.eu/news-media/news/ eu25-billion-boost-business-competitiveness-smes**

Business population

Business population estimates for the UK and regions 2011 are given at: **www.bis.gov.uk/assets/biscore/statistics/docs/b/business-population-estimates-2011_statistical-release.pdf**

Women entrepreneurs

A government SME survey of women-led businesses is available at: **www.bis.gov.uk/ assets/biscore/enterprise/docs/b/11-1078-bis-small-business-survey-2010-women-led-businesses-boost**

EU

The EU Small Business Portal: **http://ec.europa.eu/small-business/index_en.htm**

Health and Safety

For information on managing health and safety matters see: **www.hse.gov.uk/simple-health-safety/index.htm**

Government policies towards, and research into, SMEs

Department for Business, Innovation and Skills: **www.bis.gov.uk/policies/by/themes/enterprise%20and%20business%20support**

A source of wide-ranging specific information on SMEs

The British Library: **www.bl.uk/bipc/index.html**

Direct marketing

Thomson Local Directories' online information: **www.directmarketing.thomsonlocal.com**

GLOSSARY

In this glossary items that appear in definitions in **bold** type also have their own entries in the list. Common business terms are:

absorption costing   A costing method in which **fixed** and **variable costs** of production are absorbed into **products** or cost centres.

account   1. A financial record of a business transaction. 2. An arrangement to buy and receive goods or **services**, payment being made later.

accounting period   A period of time covered by the **account** in question.

accounts payable   **Debts** owed to others for goods or **services** received but not yet paid for.

accounts receivable   **Debts** owed to you for goods or **services** received by them but not yet paid for.

acid test   The test of **liquidity** which compares **cash** at hand with **current liabilities**.

advertising   Paid-for public announcements meant to sell benefits in order to induce purchasing.

agent   Someone authorized to act for or represent another person.

analysis   Assembling **data** into **information** and examining it for clues about events.

annual report   A report made yearly at the end of the financial year stating its receipts and expenditures (and hence **profits**), **assets** and **liabilities**.

asset   Any item that is owned on which a financial value may be placed.

audit   Examination of **accounts** and supporting evidence in order to assess their reliability.

bad debts   **Debts** which will not be paid.

balance   The money in an **account**.

balance sheet   A statement that shows the **net worth** of a business at a given time by disclosing and subtracting **liabilities** from **assets**.

bank statement   A periodic statement from a bank showing transactions and **balances** in the period.

bankruptcy   Being unable to pay **debts** as **liabilities** exceed **assets**.

board of directors   A body comprising elected directors which is responsible for the **management** of an organization. Electors are the owners of the company. Directors may also be owners, in whole or in part.

bookkeeping   The recording of detailed business transactions in an organization's accounting records. These used to be paper-based books and in the (usually electronic) form of today are still referred to as such.

bottom line   The final line of a **Profit and Loss (P&L)** statement which shows **profit** net of all costs.

brand   1. The name and accompanying graphic devices distinguishing a line of **products** or **services** from others. 2. A name under which a line of **products** or **services** are sold (eg: 'Ford is a major automotive brand').

break-even   The level of sales at which total income equals total expenses. With sales higher than at that point, the firm is in **profit**; lower, and it is in loss.

budget   Prediction made for purposes of planning, integration and control of income and expenditure for a future period (usually one year, broken down into months or weeks).

capital   1. Money available to invest. 2. The total **assets** available in a firm.

capital allowance   A **tax** allowance against **profits** for expenditure on **fixed assets**.

cash   Money in its most liquid form – currency or bank deposits available immediately.

consumer   The user of a **product** or service. Sometimes used interchangeably with **customer**.

contribution costing   An approach to **costing** that places the **marginal contributions** from each **product** into a pool to cover overheads (**operating costs**) that cannot be allocated to individual **products**.

copyright   Rights in written, graphic and sound creations giving weaker protection than **registered design**.

cost   The monetary value of inputs into a **product** or service.

cost centre   An accounting convention whereby **costs** incurred are allocated to particular headings, such as individual **products** or operational activities.

costing   The calculation of the **cost** of making or providing a **product** or service, necessarily based on a convention decided beforehand.

current assets   **Assets** of a business that are used in daily trading. They comprise **cash** at a bank, **accounts receivable** (**debtors**) and stock.

current liabilities   **Liabilities** of a business that arise from daily operations, including **accounts payable** (creditors) and other **debt** payable within a year.

current ratio   The ratio between **current assets** and **current liabilities**; the safe level is thought to be 2:1.

customer   Buyer of a **product** or service. Sometimes also the **consumer** but not invariably.

data (plural of datum)   Pieces of **information** that need to be assembled into a larger whole in order for meaning to be extracted.

debt   1. Money owed. 2. Funds borrowed.

debtor   See **accounts receivable**.

direct cost   The sum of all the **costs** directly attributable to the provision of a particular **product** or service.

e-business   Business carried out over the internet.

enterprise   1. A business entity ('Mitsubishi is a huge enterprise'). 2. A characteristic of an individual, a group or a firm which demonstrates initiative and creativity.

entrepreneur   A person who detects business opportunities and exploits them, undertaking all the planning, **management** and **asset**-acquisition necessary.

equal opportunities   Equality of opportunity, enshrined in law in many countries, in all aspects of economic and social life irrespective of an individual's defining features.

equipment   Tools, vehicles, furniture and machines used to conduct business operations.

equity   1. A share in a business, usually acquired via investment. 2. The total financial stake in the business held by all shareholders.

excise duty   **Tax** imposed on goods, usually (but not only) fuel, alcohol and tobacco.

exporting   Selling outside the home country.

factor   A finance company that buys **debt** in order to ease its customer's cash flow: a firm selling an item will pass the **debt** to a factor who gives it a percentage of the value of the invoice immediately and takes the risk of late payment or non-payment.

finance   Money needed to fund an activity or undertaking.

financial accounting   Systems and activity for recording the flow of money within the firm.

financial statements   Documents showing past financial results or the current financial situation of a firm.

fiscal   Financial, in the context of government taxation and spending.

fixed asset   A business **asset** to be used in operations rather than to be traded, such as a machine, vehicle or office.

fixed costs   Costs which remain constant, unaffected by business **volume**s.

forecast   A prediction, usually comprising or accompanied by numbers.

four Ps   The components of the **marketing mix** – **product**, price, place and **promotion**.

franchise   The arrangement whereby third parties pay to be allowed to operate a **service** or provide goods not owned by them. A formal agreement lays down the terms.

fraud   Deceptive and dishonest activity that gains advantage at someone else's expense.

gross profit   Sales income less cost of goods sold.

guarantee   An undertaking to repay a **loan** if the borrower defaults.

guarantor   Someone who makes a **guarantee**.

import   **Product** or **service** brought into the country from another country.

income tax   A **tax** on personal income.

information   An assemblage of **data** presented in a form from which understanding may be reached and conclusions drawn.

insolvency   Being unable to pay **debt**s when due.

insurance   A guarantee of compensation if certain defined events occur, in return for payment (an 'insurance premium').

intangible   Lacking physical form (from Latin: incapable of being touched).

intellectual property   Property comprising **copyrights, registered designs** and **patents**.

interest   A charge made by a lender for the period of a **loan**.

interest rate   The percentage rate at which **interest** is charged.

invoice   A document showing the quantity and cost of goods or **services** supplied on a particular occasion that implies a demand for payment.

law of diminishing returns   The economic law that says that increasing inputs will not be rewarded by a proportional increase in outputs. For example, doubling the amount of fertilizer spread on a field will not double crops.

liability   A **debt** that is due, or will fall due in future.

limited liability partnership (LLP)   A **partnership** whose members are not liable for the entire **debt**s of the **partnership**.

liquid assets   **Assets** that can be quickly converted to **cash**, typically financial instruments.

liquidity   1. The capacity to meet financial **liabilities**. 2. The extent to which **assets** can be converted into **cash**.

loan agreement   An agreement specifying the terms on which a **loan** is made.

loan   Money lent, usually incurring payment of **interest**.

long-term liabilities   **Liabilities** not due in under a year.

mail order   Retailing via **order**s given on the basis of a catalogue illustration and description for delivery to the customer's address.

management   1. The process of identifying and achieving business **objectives** through the use of various **resources**. 2. The activity of running a business. 3. The person or group of people responsible for running a business.

management accounting   Accounting that seeks to aid management control and decisions.

marginal contribution   The difference between the **direct cost** and selling price of a **product** or **service**.

market   1. A group of current or potential buyers or consumers who do, or might, buy a specified good or **service** ('the market for beach holidays'). 2. A geographical area which does, or might, demand a good or **service** ('the East Asian market').

marketable   Capable of being put out for sale on the **market**.

market analysis   **Analysis** of a **market** to discover business opportunities.

market development   Activity intended to increase the size of a **market**.

marketing   A major discipline of business aimed at gaining organizational goals by providing value to customers.

marketing management   1. The process of planning, supervising and conducting **marketing** activity. 2. That group within a firm responsible for planning, overseeing and conducting **marketing** activity.

marketing mix   The particular mix of **product**, place, **promotion** and price offered to the **market** by a company or **brand**, often referred to as 'the **four Ps**'.

market niche   A grouping of customers, often small in relation to the whole **market**, towards whom specific **products** and **services** may be targeted.

market positioning   Placing the appeal of a **product** or **service** in such a way that it is seen favourably in comparison with competitors.

market research   Disciplined research into a **market** designed to throw light on defined **marketing** situations.

market share   A proportion of sales into a **market** attributable to a company or **brand**.

mark-up   In **retailing**, the percentage or monetary figure by which cost price is marked-up to arrive at **retail** price.

mass marketing   **Marketing** to a large proportion of consumers in a **market** as opposed to a **market niche**.

middleman   An intermediary involved in the chain of distribution from producer to consumer.

negotiation   A purposeful discussion intended to fix the terms of a transaction or to resolve a dispute.

net assets   The extent whereby a company's **assets** exceed its **liabilities**.

net profit   Income less direct and in**direct costs**.

net worth   Total **assets** less total **liabilities**.

niche   See **market niche**.

objective   An aim expressed in SMART terms (specific, measurable, achievable, relevant, timed) which serves as a unifying focus for effort.

operating costs   Costs incurred in operating the business that are not readily attributable to a particular **product** or **service**. Also known as overheads or **operating costs**.

order   A request made of a supplier in contractually enforceable form for specified quantities of goods or **services** at stated prices and on particular terms.

outsourcing   The transfer to outside contractors of activity previously undertaken in-house.

overdraft   The extent to which a bank current account is in deficit.

overdraft facility   An agreement by a bank that a customer may take credit on the current account up to an agreed limit.

overdrawn   Having taken an **overdraft**.

overheads   See **operating costs**.

partnership   A legal relationship whereby two or more people share responsibility for, and rewards from, a business activity. In English law, partners are individually responsible for the entire **liabilities** of the **enterprise**, not just their notional share.

patent   A monopoly granted by law to an inventor giving strong protection.

payable   Due for payment.

perception   The operation of the senses to receive and interpret **data** and **information**.

performance appraisal   The periodic evaluation of an employee's work, usually by the person to whom they report, against **objectives** agreed at the start of the period.

petty cash   A supply of currency kept to settle minor expenses.

planning   The projective activity involving foreseeing future situations and creating plans accordingly.

point of sale (also point of purchase)   The location at which a **product** or **service** is available for purchase. Point of sale material is **promotion**al material placed at the point of sale to induce purchases.

principal   1. The sum on which **interest** is due. 2. The head of an organization.

probability   The likelihood of an event taking place, expressed in figures: 0 = certain not to happen, 1 = certain to happen. Decimal fractions between 0 and 1 express the percentage probability, eg 'P = 0.7' means a 70 per cent chance of occurrence.

probation   A period of assessment of a new employee's suitability in the early stage of the person's employment.

product   1. A tangible manufactured article. 2. Any good or **service** that is output for sale, tangible or not.

product life cycle (PLC)   The stages of launch, development and decline through which a **product** typically travels.

product line   A supplier's group of **products** affiliated by **brand** name or use.

product mix   The assortment of **products** offered by a supplier.

profit   The financial surplus of income over expenses.

profit-and-loss (P&L) statement or account   A statement of income from sales over a period, less the cost of goods sold, less operating expenses, to show trading **profit**, less **tax** to show **net profit**.

profit margin   **Profit** expressed as either a figure or a percentage of sales value.

promotion   The attempt to gain the attention of potential customers by means of sales **information**.

proposition   The totality of the sales offer made to potential **customers**.

publicity   **Information** provided as editorial content in independently published media about commercial offerings.

quality   The extent to which the **product** or **service** meets its specified characteristics.

questionnaire   A form used to collect **information** from individuals by post. (Also wrongly but widely used for documents recording responses to interview questions, properly named 'interview schedules'.)

receivable   Due to be collected.

redundancy   A job ceasing to exist leading to the redeployment or dismissal of the employee filling it.

registered design   A graphic design that has been registered with a government office and is thus protected from copyists. Gives better protection than **copyright**.

resources   Those tangible and **intangible assets** on which a business can call to help it achieve objectives.

response rate   The proportion of those approached who respond (eg to a survey or a promotional offer).

retail   Sales made directly to the consumer.

retailing   The act of undertaking **retail** selling.

revenue   Total sales over a period.

salary   Payment, typically monthly, to employees for work done.

service   An **intangible** output sold by a business to customers.

take-home pay   An employee's pay after all deductions.

takeover   The acquisition of one company by another.

target market That group of specified individuals, identified by socio-economic, demographic and interest factors, at whom the goods and **services** of a business are directed.

tariff A government duty, usually imposed on **imports** or exports.

tax A charge made by public authorities.

taxable Subject to **tax**.

team players Individuals who work well within a team, committing themselves to its aims and subsuming personal interests to those of the team.

teamwork Collaboration by individuals towards shared goals.

terms of sale The conditions governing the basis of a sale.

test marketing Testing the appeal of a **product** or **service** in a small, usually obscure, area to learn lessons before distribution is widened.

trade fair An exhibition at which buyers and sellers within an industry can meet.

trademark A mark distinguishing a particular supplier's **product** or **service** from those of competitors. In the UK, trademarks may be registered but not all are. The symbol ™ is sometimes used.

turf war Dispute between individuals or departments in an organization over an area of responsibility.

unsecured debt A **debt** for which the sole security is an undertaking to pay.

value 1. The relationship between price and performance. 2. Sales defined in monetary terms.

value added The amount by which sales value exceeds **cost**.

value-added tax (VAT) A **tax** charged on most commercial transactions, related to the sales price, at each stage of supply.

variable cost A **cost** that is related to **volume** of production.

venture capital **Capital** introduced to new or expanding companies usually offering high growth and commensurate risk.

volume The amount or quantity sold (as opposed to **value** 2).

wages Pay to employees for work done, usually weekly.

wholesale 1. That level of the distribution chain that comes before **retail** and supplies retailers. 2. The price charged by **wholesalers**.

wholesalers Firms buying goods in bulk and selling on in smaller quantities to **retail** shops.

working capital 1. The sum of money by which **current assets** exceed **current liabilities**. 2. **Cash** available to pay day-to-day bills.

REFERENCES

Ansoff, I (1957) Strategies for diversification, *Harvard Business Review*, 35 Issue (5) September–October, pp 113–124

Ardagna, S and Lusardi, A (2010) Explaining international differences in entrepreneurship: the role of individual characteristics and regulatory constraints, *International Differences in Entrepreneurship*, ed Lerner, J and Schoar, A, p 47, University of Chicago Press

Beshpande, B R (2011) *Small Business Analytics on the Cloud: Is There Real Value?* (online) **http://technorati.com/technology/cloud-computing/article/small-business-analytics-on-the-cloud/#ixzz1jFLG0Cxh**

de Bono, E (1985) *Six Thinking Hats: An Essential Approach to Business Management*, Little, Brown, & Company, London

Burchell, B J, Deakin, D and Honey, S (1999) *The Employment Status of Individuals in Non-Standard Employment*, EMAR Publications No 6, Department of Trade and Industry, London

Conservative Party Manifesto, 1979 (online) **www.conservative-party.net/manifestos/1979/1979-conservative-manifesto.shtml**

Drucker, P F (1974) *Management Tasks, Responsibilities, Practices*, Butterworth Heinemann, Oxford

Drucker, P F (1990) *Managing the Non-Profit Organization: Principles and Practices*, HarperCollins, New York

Drucker, P F (2007) *Innovation and Entrepreneurship*, Butterworth Heinemann, Oxford

Global Entrepreneurship Monitor (2011) *GEM 2010 Women's Report*, GEM, Babson College, MA

Herzberg, F , Bloch, B and Mausner, B (1993) (first published 1959) *The Motivation to Work*, Transaction Publishers, Piscataway, NJ

International Labour Organisation (1998) *Enterprise Creation by the Unemployed*, ILO, Geneva

Labour Party Manifesto, 1979 (online) **www.labour-party.org.uk/manifestos/1979/1979-labour-manifesto.shtml**

Labour Party Manifesto, 1987 (online) **www.labour-party.org.uk/manifestos/1987/1987-labour-manifesto.shtml**

Labour Party Manifesto, 1997 (online) **www.labour-party.org.uk/manifestos/1997/1997-labour-manifesto.shtml**

McGregor, D (1960) *The Human Side of Enterprise*, McGraw Hill, New York

Morris, M J (2011) *Starting a Successful Business* (7th edition), Kogan Page, London

Newell, H (2009) *Self-employed workers*. Eurofound (online) **www.eurofound.europa.eu/comparative/tn0801018s/uk0801019q.htm**

Porter, M E (2008) The five competitive forces that shape strategy, *Harvard Business Review*, January, pp 86–104

Schein, E (1990) *Organizational Culture and Leadership*, Jossey-Bass, San Francisco, CA

Schumpeter, J A (1975) *Capitalism, Socialism and Democracy*, HarperCollins, New York (originally published 1942)

Shaw, J (2011) *Economic and Labour Market Review*, 5 (4) April, p 58

The Times 100 Business Case Studies **http://businesscasestudies.co.uk/business-theory/ strategy/business-failure.html**

Tilley, F and Tonge, J (2003) Introduction in Jones, O and Tilley, F (eds), *Competitive Advantage in SMEs*, John Wiley, Chichester

Wiseman, R (2004) *The Luck Factor*, Random House, London

The World Bank/International Finance Corporation (2011) *Doing Business in a More Transparent World*, pp 77–138, The World Bank, Washington, DC

INDEX